MW00576932

Communication

16 Proven Methods

85 True Accounts

The Authors in This Book

The authors in this book are the presenters at the New Developments in Afterlife Communication conference held by the Academy for Spiritual and Consciousness Studies in Scottsdale, Arizona, July 11-13, 2014.

For information about the conference, the book containing conference presentations, and DVD or audio recordings, go to the Academy website:

http://ascsi.org/conference/

Editor
R. Craig Hogan, Ph.D.

Copyright © 2014 Academy for Spiritual and Consciousness Studies, and the authors as stipulated below

No part of this book may be reproduced in any written, electronic, photocopying or other copy media without written permission of the publisher or authors as described below. The exception is in the case of brief quotations embodied in the critical articles or reviews and pages where permission is specifically granted by the publisher or author.

The excerpts in this book have been included with the permission of the authors. The authors hold all rights and copyrights to the text, with no claim to copyright or ownership by ASCS or the editor.

"Aiding Lost Souls" is copyright Bruce Moen, 2014.

"Automatic Writing" is from *Phases of Life after Death—Writing in Automatic Writing* by Irma Slage, copyright Xlibris Corporation, 2000, and *Psychic Encounters—A Guide to Having Your Own Spirit Contact* by Irma Slage, copyright Spirit Publishing, 2013.

"Direct Connections" is from *Soul Shift: Finding Where the Dead Go*, by Mark Ireland, copyright Frog Books, 2008, and from *Messages from the Afterlife: A Bereaved Father's Journey in the World of Spirit Visitations, Psychic-Mediums, and Synchronicity*, by Mark Ireland, copyright North Atlantic Books, 2013.

"Dream Visions "is from *Dream Messages from the Afterlife*, by Rosemary Guiley, copyright Visionary Living, Inc., 2013.

"Guided Afterlife Connections" is excerpted in part from *Guided Afterlife Connections: They Come to Change Lives* by Rochelle Wright and Craig Hogan, copyright Greater Reality Publications, 2010.

"Honoring Spirits' Efforts to Reach Us" is from *Love Eternal* by Rhonda Schwartz, copyright FastPencil, Inc., 2011.

"Journey to the Upper Realm" is from *Journey to the Upper Realm: How I Survived the Deaths of My Sons and Learned to Communicate with Them on the Other Side* by Maria Pe, copyright Maria Pe, 2013.

"Love Language of the Afterlife" is copyright Susanne Wilson, 2014.

"Pendulum Communication" is copyright Carol Morgan, 2014.

"Receiving and Understanding Signs" is from *Hello...Anyone Home?* by Joseph M. Higgins, copyright Joseph M. Higgins, 2009.

"Reunions through Physical Mediumship—an Old Practice Being Rediscovered" is copyright Victor Zammit, 2014.

"Soul Phone" is summarized from *The Sacred Promise: How science is discovering spirit's collaboration with us in our daily lives* by Gary E. Schwartz, copyright Atria Books/Beyond Words, 2011.

"They Hear You" is from *Messages of Hope* by Suzanne Giesemann, copyright One Mind books, 2011.

"The Threshold Room" is copyright Anne and Herb Puryear, 2014.

"Understanding Afterlife and Angel Contacts" is copyright Karen Herrick, 2014.

"Voices of People in Spirit Recorded on a PC" is copyright Sonia Rinaldi, 2014.

ASCS Publications contact:

    Academy for Spiritual and Consciousness Studies
    P.O. Box 84
    Loxahatchee, Florida 33470

ISBN 978-0-9802111-7-7

ASCS Publications

Contents

Neither was it intended that the two worlds, ours and yours, should be as they are now—so far apart in thought and contact. The day will assuredly come when our two worlds will be closely interrelated, when communication between the two will be a commonplace of life, and then the great wealth of resources of the spirit world will be open to the Earth world, to draw upon for the benefit of the whole human race.

- Monsignor Robert Hugh Benson,
speaking from the spirit realm through
Anthony Borgia, in *Life in the World Unseen*

Preface

Today, for the first time in human history, virtually anyone can communicate with loved ones who have transitioned off the Earth plane through the natural life process we call death. This book contains actual accounts of people who have had afterlife communication with loved ones using one of the variety of methods available today.

The authors are the presenters at the Academy for Spiritual and Consciousness Studies 38th annual conference, July 11-13, in Scottsdale Arizona. The Academy for Spiritual and Consciousness Studies, Inc. is a nonprofit organization whose members study, publish, and teach about spirituality, the afterlife, and consciousness. Each year, the Academy holds a conference in which presenters speak on a topic of interest to the members. The topic of the 2014 conference is New Developments in Afterlife Communication. The Academy has assembled the foremost pioneers, researchers, and practitioners in the field of afterlife communication to describe the cutting-edge methods people are using today to communicate with their loved ones who have transitioned from the Earth plane to the next plane of life.

This book provides accounts of actual afterlife connections written by the presenters at the conference. The purpose of the book is to demonstrate the validity of the methods of communication they describe and to help people realize the loving, uplifting quality of the messages and experiences in these contacts. We present these accounts to encourage people to come to gatherings such as the conference to learn about the methods and hear people speak about how wonderful and life changing the experiences are.

Anyone can have rich, satisfying, continuing relationships now with loved ones who have transitioned off the Earth plane. They just have to know how. This conference shows how.

The conference proceedings, with summaries of the presenters' talks will be available in the book, *New Developments in Afterlife Communication,* and in DVDs and audio recordings of the presentations. Link to http://ascsi.org for more information.

Links to resources about the authors and methods of connecting in this book are at this link: http://ascsi.org/conference/resources.htm.

Voices of People in Spirit Recorded on a PC

Sonia Rinaldi, M.S.

Brazilian researcher Sonia Rinaldi has a Mastership Degree in Sciences of Religion. She is an author and lecturer, and is internationally recognized as one of the foremost researchers of Instrumental TransCommunications (ITC).

Sonia started researching ITC in 1988. She twice received the international Hedri Prize from the Swiss Foundation for Parapsychology for innovative research in 1995 and 1997.

In 2000, Sonia took the research to a scientific lab working with engineers, physicists, and scientists. The result of her studies of instrumental transcommunication has been the ability to record voices from people in spirit using a telephone, with incredible voice quality. She also has developed new techniques to record transimages, which are images that appear when an opaque film is waved over a person's face or some other background.

For more about Sonia, visit ipati.org. Examples of her audio recordings and transimages are at http://ascsi.org/conference/resources.htm.

1

The Phone Call Procedure

Sonia has been helping people by making phone calls to the beyond since March 2001. Most have been for parents who have lost their children. Sonia writes, "With this technology controlled by the Beyond, the call is not from the Beyond world. Those in spirit respond through our world's phone calls." Sonia has also obtained clear transimages of deceased ones.

The parents make an appointment with Sonia in advance. She doesn't charge for her work. Since the beginning, she never has had money involved in helping people. The parents are instructed to prepare 10 questions. When they call on the appointed day, Sonia has one phone in her hand and leaves an extension phone open for those in the Spirit world to participate. The telephone is connected into the microphone jack of her computer and all conversations are recorded directly into the computer.

The parents ask the 10 questions, leaving 20 seconds between each question. During the silent time between questions, no one on this side of life speaks, but the recording on the PC registers the voices of those in spirit as they respond. The parents and Sonia do not know what the person in spirit is saying while the parent is on the phone. They won't hear the responses until after the entire session is over and they listen to the recording. Then the questions and answers play back together as a conversation.

The recorded conversation lasts about 12 to 15 minutes. Sonia then listens to the entire recording, and sends the results to the parents. The person in spirit is identified not only by the voice, but also by the detailed information that only the parents know. What is remarkable about

Sonia's results is the quality achieved in both the voices and the transimages.

An example follows.

Rita Barcellos Goulart Connects with Her Daughter, Daniela, in Spirit

Rita Goulart lost her daughter Daniela at 22 years of age in an automobile accident, two years before this session. Rita arranged with Sonia to have contact with her daughter in spirit using the computer recordings of voices that come over the telephone.

The transcript of the voices in Rita's connection with Daniela follows. The recordings include 22 statements that were clear and distinct, classified as Class A voice recordings. The recordings are available for researchers to listen to.

The transcript that follows is of a test Sonia performed before Rita called in to connect with her daughter. Sonia performs this test before every session to verify the sound and make sure the speakers in spirit are available to communicate. It happens at around 10:30 a.m., one-half hour before the 11:00 a.m. time the family member calls in.

SONIA: "Hi friends. Good morning."

DANIELA: "I am here."

Daniela has answered the question before Sonia asks it, (below). That happens often in these sessions. Those in spirit know the thought before the words are spoken. Since these words are on the recording, but not audible at the time Sonia is speaking, she doesn't realize Daniela has already answered.

SONIA: "I would like to know if Daniela is getting ready to speak with Rita, and whether she is in Rio Grande do Sul or São Paulo."

DANIELA: "The attendance is the same."

DANIELA: "Mommy, I am already feeling you from here!"

SONIA: "Daniela, are you already feeling your mother?"

DANIELA: "I am holding her hands."

Daniela's mother, Rita, later reported that she and Daniela would always walk holding hands.

ANOTHER YOUNG FEMALE VOICE IN SPIRIT: "Good morning."

SONIA: "Danni my dear . . ."

DANIELA: "You are going to laugh, I am very funny."

This curious prediction came true in this phone call. Daniela became naughty in the recording, dropping the connection, and even saying that I was wearing my nightclothes!!! Danni was very funny indeed.

So that I could confirm it was Daniela, I asked a verification question.

SONIA: "Can you confirm your mother's name?"

DANIELA: "Rita."

DANIELA: "One kiss."

Daniela again answers the question before Sonia asks it.

SONIA: "Send a kiss to your mother now."

DANIELA: "Certainly, it's mine."

END OF THE TEST CALL

At 11:00 a.m., Rita called to make the connection with Daniela. This is a transcript of the connection. Sonia speaks first. Neither Rita nor Sonia can hear Daniela's responses as this session proceeds. There is a mixture of voices speaking from both sides of life at the beginning.

SONIA: "Good morning dear friends. We are online with Rita, anxious to speak with our dear Daniela."

A WORKER WITH SONIA: "They are recording everything right now."

DANIELA: "This is a message for the friend."

CHILD IN SPIRIT: "It's true. I spoke with you."

SONIA: "OK Rita, you can start."

RITA: "All right. Hi, Danni, my beloved daughter. I miss you so much. I miss our love and friendship. My daughter, what I would like to know the most is how you are, my love. Are you all right?"

DANIELA: "Answer yourself, Rita!"

Rita later explained why Daniela answered in this way. She wrote, "I knew inside that she was happy and fine that day—so, she knew that I knew! And many times she called me by my name Rita! This told me how happy she is in the Other Side."

RITA: "Daughter, how is it to live in the spiritual dimension?"

DANIELA: "Friendship. You should know more."

RITA: "My daughter, the coming of Jefferson to our family so soon after your passing, were you OK with that?"

After Daniela passed, Rita adopted a 5-year-old child named Jefferson. Here Rita asks about Jefferson.

DANIELA: "You will see at home."

Rita later explained, "We are really already seeing every day that Jefferson speaks about her as if he had known her and they had lived together. It is impressive that a six-year-old child says what he says. We adopted Jefferson after Daniella died, so they never met. But day by day he talks about her, proving that she is around and inspiring him. Just as she said in the recording, 'You will see at home.' We really see."

At this time, I interrupted Rita because she was asking questions one after another, leaving little silent time for her daughter to reply. We can't know if there is a reply until we play back the recording, so we must allow time for whatever the person in spirit may be recording that we can't hear. I usually ask the speaker on our side to wait 10 seconds between questions. Rita was so anxious that she was not waiting. But curiously, Daniela defended her mother.

SONIA: "Rita, leave more time so Daniela can answer."

DANIELA: "I am hearing!"

At this moment a problem began that would end up with the line dropping. When the problem begins, we hear on the recording a lady's voice scolding Daniela. The lady calls her by the nickname she had on Earth.

VOICE FROM SPIRIT: "Oooo Danni!!! Don't touch it!!! Leave it normal!"

I do not know what actually happened, but at this point, I didn't hear Rita anymore. I asked her to continue, but she was silent.

SONIA: "You can go on, Rita."

DANIELA: "I give you a hug. I am getting out."

The next statement might have suggested that Danni could reincarnate as Rita's granddaughter. She mentions this possibly again in this call.

DANIELA: "God, allow a granddaughter."

As there was nothing from Rita, the call was mute. I called Rita again and spoke, but she did not answer.

SONIA: "Rita."

What follows are voices in spirit commenting on the problem with the line. The first one says that the phone call is lost. In fact, the line was dropped. I couldn't hear Rita and she couldn't hear me. This is the exchange. I am speaking oblivious to the voices that were being recorded.

MALE: "It was lost!"

FEMALE: "OK. I saw."

SONIA: "Daniela."

ELDERLY-SOUNDING VOICE: "It doesn't work!"

ROUGH, ELDERLY-SOUNDING VOICE: "I already heard it!"

SONIA: "Did mum get out of line?"

At that moment, there was a sound, like "toin, toin, toin." Then a young female voice asked for more time.

A YOUNG FEMALE VOICE: "A bit more time."

Rita calls back again. Daniela makes a whimsical comment alluding to the test I did at the beginning.

DANIELA: "Testing again!!!"

FEMALE VOICE: "Danni forgot the danger"

SONIA: "OK you can continue."

DANIELA: "One thing is certain: I love all of you."

Daniela again replied to the question before it was asked. The question follows.

RITA: Dear daughter, send a message for Dad, for Mum, and for brother Dudu."

RITA: "For Elson, my daughter, say a word."

Here Rita asks Danni to say something she could relay to Danni's ex-boyfriend, Elson. He still loves her much and suffers greatly because of her passing.

DANIELA: "He is really sad! Mummy, you can imagine. He stopped his life."

RITA: "Daughter, is there any youngster or a child from the foundation near you right now?

DANIELA: "I am going to tell them to come here one day."

VOICE ON THE RECORDING: "The best principle is hope."

VOICE ON THE RECORDING: They came with Daniela."

YOUNG FEMALE VOICE: "My name is Margarita."

RITA: "Thank you for everything you have shown us. We love you. Our love grows nourished by the hope that we will be together. Send always lots of light for Sonia, for her to achieve all her goals in transcommunication. It becomes better each time. It comforts the hearts of so many families. God bless you and lighten you, my dear daughter. One big kiss, my love."

DANIELA: "I love you."

RITA: "A big kiss."

DANIELA: "I also want to kiss you."

Rita is about to end the call. Daniela asks her not to. This is the exchange.

DANIELA: "Don`t go away!!!"

Since Daniela's plea is on the recording, but not audible to Sonia or Rita at the time, Rita doesn't know about her daughter's request.

RITA: "OK Sonia, I am finished."

The following statement strengthens the possibility that she will reincarnate, possibly as her brother´s daughter.

DANIELA: "Shortly I will be here. Do you see how smart I am?"

Because Rita finished her questions, I said hello to Daniela.

SONIA: "Hi, Daniela."

The statement that follows confirms that the speakers from beyond see us all the time, since she says something specific that was true. I didn't have time to change clothes in the morning. I was alone at home, so I was wearing pajamas during this recording.

DANIELA: "You are wearing night clothes."

SONIA: "Let's talk a bit more ....."

RITA: "Hello, my love. Speak something to your mother."

DANIELA: "One day we will speak even more clearly. Death, Mother, you feel it in the air."

Daniela's statement matches what her boyfriend, Elson, said. He said that one hour before the car accident, Daniela was strangely insistent on trying to call her family, as if she was going to say goodbye.

RITA: "How can we help you to be fine always?"

DANIELA: "I didn`t die."

SONIA: "Daniela, let me also ask you one thing: Where do you live?"

DANIELA: "I go to Earth. It is very similar to here."

FEMALE VOICE: "I am off."

SONIA: "Would you confirm that you are always at your mother´s house."

DANIELA: "At her side. I feel like being there. Leonardo is going there, and Marcia too."

SONIA: "Daniela, who is accompanying you in this moment at the Station?"

DANIELA: "It´s my grandfather."

A masculine voice speaks, possibly her grandfather, confirming that he is there.

MALE VOICE: "I was together with ..."

SONIA: "OK, Daniela. Now Mum is going to tell you goodbye, and afterwards, we are going to close it, OK?

DANIELA: "It was good."

RITA: "Goodbye, my beloved daughter."

At this point, another phenomenon happened. Rita's voice was modulated into words she assured us she did not speak.

RITA'S VOICE, ALTERED: "I love you so much, my star."

DANIELA: "It was great."

ANOTHER YOUNG FEMALE VOICE: "Here is Cecilia."

DANIELA: "However, it was wonderful. My big kiss."

She again answers the question before Sonia asks it in the next statement.

SONIA: "Well, then I am also leaving a big kiss from our side to your side, and for the young people grouped there."

DANIELA: "You are going to bring all of them."

Her answer suggests she wants me to bring these young people to connect with her.

SONIA: "We are so grateful to the Station friends."

Rita's Response to the Connection with Daniela

Soon after Rita received the recording, she sent a letter to Sonia describing how she felt about it and to explain some of the dialogue. Her letter follows.

I don't need to tell to you the emotion and happiness that I feel. Thank you very much from the bottom of my heart for the opportunity. I listened to the CD with the phone call and recognized my Daniella, just as she was here among us. I now am certain that she is alive and her personality continues; it comforts my mother's heart so much.

My daughter proved to me it was her with her answers that only a mother could understand. For example, the fact that the telephone line had dropped I am absolutely sure was her trying to press some button to leave the clearest communication. It was Danni's style. Whenever she got a new device, she would try to touch all buttons and test all possibilities—she loved to discover more tools or functions in the appliances of our house.

But the most important detail of the recording that proves it was really her speaking is the moment she said that she had the sensation of feeling herself holding hands with me. This was a particular characteristic we both had: wherever we would go on the street, we walked hand in hand. I know this is quite uncommon between mother and daughter, and because of that, it is an important detail in this recording.

Also, when she said that it was "A MESSAGE FOR THE FRIEND," that was also an important point. We both were always admired by our friends for the relationship type that we had—we were faithful, and she always said that her best friend was the mother. For Daniella, I was not only her mother, but her best friend.

Another detail, when she commented that you were wearing pajamas, I laughed a lot because it is another characteristic of Danni to be indiscreet. I passed many squeezes with her. She was so spontaneous that she never thought twice before speaking anything. And you confirmed later that you were wearing pajamas. This proves that she was seeing you, in spite of the fact that you were alone at your home.

It is not in all sentences spoken that I can recognize her voice, but the majority yes. Some in particular it is HER own voice with no doubt.

Sonia Communicates with Her Dying Father During His Sleep and After He Passes

In February 2014, my father was near the point of passing away. I set up the communication equipment to communicate with him while he was sleeping, a week before his passing. Then, within four hours after his passing, I again communicated with him. These are the accounts of the two communications.

Recording Done One Week Before His Departure

Allan Kardec, who created the Spiritism religion in France, had written that communication between persons still alive on the Earth plane is a reality. He published some cases of communication via mediums with people while they were asleep.

I decided to confirm that by communicating with my father's self while he was asleep. During the final weeks, he slept most of the day and night. The result was the following dialogue. Many things spoken in my father's voice were things only the family knew.

I recorded into a microphone connected to a PC, making statements and pausing. I couldn't hear my father's response because it was on the recording. After I finished making the statements with pauses between them, I played back the recording, hearing my father's voice after my statements.

The dialogue follows. My father refers to my husband, Carlos, who was in the room with me.

SONIA: "Are you . . ."

My father spoke over my voice because he knew the question before I spoke it.

FATHER: "I'm fine."

SONIA: ." . . fine?"

FATHER: "Go on with your work. You will prove what is needed."

He encouraged me to continue with my work to find ways people can communicate with the afterlife.

FATHER: "Thereza."

SONIA: "Who is with you now?"

He has already answered me: "Thereza." Thereza is my cousin, who passed about 10 years before.

FATHER: "Paschoal comes to toast . . ."

Paschoal is an uncle who passed about 40 years before. Although Father is in his frail body, he is spending time in sleep with people on the other side.

FATHER: "They give us a mug. We have to use it."

My father had been fed through a tube inserted into his stomach, so for some months, he received no real food and could not eat by himself. The mug is possibly training for learning to eat by himself on the other side.

SONIA: "You are worried about Oswaldinho, aren't you. But Oswaldinho is fine."

FATHER: "Yesterday I was there, at the beach."

He was referring to going to where Oswaldinho lived, at the seashore. My father was indicating that he was taken to the beach the day before. It confirms that guides take people partially in both the Earth plane and next plane on tours.

SONIA: "We are also well."

FATHER: "Gets up. He is not fine."

In response to my statement that I and my husband Carlos are fine, my father responded that Carlos is worried about my father, so he has difficulty sleeping. In fact, Carlos often went to my father's bedroom (that was in my house) to check on my father. It showed that although he was in a coma-like sleep most of the time, he was aware of what was going on around him.

FATHER: "My coming has made you more work."

SONIA: "Do you see what is going on in our house?"

My father answered before I asked the question. He was saying that his being in the house required 24-hour care, with more laundry, medical consultations, special shopping, and other duties.

FATHER: "Brother, I am in the Station."

A lighthearted slang phrase meaning, "Man, I'm in the train (or bus) station ready to depart."

FATHER: "I'm stuck."

CARLOS: "Listen to these people."

Carlos, my husband, told my father to listen to the people communicating to him from the other side."

SONIA: "Can you leave a message for Oswaldinho?"

FATHER: "Vadinho counts on me too."

He referred to my brother by the nickname he had as a child, Vadinho. It was a nickname I had forgotten about. Oswaldinho wept when he heard this on the recording.

SONIA: "Dad, you have ugly wounds. You are fed through your belly. Isn't it time to leave this body?"

FATHER: "To wake up? Yes, I would rather."

My father referred to going to the other side as "waking up."

SONIA: "Can you see aliens? Why don't you go with them?"

FATHER: "I want to."

FATHER: "Hairdresser!!!"

SONIA: "Carlos will speak a word to you, Dad."

My father responded before I made the statement. He jokingly referred to a hairdresser because Carlos is totally bald.

CARLOS: "We have seen . . .

FATHER: "They blame me."

CARLOS: ". . . their status."

My father interrupted with the comment that he was blamed for his indebtedness.

CARLOS: "We believe the wounds bother you so much . . ."

FATHER: "Yes, they are painful."

CARLOS: "When we see you restless and agitated, is it because you see people?"

Occasionally, while he was sleeping, my father seemed to be seeing people.

FATHER: "Remember the Station, bro!"

My father interrupts him, again referring to leaving at the station, possibly meaning he was seeing the people coming for him.

CARLOS: "The people from the other side are there to explain to you what it will be like to leave the body."

SONIA: "Dad, I want to thank you . . ."

VOICE: "He is coming."

VOICE: "I came for him."

An unknown voice confirmed that my father would depart soon. In fact, it would happen a week later. Another voice confirmed that they were there ready to receive him.

SONIA: "A kiss . . ."

FATHER: "I didn't enjoy life."

SONIA: ". . . and a big hug."

FATHER: "Pass on my messages."

Recording Done Four Hours after His Passing

My father passed into spirit a week later on February 13. I discovered that he had passed when I went to feed him at 7 a.m. His body had been lifeless on the bed for hours. His nurse came to dress him, and we waited for the hearse until 4 p.m. that afternoon. Such delays are common in Brazil.

I recorded the following audios a few meters below my father's body within four hours after his passing.

SONIA: "So you're gone, right Dad?"

FATHER: "I'll take you."

I understood that he would carry me in his heart, thanking me for the last years I cared for him.

SONIA: "I knew you'd be relieved, Dad."

FATHER: "Tomorrow, I will be there!!!"

We had started to organize his funeral in the morning, planning to bury him the same day. We would have had time to arrive at the graveyard because it was open until 4:30 p.m. My brother was going to help me with the documents so everything would be ready on time. I recorded this at about 11 a.m., so when I heard him saying,

"I will be there tomorrow," I thought "Where will he go tomorrow?" I let it go. But as the day progressed, the delay in the hearse's arrival meant the funeral had to be postponed until the next day. He was saying he would be at his funeral to watch and say goodbye to his family.

SONIA: "Are you OK? Are you relieved?"

FATHER: "I'll film!"

Again, with his witty sense of humor, he says he will appear in one of the videos I am able to make of the images of people in spirit. I hope he does.

SONIA: "Is he with you?"

FATHER: "I would like some coffee."

I ask about my husband in spirit, Fernando. My father continues his light-hearted mood. When he visited relatives, he would always enter the house asking for coffee, just as a joke. He is joking about arriving at his destination.

SONIA: "Are you with him?"

FERNANDO: "We have contact . . ."

SONIA: "Can he talk?"

I ask my husband in spirit, Fernando, if he was beside my father. He confirmed that they were in touch.

SONIA: "Hi, Fernando."

FERNANDO: "Contacting Earth . . ."

SONIA: "I want to know from you if Dad has arrived safely."

SONIA: "Dad, I want you to give us good news, that you are happy with Mom."

Mom was still alive. They had issues with each other.

FATHER: "I will come to Earth."

SONIA: "Dad, I was very happy for you that you passed. Happy you got rid of that bed."

FATHER: "I love you."

FATHER: "Your mother has forgiven me."

Self-Guided Afterlife Connections

R. Craig Hogan, Ph.D.

R. Craig Hogan, Ph.D., is director of the Center for Spiritual Understanding, devoted to helping people develop spiritual understanding through afterlife connections. He is the author of *Your Eternal Self*, presenting the scientific evidence that the mind is not confined to the brain, the afterlife is a reality, people's minds are linked, and the mind affects the physical world.

Craig co-authored *Induced After-Death Communication: A New Therapy for Healing Grief and Trauma* with Allan Botkin, Psy.D., and *Guided Afterlife Connections: They Come to Change Lives* with Rochelle Wright, M.S.

He is on the boards of the Academy for Spiritual and Consciousness Studies, Association for Evaluation and Communication of Evidence for Survival, and American Society for Standards in Mediumship and Psychical Investigation.

The Self-Guided Afterlife Connections Procedure

Craig developed the Self-Guided Afterlife Connections procedure for the Center for Spiritual Understanding. It teaches people how to guide themselves into a connection with loved ones in the afterlife. The procedure is available on the Internet for free at http://selfguided.spiritualunderstanding.org.

The Self-Guided Afterlife Connections procedure uses relaxation activities with guided meditations presented in eight training stages. At each stage, the participants learn to become more adept at allowing the natural unfoldment from their subconscious through which they will receive messages from loved ones living on the next plane of life. The training results in the participants' becoming open to the messages coming from loved ones in spirit, culminating in their being able to sit quietly anywhere, without the guided meditation, and connect with loved ones now living in the afterlife.

In a study of 22 participants who had gone through at least the first four stages in training, 86% of participants had an afterlife connection. To learn more about the Self-Guided Afterlife Connections procedure and to read journals of people who have gone through the procedure, go to http://afterlifeconnections.org.

After each training stage, participants fill out a journal describing what happened during their session. They have given permission for excerpts from their journals to be made public. A small sample of the descriptions follows.

For more about Craig, go to afterlifeconnections.org or youreternalself.com.

~ Participant Journal Excerpt ~

Even as I started paying attention to my breathing, I felt that my daughter was reminding me about how she had done in a class that she had taken a few years ago.

Then as I pictured a place of beauty, I was with Linda at a park. She was dressed in warm weather clothing. She seemed amused that I would be concerned about temperature and she enjoyed the idea that she was teaching me. We then were up in the air looking down at the treetops briefly and then were back sitting together on the bench. We communicated for a while about our feelings for each other. My father came from our left and stood to the side. I could sense my mother and nephew there also, but their form was not as solid as Linda's. My dad indicated that he just wanted me to know that he was proud of me, but wanted to allow me to spend this time with Linda. Linda let me know that she was glad that I was trying to stay connected with her and kissed me on the cheek to say good-bye for now.

~ A Second Journal Excerpt by the Same Father ~

I talk to my daughter throughout the day. The last couple of times that I've done the exercise, I tell her ahead of time that I will be doing it and the time I plan. She seems to be waiting for me when the time comes.

This time as I sat down on the chair to begin, I felt that she was letting me know that she notices when I eat foods that she enjoyed and that she likes that I do it.

As I began the exercise, Linda was there. I didn't even go to a place of beauty to get started. Other than the idea that any place where Linda is will always be a place of beauty for me.

We were floating in a rich black sky with stars above us. We watched three or four shooting stars. She really seems to enjoy being my guide and being able to show things to me. I enjoy it also. Then I felt that we were sitting on the hood of a car with our backs resting on the windshield. Then there were fireworks above us. After watching a few, I think that she did something with her hand and some of the sparks did loops and designs. She looked over at me as if to say, "See what I can do." She laughed about it all.

While I was thinking about having fun together, she leaned over and gave me a big hug and said that our time together meant a lot to her. I let her know that I will continue doing this. She replied, "Tomorrow?" I said that it would be sometime soon. To which she replied "TOMORROW" in a slow clear voice.

~ Participant Journal Excerpt ~

Before there was any mention of going to a place where love is, I saw a scene. It was a huge field of daffodils with the sun shining on them and butterflies all around. In the sky some clouds had come together to form the shape of an elderly man's face and he was smiling down at the field, his face full of love. I walked through the field and the butterflies followed me. Then I had a feeling of my horse and my dog that had passed away many years ago. Satin was my very first horse and he had taught me how to ride. Teddy was a miniature collie and I was closer to him than any dog I had ever owned. The feeling was more like the feeling you have for a human friend than for a dog. I had not thought of either of them prior to the session, nor had I planned to connect with them.

I felt the presence of both of them. I remembered how I used to ride Satin in the woods with Teddy trotting behind us. I caught glimpses of both of them in the field of daffodils. I was enjoying it when I suddenly caught a glimpse of part of a cat's face. I wasn't sure if it was friendly and a tiny bit of alarm went through me. Then suddenly I felt it against my arm, not in the field of daffodils, but against my arm in the chair in which I was reclining. I instantly relaxed again as I recognized it. It was my cat Saturn. He had died many years ago when he was 25 years old. His face had been a bit wild looking, not cute like the average domestic cat and when I first caught a glimpse of him, I had not recognized him. Now I knew exactly who it was. I could feel his fur against my arm which was resting on the chair. Then I heard his purring quite loudly. He sounded so extremely happy. He dominated everything. I was only aware of his fur and his purr, nothing else, not the horse, not the dog, not the daffodils, just him.

The session then ended.

The sensation of touch from the cat's fur was so real and much more real than I had imagined a sense of touch to be as well as the loud sound of purring. It was like he was purring in the room. It was amazing.

~ Participant Journal Excerpt ~

Once again, my father appeared even before the instructions came to go through a Heavenly door. He greeted me and said that it's good that I'm coming back here again. Then when the voice instruction broke through to go through the doorway, my Dad said to me "Well, listen to your teacher and do what he says"; so I walked up to this door and walked through it, and Dad stood there, smiling as if to say, "That's good."

He said, "Look who's here with me again," and then he was holding my pet rabbit, Anubis, who was happy and peaceful. Dad said to me "Hold her," and I did. I felt her in my hands. I started to cry again and Dad told me not to cry, that there's no reason to cry, that I can see that they are there. I patted her and kissed her. Dad said that I was on the right track to be pursuing my spiritual journey. I told him that I found it hard at times, that I didn't always know what to do or where to go for information or answers. He said to take things in steps, one step at a time—that it's all about steps. I said that we used to take walks together while he was alive and he said this was like taking walks, one step at a time; that this is what we will always do, taking steps, moving forward.

I told him that others in the family don't believe in this spirit stuff, that they often think it's all nonsense or imagination or bogus and that it frustrates me. Dad said that it is because of fear, that people will often just go with what they know because it feels comfortable to them, like always choosing the same meal on a menu over and over again rather than picking a new dish for fear you may not like the new meal. So you choose what you know to be safe and familiar. He told me not to feel angry or frustrated with this, but to understand where they're coming from. That they're just wanting to see the world as the only place of being comes from a need to feel safe with what is familiar and known.

I saw other pets just lounging around on this oak island; the mosses were so thick and lush, everything green and warm. One of my cats from the past, Tiger, actually smiled at me.

I asked Dad if I could hug him. He said yes. I did hug him and felt the material of his shirt and his bones pressing against me and the scratch of the hair on his chin. He said that this was probably enough for now, to not try for too much all at once and that it was good to come back there. I also told him that I would like to connect with my mother who crossed over just a few months ago, and that I felt disappointed that she had not made much connection yet. He said that she had been busy meeting with many people and other beings since she crossed over, that she means to connect, but that it's like I can find days here on earth where there's so much on the agenda that I don't always get to everything I'd like to do in a day. He said it had been much like that for her, but that she wants to make the connection. That I'm to just give her time.

Then things faded out. I didn't do the five to one count to come out of the relaxation; the image of them just faded out.

~ Participant Journal Excerpt ~

This session is one of many a woman has now had in which her husband Karl in spirit takes her on his rescue missions to the Earth plane where he ministers to people who are newly passed away. In this session, Karl is instrumental in a little girl's near-death experience. The woman explained in an earlier session that when Karl appeared at his age when he passed and in a trench coat, that meant he was going to take her to the Earth plane on a rescue mission.

Karl was just waiting for me, 67-years-old, trench coat, quickly a kiss. I noticed that when I am going to accompany him on a mission, I immediately feel an energy flux directly into my left thigh, with little but strong current impulses, being rather painful.

"Another accident, Karl?" "Yes, right!" nodding his head.

Superhighway, accident just happened. Occupants: a mother with her little daughter, 5 years old, named Carina! Mother lost control of the car and it began lurching about, finally going head over heels, slithering for another hundred meters on its top along the breakdown lane. The mother freed herself and came out suddenly, being only slightly injured. Carina was still fastened in her seat belt in the upset car.

Arriving at the scene of accident, we're seeing the police and this time a large-capacity-ambulance. Karl said that Carina was just taken out of the car in trauma. She was in the ambulance, being resuscitated.

Then in an instant we were in the ambulance too, because Carina was flat lining! I was sorry to notice the well-known light foggy blue haze.

Craig's note: In earlier sessions, the woman learned that the blue haze means the spirit is separating from the body. Carina was dying.

Carina was coming out of her little body so easygoing, with amazing, wondering, wide-eyed child's eyes, pallid blue shining, holding strongly her teddy bear in her arms. Karl was smiling at her. She responded with a delicate smile too, and then floated directly into his wide opened arms!!! A tender, heartwarming moment! How much love was in the air! Enough love for me to watch that scene teary-eyed.

Then just we three were in another place…in another world…in a world of fairies and brownies…awesome!!!!…in a World of Magic!

A beautiful, mystical place, colored in a mild-pink light, soft music sounding out of all these hundreds of so sweet smelling flowers, growing on a soft, green meadow; not far away, hearing the loving whooshing of a little stream, all surrounded by big, mighty oak trees, waving with heavy treetops. And in the middle of this magical atmosphere, there was standing the most beautiful woman I'd ever seen: MARIA!

*Craig's note: Maria had been involved
in these rescues before.*

She was wearing a long, white glimmering and shining dress, her wonderful golden-red hair long, falling down curly to her hips. She was there expecting Carina, so she was kneeling down welcoming the little girl with wide-open arms. Carina, with no sign of fear, was approaching Maria trustfully… then touching her face and caressing her long hair tenderly, asking, "Are you an Elvin?" "She is the Queen of the Elvins!" Karl explained smiling while Maria, blushing at Karl's compliment, was caressing the girl daintily, smiling, full of love and compassion.

Carina, continuously gazed at Maria's face: "Can you even perform magic?" Maria kept on smiling, and so Carina was smiling too: "How lovely you are, Queen of the Haunted Forest!"… giving a kiss to Maria…"But where is your magic wand?" she asked, curling her lips.

Maria was laughing silently: "Look, I'm doing it with my fingers!" … and so touching a blossom nearby, hundreds of little silver stars were sprinkling out immediately. Then touching some green leaves, they were becoming pink at once.

"Would you like to try it too?" Maria tenderly asked the little girl with the wondering great eyes. Carina nodded her head lightly; what she had seen has left her speechless. But Karl was giving Maria a sign… time to return into the body!

So Maria was standing up, carrying the little girl in her arms. "And now Carina watch! Karl will perform great magic." Karl said, "Now I'm conjuring you back to Mommy! She's just waiting for you ever so wishfully!"

We were back again in the great ambulance. Karl and I were watching the little girl awaken with wondering great eyes, smiling greatly to her beloved Mommy, saying, "You know, I have seen the Queen of the Haunted Forest. She has conjured me back to you!"

~ Participant Journal Excerpt ~

I walked into a meadow with wildflowers in the tall grasses. I could smell the scent of the wild flowers and feel the warmth of the sun on me. I saw some trees and horses in the near distance. Behind me on a small hill were a farmhouse and a barn. There were more horses and some other animals there. I heard the horses whinny and snort. They were running and seemed to be enjoying the freedom of running.

I was walking on a path through the meadow and I saw my friend Jean coming toward me, leading two saddled horses. I was so excited to see her. She passed several years back and I had not seen her for several years before that. I said hello and that I was so very glad to see her and she responded that she was glad to see me also. She asked me how my life had been in the years we had not seen each other and I told her it was good with my husband, children and grandchildren. I asked if she had been happy with her husband and she replied it was good.

She asked if I remembered all the fun we had in years past when we would laugh for no reason and we would go to dances when we were both single gals. I said I remembered and missed that contact of being best friends and doing all those crazy things we did. I asked why we grew in different ways and why we went different directions. She responded that it was time for us each to grow with the men that came into our lives. The men we each fell in love with had different likes and of course we each pursued those with them. It was not that we didn't care about each other anymore. Our bond of friendship has survived the physical life and is still intact. She said she wants to stay in touch with me now as when we were young. I said to her I never told her how much she meant to me or how I loved her personality and laugh. She said she knew how I loved her, as she felt the same about me.

I told her I had planned on coming to see her at the hospital the day she died. She said she did not want me to remember her the way she looked, so that was the reason she passed before I got there.

We rode the horses she brought for a bit and I asked what she did here. She replied that she has the horses to ease the transition for some children who struggle in their journey to this realm. She said they enjoy being with and playing with the animals. I told her she always had a way with animals and children.

My friend had had an abortion when she was a teenager. Now she introduced me to her daughter, Pamela.

She had no other children in her physical life. I thought it was wonderful that she was reunited with this child that she had to give up and that she can now be a mother to this child that she didn't get to enjoy in this Earth plane.

> *Craig's note: Unborn children or newly born children who pass grow up on the other side and are reunited with their parents when the parents pass, having grown to the age they would have been on the Earth plane.*

We rode back and I told her goodbye, that I loved spending time with her again and then made a personal joke we both understood and we laughed until tears ran down our faces. She said, "Return to your place of love and I will come to share more laughter and love with you."

As I came back, real tears came to my eyes as I have missed my friend so much and it was a blessing to laugh with her once again! What a beautiful experience.

~ *Participant Journal Excerpt* ~

As I lay in bed, trying to quiet my mind, I felt an urgency to get up and resume the Self-Guided Afterlife Connection program and do Stage 4. I felt my husband, Barry, was telling me that it was time.

It was pretty easy to find my quiet place and even though I haven't thought once about the peaceful tableau that is my place of connection, it came back to me as if I had just been thinking of it. My peaceful place is a cabin on the edge of a lightly wooded area, on the shore of a lake, with mountains in the distance. My place of connection is on the back porch with wooden chairs all along the back, as if we can all gather there. As I started listening to the meditation, I felt Barry just waiting on the sidelines for me to be done and to connect with him. When you, Craig, said to go to the place of Love, I didn't feel it right away, but then when you started the countdown from 20, I soon felt disjointed with my body and tears started pouring down my face.

When the prompt said to cross over to the afterlife, Barry took my hand and we walked off the porch. Our dog, Rinnie, was there running to greet me and was so excited that I was there. She jumped up on me and ran around Barry and me. Barry then led me to a neighboring cabin and said that this is where he lives. I asked who he lives with and he said his Grandpa Gene, my stepfather. I was extremely close with my "Dad" and he and Barry almost always come together when we have a reading with a medium. My dad was there to greet Barry when he crossed over.

Barry and I walked around the back of their cabin and my Dad was at a skill saw with goggles on. He saw me and we enjoyed a very strong hug. He said that he had built the cabin. My Dad was a general contractor in his Earth life and it doesn't surprise me that he is still building over there. He was very creative. I asked what he was building now and he showed me a sort of picture frame and another finished one on the inside of the cabin. The picture frame held a collage of pictures of our family. He/they said that just as we have pictures here to glance at lovingly, they like to have pictures there. It is as if we are with them.

We left my dad and walked along the shore of the lake. I asked Barry to show me around and we walked into the lake and swam down. Even though we didn't need them, we wore some sort of breathing mask underwater, but it wasn't connected to anything. I think this was to make me not anxious about being under the water. Also we scuba dived as a family and that was a good memory. We surfaced in a cave grotto and sat on the side, then lay back with our feet in the water. Above us, the sky was exposed and we saw stars and Earth. I had/have so many questions for Barry and was asking him question after question.

I had a miscarriage between my two children and I have begun to question and think about this soul we never met. I was 3 months along when I found out the baby had died, so it was a later miscarriage and I had to have a D&C. At the time, I was sad and even gave the baby a name of sorts (I didn't tell anyone), and have felt guilty lately that I don't remember the name. It has been over 21 years and when we got pregnant with our daughter, I didn't really think about the miscarriage anymore. I have now started thinking about this baby and have wanted to connect. I never knew if it was a boy or a girl and I asked Barry if I could meet this soul. He pointed out a dark haired girl and I gave her a long hug. I asked her what her name was and she said Jade. I tried to think of a different name, thinking that I would never pick Jade, but then realized that I was trying to direct what was happening. I then thought that maybe that is why I like the color green so much. Barry and I were going to continue on, so I took Jade's hand also.

~ Participant Journal Excerpt ~

I remembered the place of love I had been to before which was a beautiful field of daffodils full of sunlight. I saw myself walking in the field, but I was younger, about 16. Suddenly a big gust of wind pushed me backward and I couldn't keep my footing. It continued until it had blown me out of the field.

I found that I was standing still looking at a bright red engine. It was the engine of a model railway. It was on a floor and running on a track. It looked familiar, but I couldn't place it. Then I looked up and saw my father smiling down at me and I remembered that this was the model railway that he had built for my brother in the cellar for a Christmas gift and that I had come down to the cellar when I wasn't supposed to and I had seen it. I suppose I was about five or six at the time, but now I was a grown woman. My dad looked young, in his early 40s, and he was dressed in clothes from the 1940s. He looked much the way he had looked in pictures of when he and my mother were first married. They had married late in life. Dad had been 40 and Mum had been 35.

He was beaming at me. I asked him how he was and he said they were fine. Then I saw that my mother was standing next to him looking very pretty and very happy. She was also dressed in the style of the 1940s and looking very young. She looked extremely happy. Her name was Emma and Dad had always called her Em for short. He said, "Go on, tell her Em." She looked at him and smiled and then she said to me, "We Dance." I said to her, "You and Dad always did dance together." She said, "No, I really dance, we both do." I looked at her with a question on my face. She said, "I ballet dance." As she said that, I could feel myself tingle all over with excitement. She said, "And your father dances with me." Dad turned to me and said, "I have learned how to do it."

I was speechless; I didn't know what to say. I just smiled at them in wonder and excitement. Mum's face started to change and not be her face and I knew it was all fading away. Then the session ended.

It was a perfectly lovely experience. I'm still tingling writing this journal entry.

~ *Participant Journal Excerpt* ~

A man has a connection with his wife in spirit.
He has connected with her before in the same setting.

I am standing on the veranda of our house. She comes out of the front door. She's dressed in Victorian style again. She comes over and stands in front of me, head slightly tipped to her right. She smiles. I don't see her speak, or see her lips move, but she asks me how I'm feeling. I tell her fine, now. Again, that smile. She moves to my right side and hooks her arm in mine. We stand there looking at the green countryside before us. I realize that I am also dressed in Victorian style.

Then I hear the instructions about an opening with light coming through. I don't know how this can get any better; but I step through. I remember the Web page saying to let them run the show. It does get better.

We are swimming, or rather standing in water about shoulder deep for her. She is smiling at me and I feel her asking me if I remember being here with her. I can remember. It was shortly after our first anniversary, about a year before she died. It was a beautiful day, a beautiful time together. She smiles and says she is still here. That makes me feel better somehow. She kissed me on my right cheek. She placed the tips of the index and middle fingers of her right hand very gently under my chin and she kissed me. It was so familiar. I know it was something she frequently did when we were together. I don't know how I know it; but I do.

She "tells" me to concentrate on my current life. Our time will come, soon enough. She is always ready to listen and, if I need it, give me help. My current life must remain my main focus though. She knows me well. I want to follow up on this and develop it. As I am effectively on my own, I'd likely concentrate most of my energy on doing so.

The scenery, the view from the veranda was "correct" again. The city was gone. I felt relieved and very happy about that. I live in Paris, France. There is a lot of urbanization going on here. Perhaps seeing the city was a carry-over from that.

She came out of the house. I was close to tears, I was so happy seeing her. I know I'm seeing her true self, not a physical being. She is indescribably beautiful. She had her hair up when she was standing on the veranda with me. It was down when we were swimming. It is long, almost black and wavy. Her eyes are mostly green with some light brown around the iris.

When we stood on the veranda and the opening appeared, she looked at me with this smile. She was holding the right side of her lower lip in her teeth and the left side of her mouth was pulled slightly up. It was a smile full of mischief and fun. It was as if she was just waiting to see what I'd do.

While dictating my notes onto my recorder, I once again felt repeated "touches." It was like being told again that she's always there.

~ Participant Journal Excerpt ~

A woman connects with her twin brother who
passed into spirit on the day of their birth

I met my twin brother Kevin tonight; although I've had vague images of him in the past and have always felt him close by, I've never seen him up close like I did tonight. He has longer reddish brown hair that is parted in the center and reaches his chin in various similar lengths. He has a short beard and moustache. He looks like my dad, but he also looks like me. His eyes are blue like my dad's, and yet although I got my mother's darker looks and eyes, we have similar features. He is taller than me; he is about six foot one, and he leans over a little. We hugged each other. He's tall and reedy as a man, similar to my father. He was wearing a blue cotton shirt with a white t-shirt underneath and a pair of blue jeans. We met at the picnic table on Deer Island. He looks about mid-20s. He sees me as I am now, in my mid-50s and yet I don't feel that age meeting him; I feel as if we are on par.

I told him it was so good to see him. We sat on the top of the picnic table, him to my left, and we held hands, my left hand holding his right hand. I told him that I've missed him all my life, even though I've felt his presence often. He told me that he's always with me. I asked him about when we could be together again, when it would happen. He told me that it would happen, but that he could not elaborate why. He told me that there is knowledge in Spirit that, if I knew it now in my mortal form, it would "blow my mind"; that there are things that those in Spirit simply cannot reveal to those of us in mortal form while we are here, but that 'it will all make sense' when we cross over.

I am left with an impression that just this first meeting is all I can have tonight and I come out of the meeting with deep emotion; the image fades immediately. I feel tears on my cheeks to have actually held my brother's hand and to have hugged him. I miss him so much. I haven't seen him since I was one day old; he is my twin, my other half.

Having gone through these steps, I go immediately into contact as soon as I begin the countdown from 20 to 1.

It is wonderful being able to "be there"; I want to keep going and to go more deeply into these experiences and hopefully have them last longer. I keep seeming to get segments of info from loved ones, like little chapters, before the contact is cut off, sometimes instantly.

Validations

Many of the experiences result in validations that the Self-Guided Afterlife Connections are real connections with loved ones in Spirit. Below are three of them.

~ Participant Journal Excerpt ~

A woman finishes a connection with her
daughter, then sees the daughter of a friend.
This begins in the middle of the journal.

Then I saw a young girl/teenager. She had familiar features. The name Brenda came to me and I realized it's a friend of mine's daughter. She died in a rollover crash where she was pinned and asphyxiated. The kids with her were allegedly responsible for her being abandoned at the wreck. The feelings I got from her had nothing to do with that wreck or the people around her then. She hovered with me, morphing a bit so I saw her in different stages, ages. I saw her exploring. I heard her say, "I love mom. I miss mom." I saw some food item, rolled. It looked like a lobster roll, but with jalapeños. I was focused on it too much and it disappeared. I looked to the side and saw her as a little girl, rolling out dough, working on a red checked tablecloth, working so hard. She was darling! Then, I realized, "Oh, she misses doing this stuff with her mom." At least that's what I got from it.

Craig's note: The participant wrote the following in an e-mail a day later.

Well, how dee doo? I wrote Lauren [*mother of the little girl in the afterlife connection*] and told her the first part of it and how confused I was with the roll-ups that had jalapeños in them. I kept thinking, what on Earth! So, I wrote Lauren unsure of how much to tell her. I can never remember who is a believer and who isn't. Guess what? She writes back and says it makes sense to her. Yes, they made jalapeño roll-ups. WHAT.... I've NEVER heard of such a thing. Look, if I ever thought I was making this stuff up, well, I completely believe now. Where the hell did jalapeño roll-ups come from?

~ Participant Journal Excerpt ~

This woman saw a picture being moved in her experience, and later found out about the picture.

I first noticed I was in a park like setting—a beautiful fall scene with lots of reds. There was a park bench off to the left. Suddenly, a small boy, old enough to walk but not talk was in front of me looking up. He was wearing only a little green football jersey and a diaper. His jersey had the number 23 on it. It was green with white stripes. He had blond hair. He was shy, but wanting my attention. I noticed that while he looked at me, his little toes were pinching at the grass. He was holding someone's hand but I couldn't see the person.

Suddenly a little girl appeared, who was Asian, perhaps three or four years old. She had a picture in her hand. It was a picture she had been coloring. It was amazing! The detail, while abstract in nature, and the many colors she chose and how she used them was really, truly amazing! She was carrying it around like any child her age would do. It was getting bent and folded from the wear and tear of being carried around — and I was thinking, "Oh no! That's amazing! It should be framed and perhaps presented to an art school for display!" She was so excited. She took me by the hand and led me to the park bench where she had been coloring and I could see all her art pencils scattered around on the bench. She didn't talk with words. But I could feel her excitement and she was very comfortable with me.

Next, I saw an aunt on my dad's side that I've always felt very close to even though we didn't really have a chance to know one another in life. I was named after her. However, she died when she was 18 years old — and I was only 3 at the time. She was not talking to me, but showing me scenes from her lifetime. I saw her at her wedding, and then I saw her sitting at a table, somewhat bored looking, and then I watched her make a peanut butter and jelly sandwich, and before she ate it, she smashed it all down really flat. I have no idea if she liked her sandwiches that way, but I hope to find out. In any case, the next thing I know I'm at my grandmother's house (her mother) and I'm seeing this giant portrait of my aunt (that's really there!) and I see it being taken down, and being moved around...but then I became aware that this was difficult for someone, that they wanted to move the portrait but couldn't bring themselves to do it. I wasn't sure what that meant.

I was talking with my mother the next day and I told her about what I had seen. As it turns out, my sister's daughter was visiting. She and my sister live in my grandmother's old house and my niece and my sister had talked about moving my aunt's portrait because they had something else they wanted to hang but my sister just couldn't bring herself to do it. The house has pretty much remained the same since my grandmother passed in 2005. I haven't been to the house since my grandmother passed. Anyway, my niece said that when her mother wasn't home, she took down the portrait of my aunt....and so the portrait has been removed and this picture from Italy is now in its place. My niece felt horrible when my mother told her what I had seen, but my mother reassured her that it was not that my aunt was unhappy about the move of her picture, but that this was something that would be validated for me.

I was very excited! I mean, how cool!

~ Participant Journal Excerpt ~

The participant meets and learns the name of someone she doesn't know, and her grandmother validates who it was.

[*Before the session*] I told my grandmother [*still living on the Earth plane*] about my first experience and she was very open and interested. The fact that my grandpa in spirit had said "My Camille" meant something to her. She asked me to try to meet her mother next time I did this.

I had another connection with my grandfather. I followed pretty much the same steps as the last experience. Towards the beginning I sort of felt like I was on the edge of fully being there with him and not being there at all. He grabbed me and I had a sensation of movement, sort of further into his realm. And he said to me that the difference between where I was a moment ago and where I am now was just an illusion. He "moved" me deeper in, but said that it was only a representation for the mind, nothing more.

Grandma had asked me to try and meet her mother next time I did this. So once I was connected with my grandpa again I said that Grandma wanted me to do this.

Nothing happened except that I saw in my mind's eye an photograph of a woman. Then I heard Mabel, Mabel, Mab This went on about five times. I was thinking that maybe that was my grandma's mother's name. So I asked my grandpa, "Who's Mabel?" He suddenly had his arm around a teenage girl and he said that this was my grandma's sister who died when they were girls. Mabel was nice and the three of us talked for quite a while. I imagined a tree and it appeared. We all sat and laid under it for a while. They answered many of my questions, mostly pertaining to spiritual topics.

Once the session ended, I went and talked to my grandma. I said I was with Grandpa and was going to try and meet her mother but then heard the name Mabel several times. As soon as I said that name, my grandma said "Oh, my sister. She died when she was 16."

It was a great experience!

Links to More Journals and Information

Links to many more journals, the study of Self-Guided Afterlife Connections, and explanations about the procedure are online at http://ascsi.org/conference/resources.htm.

Meditation Connections

Maria Pe, Esq.

On June 21, 2011, Maria Pe experienced the unimaginable—the murder of her two teenaged sons, Sean and Kyle, by their own father. In her struggle to survive the overwhelming loss, Maria embarked on a profound spiritual journey to find her sons and continue her relationship with them. Well-educated and trained as an attorney, Maria was skeptical, but she began learning everything she could about the afterlife, meditating, and keeping a journal. Starting with simple meditations and opening herself to the possibilities of existence beyond the physical body, Maria learned how to connect with Sean and Kyle through her "journeys" to the Upper Realm. With her sons' help and encouragement, Maria not only survived her tragic experience, but learned how to embrace life on Earth again.

By sharing her experiences day by day in her book and this chapter, Maria shows us that we all have the ability to communicate with loved ones on the other side and to learn and receive guidance from them. And through her story, Maria shows us that from unbearable pain and loss can come self-discovery and the strength and courage to continue life's journey.

Maria I. Pe was born in Manila, Philippines, and raised in the San Diego area. She received her bachelor's degree from Harvard University and her law degree from the University of San Diego School of Law. She has practiced law and worked in business and government for 30 years. She currently works in local government.

The author's profits from book sales will be donated to the Sean & Kyle Imagine Fund. Visit the website at seanandkyleimaginefund.com for more information about Sean and Kyle, and to learn about the projects that promote their ideals of peace, love, excellence, and integrity. The book is also available for FREE in PDF or Kindle versions on the website.

Journey to the Upper Realm

Excerpts from *Journey to the Upper Realm: How I Survived the Deaths of My Sons and Learned to Communicate With Them on the Other Side*

by Maria Pe

Prologue

On June 21, 2011, my two sons began their transition to the Other Side. At the time, I didn't see it that way.

Tuesday, June 21, 2011, was a normal morning for me. I finished getting ready for work and was just about to leave the house. I was ready to click the TV off when the news story caught my attention: Murder-Suicide in Bonita. The camera panned to a neighborhood and I saw the house across the street from my ex-husband Tom's house. My heart began to beat faster; panic began to set in. The news reporter indicated that a man and two young boys had been killed.

My heart began beating even faster. I called Tom's home phone. No answer. I called Tom's cell phone. Voicemail. I called Sean's cell phone. Voicemail. I called Kyle's cell phone. Voicemail. No. No. No. No. I rushed out of the house and got into my car. I drove the six miles to Tom's house. I was in a state of panic and disbelief. There is no way this could be my sons! I got to the neighborhood, which was filled with news crews. The area was cordoned off with yellow crime scene tape. I parked my car in someone's driveway and ran down the street to the first police officers I saw. "Tell me that it's not my sons," I begged them. "Please tell me it's not my sons." They escorted me to the house across the street. A man came and asked me my ex-husband's name. My son's names. Sean. Kyle. He confirmed that it was their house. Then he said that there had been gunshots. No! No, no, no, no, no! I crumpled to the ground. There were no words. There were no words possible.

My ex-husband, Tom, had killed my sons, Sean and Kyle. He had given them sleeping pills to make them fall into a deep sleep, then he had shot them while they slept in their own beds. Then he had shot himself.

This is how my journey began.

The book is the story of my journey—my "Journey to the Upper Realm." It is the story of my experience during the 13 months after my boys were killed, day by day, as it was happening. It is my story of how I survived the deaths of my sons and learned to communicate with them on the other side. And ultimately, how I found myself on the road to forgiveness.

This chapter contains excerpts from the book that show the milestones along the journey that I took.

Prior to my sons' deaths, I had never kept a journal, but I started writing in a journal shortly after my sons died. I didn't really know why, but I felt that I had to record my thoughts, feelings, and the things that I learned along my journey. Through the process of writing the book, it finally became clear to me why I had been keeping daily journals about my experiences. I was "guided" to write the book by my sons, and by Spirit. I understand now that the book is part of my remaining work here and my contribution in this lifetime.

This is my journey. It is my Truth. And the gift that I received.

Day 5 — June 26, 2011

Email from Susan: I'm thinking and praying for you and your family. I may wait until after the burial to pay my respects at the cemetery for the boys when it's more quiet....if that's ok. I know it's not the same, but my collie Dillon (who would become an important figure in my journey) recently passed away and I have been terribly depressed for a few weeks; then with the boys now, it's made it worse. I'm a pretty private person, so I would like to go to the cemetery after. I went to the little memorial their friends put at the house....they were very loved, and hopefully your niece and Tony told you I called twice. It's heartbreaking for those left behind when you lose those you loved.

Day 20 — July 10, 2011

When we got home from Mexico today, I was feeling the most intense pain and grief. It was unbearable. Then a thought popped into my head: "Marcie." Shannon said that her sister Marcie had "checked on the boys" and they were doing okay. Marcie is a shamanic practitioner, but how could she "check" on them? Did she really see them? Did she talk to them? What did they say? I need to talk to her. I need to find out if there is a way for me to still have a relationship with my sons, to still see them and talk to them and touch them. I don't know how, but I need to find out if there is a way.

Day 22—July 12, 2011

Woke up in anguish. Thoughts of you, Kyle, filled my head and the pain of loss filled my entire being.

I called Marcie to see what she had learned when she "checked in on the boys."

Notes from my phone conversation with Marcie about her meeting with the boys:

- I was with the boys on July 5. They are not with their father and they will not be with him; they are with family members and other loved ones they knew. There is a dog with them that seems to support them.

  Sean had more awareness of what had happened and the shock had decreased; he had more understanding. Their guardian angels were with them, but they had not gone to the other side yet. They were feeling the pull to go to the other side, and they understood that they could still reach you, but you will need to be able to receive their energy. Their guardian angels will teach them how to connect with you.

  They were very concerned about you. They were worried that you would leave this realm before your time. Kyle did not want to go until he was assured that they could still talk to you after they crossed.

And Sean did not want to cross over without Kyle. Kyle wanted to connect with you and your energy, but there were so many "people around" and he was having a hard time getting through to you. He asked me, "Why are there so many strangers?" I explained to him that there are many people who love them and want to help, and that those people are sending love and healing energy to them. I showed him how to block out the other energies and how to feel only your energy. I told him to put up a shield or a barrier and to focus on what he wanted to feel and receive, and then only your energy would be allowed through.

They understood then that they could still reach you in your realm, and I assured them that they could talk to you directly sometime in the future. They know that you are working on it, and I told them that you have a lot of support. They will want to hear directly from you and they are watching over you. They are very concerned about you and about maintaining your bond together.

Marcie then assured me that I could have my own contacts with my boys. I just needed to learn how, be patient, and practice. She gave me the following instructions.

- As humans, she said, we need to balance our four "bodies" — the physical, intellectual, emotional and spiritual bodies. The spiritual body is how we connect to the other realm. I need to get my spiritual body balanced with the others, so it is not dominated. I need to trust that my spiritual body is as real as the other bodies.

- How do I get better on the spiritual side? Teach my conscious mind to shift, and keep the four bodies in balance; balance the spiritual body with the others. In this realm we tend to shut the spiritual body down. We will do emotional body healing work to release emotions, then get the spiritual body balanced with the other three bodies. We will use guided meditations and learn new skills.

- Homework—spend time sitting quietly, eyes closed, then just listen and feel. Write down whatever you hear or feel, and don't judge it.

I did my first short 10-minute meditations in my backyard, sitting quietly in a chair with my eyes closed. I recorded my experiences in my journal immediately afterwards. This is my first journal entry:

Meditation journal: *What I <u>heard</u>: leaves rustling in the wind; wind; leaves brushing up against the planter; small planes; large planes; a bird chirping; children's voices; a car; clanging; machinery beeping; buzzing fly; wind chimes; a dog barking; birds wailing; helicopter. What I <u>felt</u>: the breeze; chills; warmth of the sun; the boys through colors (deep purple with blue veins, shots of neon green with a blue dot; bright orange; many colors); energy from the sun; calm; peaceful; serene; comfortable.*

Day 25—July 15, 2011

Sean and Kyle, I will do what I need to do to continue to receive your gifts of love and beauty. I am with you always, always, always in my heart, soul and being. Your mother and friend forever. Love, love, love you!!

I then performed two 10-minute meditations.

Meditation journal entry: _Heard_: birds, footsteps on the path. _Felt_: anguish in stomach, sadness, anger, hopelessness, asking why, why did this have to happen? Why do I have to stay here another day? I just want to be with you! Why can't I just be with you now? How much pain and hurt and anguish must I endure? It is so hard, it hurts so much. Sometimes I fear that I cannot endure it. Oh boys! I need your help. I am seeking and receiving help here too. Please continue to send me your energy. I will keep trying, I will endure the pain if it is what I must do to be with you again. I miss you so much, please be with me.

The second meditation journal entry: _Heard_: strong wind gusts; plane; leaves rustling. _Felt_: Sean, very strong, talked with him. He showed me my power and strength in pink. He said he is OK and Kyle is OK. Told him that Kyle and he are lucky to have each other. He said everything is right, this is right. "Keep trying, Mom, promise me you will keep trying." "I promise, Honey, I promise, but it hurts so much. Why does it have to hurt so much?" "You will see, Mom; it is the right thing, the right way. Trust yourself." "I need your help, Sean." "Mom, I am always with you, and you are always with me and Kyle. We are always with you; we are in your cells." "I don't want to open my eyes, Honey. I just want to stay here with you just like this." "It's OK, Mom, you can be OK in this realm. It's OK for you to open your eyes. I will still be with you." "Oh, I love you, Sean, I love you." "I love you too, Mom."

Day 27—July 17, 2011

I AM HERE
I AM WITH YOU
I AM PEACE

The meditation work is difficult. I try to connect with Spirit and honor my intellect/ego so I will continue to have complete faith in the Universe and erase all doubts and fears that continue to pop up in my human ego. The human condition is a painful one at times, yet mysteriously peaceful at other times when Spirit is strongly present. My "human" being hopes that my number will come up soon. The ache immobilizes me. The sadness is greater than anything I have ever felt. Why do I continue to yearn for Sean and Kyle in their human physical forms? It is so hard to be satisfied with connecting with them in Spirit even though I now know that Spirit is the only lasting reality. It must be part of the learning process in human form. I know so little about the vastness of the Universe and its plan, and I accept that I will likely never know in this realm. I must accept and keep faith that Spirit will lead me where I am meant to be.

Today's meditation journal: *What I heard—planes, wind, metal sign clanging against fence, leaves rustling, cars. What I felt—sadness, anguish, Sean and Kyle. I saw my bright pink being supported by the vibrant green and blue of my boys; showing me my strength and that they would support me, protect me, lift me.*

Day 36—July 26, 2011

Sean and Kyle are with me as I wake, almost as if to try to prevent or lessen the pain of loss that creeps into the pit of my stomach as I awaken from sleep. The growth of my spiritual being has skyrocketed. I think it is an incredible price to pay for the evolution of my consciousness, too high a price for anyone to pay. That's why it feels so unfair and somehow wrong. I find myself wishing it was not true, not real, but I know that is a waste of time because it has happened and I am left here to survive and endure. It sucks.

Today's meditation journal: *Heard—planes, cars, leaves, dog barking, cat collar bell, brother in kitchen. Felt—lots of chills, itchiness, tingling, warm sun, nice breeze, told the boys I am confused, but I know they know what they are doing. Asked Sean for help. "Trust, Mom, trust yourself. You know what is right, what feels right. Go with that and <u>KNOW</u> what is right." Bright pink colors showing my Spirit energy. "You see, Mom, you are strong; you know what is right for you." Felt peace, and calm.*

Day 37—July 27, 2011

My only hope now is that I will be able to learn how to go to the boys' realm and be with them. I feel that it will be the only way for me to get any comfort in this cruel Earthly existence. I miss you guys so much. Please be with me, stay with me. I ache with loss for you. Help me to stay strong, trust, and keep faith that all is as it should be and that I am doing the right thing. I love you, I love you, I love you!

Today's meditation journal: *Heard—voices, laughter, leaves in the wind, planes, traffic. Felt—strong powerful breeze (the boys showing me their Spirit strength), love. "Mom, do you see you are a magnificent Spirit? Do you see how strong you are? You taught us so much and now we are strong." Blue dot bigger now, with green neon around it. Sean and Kyle are together as always; they will always be together; they are meant to be together. They are bonded Spirits with incredible love and respect for each other. They make me so strong; my bright pink Spirit is so powerful and getting stronger every day. My boys are amazing!*

Day 41—July 31, 2011

I love you Sean, I love you Kyle. Please keep guiding me, please keep helping me. I need you now more than I have ever needed anything in my life. I need you to sustain me so I can do what I am meant to do here, to honor you, to honor you as boys, as young men, as amazing role models and leaders, and as tremendous and powerful Spirits. I am so humbled and honored by you. I cherish my role as mother to you. Oh how I love you.

Today's meditation journal: *Heard umbrella cover blowing in the wind, planes, leaves, breeze. Felt breeze, lots of chills, especially in my midsection, peace, love, comfort. Boys were everywhere in front of me. Sean first with his wash of green. Kyle's image/silhouette inside of my pink Spirit. Blue and green ribbons and veins of color, so beautiful and so comforting. I thought about Lina, the boys' caretaker during the first five years of their lives, because she has passed into spirit. "Is Lina with you, boys?" Pink heart.*

I was having lunch with Susan today. We were talking about the boys and her dog, Dillon, who had passed away on May 27, about three weeks before the boys were killed. When she said that Dillon was so mellow and that he was like the dog version of Sean, it suddenly occurred to me that the dog Marcie had mentioned in our conversation on July 12 was Dillon. Susan said Dillon was a brown and white collie. I made a mental note to ask Marcie about the dog the next time I talked to her.

Day 42—Aug. 1, 2011

I was having a really hard time this morning. I talked to Marcie and felt a lot better, hopeful about what I am going to learn and experience soon. I asked her about the dog that was with the boys when she saw them on July 5. She said that it was standing between the boys and tended to stay close to Kyle. I asked her what it looked like and she said that it was brown and white and looked like a collie! There are no coincidences! It gives me comfort knowing that Dillon is with Sean and Kyle. He was very calm and peaceful, and I am sure he is comforting to the boys, especially Kyle.

Today's meditation journal: *Heard planes, breeze, leaves, church bells. Felt Sean's incredible bright green dot, then his image/outline; then it was inside of my pink Spirit. "Sean, you are amazing and powerful!! I love you buddy, I love you so much!"*

Day 52—Aug. 11, 2011

We arrived at Marcie's home in Alturas, California this afternoon. The tears began to flow as soon as I saw Marcie. I feel so much emotion, and so much hope.

Day 53—Aug. 12, 2011

More information from Marcie about her meeting with the boys on July 5:

- The boys were accompanied by two men dressed in suits. Their mannerisms and appearances were identical to each other. They did not say anything. They just stayed close to the boys, behind them with their hands folded over each other, very business-like and professional.

- At the vestibule, the boys were greeted by two women and a man. The woman who stepped forward was petite, had a round face, and looked like she was related to me. She was smiling and very inviting (Lina!). The other woman also looked related to me (my mom?). The man was older and Caucasian. The boys were comfortable and happy to see them. They crossed over and the collie (Dillon) went with them. She said Dillon was in the Animal Realm.

I asked Marcie about the Animal Realm and she invited me to lie on the floor with her and meditate together to go to the Animal Realm ourselves. We lay on the floor holding hands and went together to the Animal Realm.

The way to the Animal Realm was through a meadow to a large tree. We had to get into a hollow in the tree and climb down to the Animal Realm.

Dillon was in the Animal Realm when we went there, but I did not see him. Marcie talked to him. He said he was with the boys when they crossed over because it was what he was supposed to do. He was waiting for the boys until they arrived at the transition point. (Marcie had never seen a dog crossing over with people into the other realm.)

Later that day, I went back to the Animal Realm alone in my meditation.

Today's meditation journal—Journey to the Animal Realm:

Started in the meadow. Walked down the path to the large tree and climbed into the tree, then went down. Landed in a lush tropical jungle. Saw a yellow snake that scared me. Saw a black panther, then a tiger. The black panther stayed with me. We lay down on the grass. I asked him if he was my animal guide, and he said yes. He let me pet him for a while, and he stayed with me. Then he said he had to go. He jumped onto a high tree limb, then said again that he had to go. I said, no, wait, don't leave me, and I started to cry. I felt so alone and scared. I made my way back to the tree, climbed up and out, and walked back up the path. I was OK by then.

Day 55—Aug. 14, 2011

Marcie told me that today's meditation would be very special. It would be my first meditation to go to what she called the Upper Realm, where I would be able to meet with the boys. She said that I would not meet the boys the first time I went there. I would meet my guide first and create the sacred space where I would be able to meet the boys. I would then leave, but return in the next meditation to meet the boys.

Two others would be there: Snowball, my cat now in spirit, and Black Panther, whom I had learned is my animal guide. Marcie told me that I would arrive in a meadow and would see a well. I was to cast into it all Earthly cares and burdens before entering the Upper Realm. I would then go to the edge of a cliff, get onto a cloud, and travel up to the Upper Realm. There, I would meet my guide.

This is my journal account:

Today's meditation journal—Journey to the Upper Realm:

Walked from the meadow to the well. Dropped a heavy object (kind of like a bowling ball) into the well. It symbolized my troubles that I was leaving behind for this meditation. I turned around and walked through the meadow to the edge of the cliff. I got onto a cloud and travelled up to the Upper Realm. I landed in a garden and got off the cloud. I walked to a white marble bench and sat down. A man sat next to me and put his arm around me. He said his name was Michael, my guide! I leaned against him, feeling comforted. I suddenly remembered that one morning I had been wakened by a clear, distinct voice asking for "Michael."

We got up and walked a short distance out of the garden to a grass area where there was a big leafy tree. Under the tree, there was a picnic area with a U-shaped bench and a table. Just enough room for three people to sit around the table—the sanctuary. There were plates of fruit. Snowball, my beloved cat, was there sitting on the cushion on the bench. Black Panther lay down behind the benches. It was as if we were just waiting for the boys to come. I could feel Sean's energy and I could picture him sitting with me at our picnic table. I sat holding Snowball. I was so happy to see him again, and he was happy to see me. I felt the old familiar feelings of love and comfort toward him. Michael stood nearby watching quietly. I pictured the favorite fruits and sweets of the boys sitting on the table just waiting until they arrived.

But this visit to the Upper Realm was not to be the one where I would meet with my boys. After a little while, Michael said it was time to go, so I walked back to the garden. Michael stayed near the picnic table and bench, watching me as I left. I got back on the cloud and came back to the cliff, then to the meadow and back to the physical realm.

Second meditation journal—Journey to the Upper Realm:

Started in the meadow, walked to the well and dropped in my troubles, some small stones. Walked up the path to the cliff edge and got onto the cloud. Got to the garden and went to the bench. Michael arrived and asked me if I was ready. I said yes. I was very excited. We walked hand in hand to the sanctuary. I looked at the picnic table but the boys were not there yet. I turned to my right and the boys were there. They came to me and hugged me. I took Kyle's face in my hands and kissed him. I hugged Sean and he held me and looked down at me. I was so happy to see them. We walked over to the picnic table and sat down, me in the middle, Sean on my right and Kyle on my left. They showed me that they had left a small corner of agar for me. They were eating the fruit on the table.

Sean said, "Mom, remember when we had these in China?" and he held up a fresh lychee fruit. I said, "Yes!" Then I asked Kyle if he knew about Coach Gil's message and he said, "Yeah, Mom, I know." I asked them if they had any regrets. Kyle said he misses playing football, but he is watching all the games and the start of

the new NFL season. Sean said he still plays the guitar. I asked
Sean if I should give or loan the drum set to Andrew because
Andrew is starting a band called Sean's Band. Sean said, "It's up
to you, Mom. I'm ok with it, but you need to decide if you want to
do that."

I touched their hands and their faces and kissed them. Then
Michael said it was time to go. The boys said they would come
there again. Sean said, "See, Mom, see how great it is for us here?
You are doing really great, Mom." We got up from the table, and
they started to walk away to the right. I ran to them for one last
hug. They both held me and kissed me. Michael took me by the
hand and led me back to the garden where I got back on the cloud
and came back down to the cliff, then the meadow.

Day 60 — Aug. 19, 2011

Very early this morning, the boys came into my room
to hug me and kiss me. There was also a little girl with them.
It was so REAL, so tangible. I could see and feel them so
clearly. They were so loving. I was hugging the three of
them and telling them they were my favorite "three little
ones." It was so real, so tangible — their skin, their hair, their
faces, touching them, kissing them. It was amazing.

Today's meditation journal: Journey to the Upper Realm:

Started in the meadow, walked to the well, dropped in
gravel of troubles, turned and walked up the path to the cliff edge
with Panther. We both got onto the cloud to the Upper Realm and
landed in the garden. We walked to the bench. Michael met us
there and greeted us. We all walked together to the sanctuary. I
started to cry with tears of joy and emotion as I anticipated seeing
the boys. They came running from the right. They hugged and
kissed me as I cried and cried. Kyle squeezed me tight. We walked
to the table. Sean sat in the middle this time, Kyle on the right, me

on the left. Snowball jumped up onto Kyle's lap. The boys were happy to have Snowball. I asked if Dillon came to see them. They said yes. Then I said that Snowball would probably like Dillon and they said, "Yeah, Mom, he does."

It was so nice just to sit with them and feel their energy. We sat together petting Snowball. As we looked at Michael and Panther standing nearby, Sean asked, "Mom, do you like your animal guide?" "Yes!" "It's pretty cool, huh, Mom. Panther is like a bigger version of Snowball." We smiled and laughed. I asked them if they could help Conner because he is having a hard time. Kyle said, "Tell Conner that we are OK, Mom, and that we will help him. Tell him that he will be OK." "I will tell him, Honey, but if you can show him as many signs as possible, I think it will really help him a lot." They said, "OK, Mom."

Michael was standing nearby with Panther who was sitting patiently next to him. Michael said, "It's time to go." I was not making much of a move to go. I wanted to sit with my boys. When my alarm went off, Michael said, "Ok, it's really time to go now." I got up from the table. Kyle hugged me first and lifted me up. Sean hugged me and patted my head in a cute teasing way since he is taller than I am. I left with Michael and made my way back with Panther. As we got into the meadow, I patted Panther and said goodbye, then made my way back to the physical realm.

Day 68—Aug. 27, 2011

Today's meditation journal—Journey to the Animal Realm:

Walked quickly to the well and dropped in pebbles. Panther was waiting at the tree for me. I went down with him and landed in the jungle. I saw lots of big cats around. There was a stream with an alligator. I sat in the clearing with Panther and asked for Dillon. He appeared and sat down with us. I asked him what he was doing with the boys. He said he was their power animal and was supposed to wait for them when they came to the Other Side.

I looked down into an area of the jungle that was dark and cold. I asked Panther what it was. He said, "It is a dark place that you will go to see one day, but not now." I was not worried but trusted what he was telling me. I enjoyed a little time with Dillon and Panther. Then I had a lot of thoughts about the mundane Earthly realm. I pulled myself back into the journey. When I came back up the tree trunk, I entered the meadow and came back to the physical realm. I noticed a sharp pinprick type of sensation in my left index finger while I was down there, and on the return, I felt the same sensation in my right index finger.

Day 70—Aug. 29, 2011

Today's meditation journal—Journey to the Upper Realm:

Started in the meadow, walked to the well, dropped in a heavy, dark object and watched it plop. Panther joined me and we walked to the cliff and boarded the cloud. We went up, and I could see the Earth below us, lots of tiny trees, houses, etc. We passed through clouds and landed at the Upper Realm clearing. I walked to the white bench. Michael appeared from the right and greeted us wordlessly with a nod. We all walked to the sanctuary.

The boys were standing to the right. I walked to them and we hugged quietly, Sean on my right, Kyle on my left. "Hi, Mom." "Hi guys." We turned and walked to the table. Sean scooted into the seat first, then me, then Kyle. They started eating lychee fruits. Kyle was touching my face and hair, and hugging me. He said, "You look so pretty, Mom." "Thank you, Honey." I smiled at him.

I told them what I had decided about Ping, their cat. "I want to give Ping away. I want to simplify my life and get ready to come to you." Sean said, "Do what you feel is right, Mom, just find a good home for her. If you feel like it's the right thing, it's OK with me. You have been trying to do the right thing all along, haven't you?" "Yes, Honey, but I know I just want to make sure you guys are OK with it." Kyle said, "It's OK, Mom." Sean said, "Mom, you know you will be with us soon. It feels like time passes slowly there, but here it is fast. We will be here waiting for you, but you still have a lot to do there. We are doing our work up here and you are doing your work down there. You will see. Someday you will know what we know. You will know as much as we do and you will understand. So keep doing what feels right. Trust yourself, Mom."

"Thank you, honey, I am trying. I will do my best. Dillon says he is your guide." "Yes, Mom, we see him." They called Dillon out, and he appeared, came over to Kyle and put his head on the seat next to Kyle. Kyle petted his head gently. Dillon was very calm and serene. He lay down in front of the table. "Susan says he likes to be called Dilly Dil." "Mom, he watches over her and Annie too." "Yes, he is a good dog, and a good guide for you." "Yeah, Mom, we really love him."

Michael stepped up to the table and said, "It's time to go." I turned and hugged and kissed Sean. He touched my face and held me. "I love you, Mom." "I love you too, Sweetheart." Kyle scooted out, then me, and we embraced. He touched my hair and face again. "I love you, Mom." "I love you too, buddy." He sat back down and he and Sean stayed at the table eating fruit. Dillon got up and I held his face. "Take care of my boys." "I always do."

I walked with Michael and Panther back to the garden. Michael stood by the bench as Panther and I continued into the clearing to the cloud. Michael gave me a comforting, knowing look. Panther and I boarded the cloud and went back down to the cliff. We walked back to the meadow. I got down on my knees and hugged him goodbye. I AM HERE. I AM LOVE, he seemed to say to me. Then I turned, went to the meadow and returned to the Earth realm.

Day 75—Sept. 3, 2011

Lately I am really feeling the loss of my boys in this realm and their physical beings. I struggle with it, especially in the mornings when I open my eyes and see their pictures. Please come to me my boys, please help me. I still need your help so badly. I feel like a very weak human being even though I am supposed to be a strong spirit.

My work is to move the love I have for my sons from the outside to the inside. As painful as it is to no longer be able to see, hear, or touch my sons physically, I must learn to feel my children as part of my heart forever, knowing that LOVE never dies. Grief is the price I pay for having loved, and my pain is none other than the result of the joy with which my children have blessed me.

Today's meditation journal—Journey to the Upper Realm:

Started in the meadow, walked down to the well, noticing the tall delicate grass and the small flowers. I held a glowing ball of energy over the well, which was rushing with water. I dropped the ball into the water and a bright glow emanated up when it hit the bottom. I turned and walked by the tree trunk. Panther emerged and we greeted each other. Then we walked to the cliff edge and boarded the cloud. It went up and up through the mist to the Upper Realm. As we rose, I recalled that I had dreamt about Rosemary Smith's sons, Drew and Jeremiah, last night in my sleep.

We got to the garden and walked through the clearing. Michael was standing to the side of the bench, partially obstructed by the plants. He said, "You're doing better now." I said, "Yes." I could see the sanctuary and the boys already seated at the table. We walked there and the boys greeted me, "Hi, Mom." "Hi buddies!" Kyle got up from his seat on the left and hugged and kissed me.

Dillon was lying in front of the table. I walked to the other side of the table and Sean got up and hugged and kissed me. I held his face in my hands for a few seconds. I saw that Snowball was sitting on the bench, so Kyle said, "Mom, get in on this side because Snowball is over there." So I scooted into the middle. Then Kyle sat down again.

I asked them, "What have you been doing?" Sean said, "Mom, we are so busy learning so many new things." Kyle said, "Yeah, Mom, the stuff we are learning here is incredible, stuff about the Universe, how everything works. It makes the science and math we were learning down there look like total elementary beginner stuff!" "That's so great, guys." I asked them about Lina and told them that I want to see her sometime.

Then I told them, "I'm sleepy and tired, guys, and so I better go back." "Okay, Mom." I hugged and kissed Sean, then Kyle, then made my way back to the garden and the clearing with Panther and Michael. Michael held my hand briefly as we extended our arms. Panther and I got back down to the cliff, and the meadow. I said goodbye to Panther and held his chin in my hand.

Day 124—Oct. 22, 2011

I wake with emptiness, but the boys are once again with me, especially Sean. His neon green fills my field of vision so often. His presence is clear. Sean, my lovely sweet boy, you and Kyle will sustain me through this, won't you? I know you will keep me going and keep me strong.

Today's meditation journal—Journey to the Upper Realm:

Started in the meadow. It was very bright. The sun was shining, the grass was green and tall, and there were butterflies all around. I walked down to the well. I felt youthful, having the sense of a young mother. I recalled sensations of welcoming my sons into the world. I held my hand out over the well, and a ball of bright yellow/white energy hovered above them. I dropped it down into the well and when it hit bottom, light shot up into the sky. Everything turned a white light, almost translucent. I turned and walked up the path to the tree trunk. Panther came out and Tiger with him. I had met Tiger in the Animal Realm.

They walked with me up the path to the cliff and I got onto the cloud. They followed. We rose up into the sky, which was dark like space, but sparkling with stars and lights. We got to the Upper Realm and they got off the cloud first, then me. We walked around the clearing and met Michael on the other side. He looked at Tiger and seemed to say, "Oh, you brought another friend. Very nice." We continued on to the sanctuary.

Panther and Tiger lay down on the grass off to the side. I waited, looking at the mist, and a few seconds later, the boys emerged and Dillon was with them, staying close to Kyle. They walked over to me and said, "Hi, Mom!" "Hi, guys!" We hugged briefly. Then Kyle took off into the grass area with Dillon. They were playing, running, and jumping, and Kyle was flipping.

Sean stood close to me with his arm around my shoulder. "Look how tall you are now," I said to him. He smiled. He had his head leaning on mine and there was a sense of his protecting me, taking care of me. "I am always watching over you, Mom, just like this." "Thank you, Honey. I know. I feel you." We stood watching Kyle and Dillon, enjoying their playfulness and energy. After a little while, Kyle came over and put his arms around my waist and held me tightly while Sean stayed close on my right side. He rubbed Kyle's head playfully, and Kyle said, "Hey!" They laughed.

Then they said, "Let's take Mom for a ride." I said, "OK, but not too high. You know I am a chicken." "We've got you, Mom." They lifted me up into the air and we floated around the sanctuary, not too high. We floated over to Michael. Sean said, "Hey Michael, isn't my mom doing great?" Michael nodded, smiled and said, "Yes, wonderfully, wonderfully." We floated around to the other edge of the sanctuary where Dillon had lain down with Panther and Tiger.

Kyle said, "Come on, Dillon, it's time to go." Dillon got up and walked over to Kyle. We all walked to the edge of the mist. The boys turned to me and hugged me. "See you later, Mom. I love you, Mom. Love you, Mom." "I love you, my angels." They both smiled at that. Then I did too, realizing how accurate that title was for them. I used to call them "angel" when I put them to bed. I would say, "Goodnight, Angel." They truly are now.

I watched as they disappeared into the mist. Then I turned and walked over to Panther and Tiger, and they got up and we walked over to Michael. We walked back to the garden. Then Michael left us. We walked back to the cloud and got on. Tiger sat next to me and Panther was at my feet. We went back down to the cliff edge and got off the cloud, them first, then me. I walked with them down the path. Then the two of them "hugged" me and went down the tree trunk.

I walked back to the meadow and stood for a few moments taking in the beauty, and marveling at the feeling. It was so beautiful, so peaceful, such an amazing reality. But I knew I had to return to my body and the physical plane. I came back slowly, then opened my eyes.

Day 148—Nov. 15, 2011

Today's meditation journal—Journey to the Upper Realm:

Started in the meadow. The grass was tall. I walked down to the well and held my hands out above it. Fine white sand slipped from my hands down into the water. The sky was pale; everything was still and calm. I turned and walked up the path to the tree trunk. I waited a few seconds. Panther came out. I knelt down and hugged him. I could feel his loving energy. He knew that I have been hurting. We walked up the path to the cliff. He got onto the cloud first, then me. We rose up into the sky.

We reached the Upper Realm and got off the cloud and walked into the garden clearing. Panther lay down on the ground, and I sat down on the bench. Shortly, Michael appeared. He looked at me with love, understanding and compassion. He also knew that I have been hurting. We walked into the sanctuary. It was very peaceful. There were birds and insects all around; it was full of life. We stood to the right, waiting and looking at the mist.

Then the boys came out. They put their arms around me. "Momma," Sean said quietly. I started to cry with love and emotion. We stood together with our arms around each other. I had my head on Sean's shoulder, and Kyle had his arms wrapped around my waist. It felt so good to hold them. I looked into their beautiful faces, touched their hair, held their faces in my hands, kissed their cheeks.

Sean said, "Mom, you should go on that trip to India with Gina. You love to travel. We are so happy that you are doing the things you love again." They lifted me up so we were floating above the ground a few feet. Kyle was laughing with delight. They took me around the perimeter of the sanctuary, counter-clockwise. Then we ended up at the table. They lifted me a little higher. Then we came down gently into the seats. Sean was on my right and Kyle on my left. Kyle smiled and reminded me mentally of the "21" on the cable box. They conveyed that they are all around us, in Alicia's dreams, near Uncle Bert, always helping us and loving us.

Sean said, "Mom, you will be back to yourself, only better." I asked him to tell me about myself. He said, "Mom, you are an amazing soul, amazing being. You have done so much good for the world and the Universe. You are a great teacher." They held me close. I was leaning up against Sean, and Kyle was leaning up against me. Their energy was filling me up and permeating my being. It was rejuvenating me with so much love and light. I touched their faces again and stroked their hair, and they touched my face and hair too. Sean kissed me gently on the cheek. Then Kyle gave me a quick little peck on the other cheek.

I asked them if Grandma tried to come through to me, but the answer was not clear. I asked them if they were with Grandma and they said, "Yes, and Lina too."

After a little while, Michael came over to the table to let me know it was time to go. Panther stood next to him. The boys said, "Hey, Michael." We lifted out of our seats and the boys set me down in front of the table. I turned to Sean and hugged him tightly. Then I turned to Kyle and hugged him. Kyle looked at me with his beautiful bright eyes and smile.

Then Michael took my hand and started to lead me out of the sanctuary. The boys started walking toward the mist. Kyle said, "Bye, Panther." Then Dillon appeared near the mist, waiting for the boys. Sean and Kyle had their arms over each other's shoulders. I turned my head to look at them, and they turned their heads to look at me. "We love you, Mom." "I love you, my angels." They continued into the mist, and I walked with Michael and Panther into the garden.

Michael kissed my hand with love and protection. Then Panther and I continued on to the cloud. We came down to the cliff and got off the cloud. We walked down to the tree trunk. Panther said goodbye, then went down. I walked into the meadow and looked around, taking in the beauty. I could sense myself, my energy, above the Earth. Then I came back to the physical realm.

Day 367—Jun. 21, 2012

Today is the one-year mark. There are no words to describe the depth of my love for you, Sean and Kyle! No words, only pure and absolute love. Thank you for blessing me with your love, your presence in my lifetime, your gifts, your wisdom, your truth, and for showing me our eternal nature, our beautiful and everlasting essence! I will carry on and continue to do my work and make you proud. You are forever with me. I feel it and I know it.

A Medium Reading Validates the Boys' Activities and Dillon's Presence

On June 21, 2012, the one-year anniversary of Sean and Kyle's transition to the other side, I had a reading with medium Tim Braun. He described to me what my boys were doing with our cat that had passed, and Dillon's presence. It validated what I had been experiencing. A portion of the reading follows.

Tim: [Well into the reading.] And there's actually three pets over on spirit side with them, one of which I do feel like they knew. Was there one cat that passed over before them?

Maria: Yes.

Tim: What the younger one does is, he lifts up this cat and he goes, here, give it to her. And it's almost like either he doesn't know how to pick up a cat or doesn't really know how to hold a cat, but it would be kind of like a guy who picks up a baby. The youngest one does this with this cat that passed over before them. He puts it out like this and he smiles and he says give this to my mom and let her know it's over here with me. The older one says, she doesn't want to hear about the cat, she wants to hear about us. They're arguing a little bit. Things haven't changed. And arguing is not a bad thing, it's just they're in disagreement. He's telling him to put the cat down and he says, no I want to bring the cat in. So I just want to tell you that one is not giving up.

I feel, in life, the older one might have had a little bit of influence or a little bit of control. Not in spirit side. Because he's telling him to put the cat down and he won't. He says I don't want to, I want to bring this in for my mom. And I'm letting him, and he puts that right there in your lap. I don't know how soon the cat passed over before, Maria, but I can tell you that when this youngest one went to the spirit side, he opened his eyes, this cat was actually there, being there with him. And he just shows me, I closed my eyes, I went to sleep, I opened my eyes and there was the cat. So the youngest one, what was important to him, or what made him feel comfortable was the cat that greeted him.

On top of that, there are two other pets over there. One is actually a rabbit, which I don't feel that they ever had. And another one's a dog over there which I don't feel that they would have had. So just know that there are these pets over there with them. And when pets come into a sitting, usually it's the highest amount of love that comes into a session; it's pure love. . . . The older one likes being in control as far as telling the younger one what to do, but it's not working anymore because now the younger one's coming over here and he stands and cuts right in front of the older one and then wraps his arms around. . . . What's Dillon mean? Dillon?

Maria: That's my friend's dog.

Tim: Ok, that's the other pet that's over there, is Dillon.
They're saying something about Dillon. Dillon. So
Dillon is the dog that I saw earlier. . . . Your oldest
one's playing with the dog. There's a little
competition here. The one keeps putting up the cat,
holding up the cat, and so he's not putting it down,
and it's frustrating your older son, so what he's
doing is he says, see well I've got the dog. So he's
basically saying see I can do what you're doing. So
they're a little bit in competition with each other, in
a good way, in a very, very good way. . . .

Guided Afterlife Connections

Rochelle Wright, M.S.

Rochelle Wright is a licensed mental health counselor, licensed chemical dependency professional, national certified counselor, EMDR certified therapist for 14 years, and designer of the Guided Afterlife Connections procedure. She has been a state-licensed grief and trauma psychotherapist for 23 years.

Rochelle developed the Guided Afterlife Connections procedure that uses bilateral stimulation to enable people to have afterlife connections while in a psychotherapist's office. The Guided Afterlife Connection method is a psychotherapy procedure that can be administered only by a seasoned, state-licensed psychotherapist. It is a cutting-edge therapy method that does more than simply connect the client with loved ones in the afterlife; it heals grief and trauma in as little as one session.

For information about having a Guided Afterlife Connection session or being trained to administer the procedure, visit Rochelle's website at RochelleWright.com.

Guided Afterlife Connections

Excerpted in part from *Guided Afterlife Connections: They Come to Change Lives*

by Rochelle Wright and R. Craig Hogan

We now know how to help people have their own afterlife connections with loved ones while they sit quietly, comfortably, and peacefully in a state-licensed psychotherapist's office. All the psychotherapist does is to guide the experiencer into the frame of mind that will allow the afterlife connection to occur naturally. The psychotherapist doesn't act as a medium and doesn't make the afterlife connection happen.

The procedure uses bilateral stimulation, in which the left and right sides of the brain are stimulated alternately. It uses two senses for the stimulation: auditory, by having music and various sounds alternate in volume between left and right speakers of a set of headphones, and visual, with the psychotherapist having the client rhythmically move his or her eyes in a motion rather like the eye movement in deep REM sleep.

After a short period of this bilateral stimulation, the clients close their eyes and have experiences. When the experience ends, the clients open their eyes and tell the psychotherapist what they experienced. The psychotherapist repeats the process for the remainder of the session. In 95% to 98% of the sessions, the procedure results in a life-changing afterlife connection.

To date, over 40 psychotherapists have learned the procedure and are using it successfully with clients.

Following are actual accounts from the psychotherapists' notes, printed here with the clients' permission.

The process of the clients' having the bilateral stimulation through eye movements and audio, closing their eyes, and having experiences is referred to in the accounts that follow as "the procedure."

Connie, an RN, Connects with Her Mother

Connie, an RN, had a Guided Afterlife Connection session to connect with her mother, Fern, who passed into spirit in 1995 at the age of 79.

"My mother was a strong woman, the leader of our family," Connie began. "She was a perfectionist; everything in the house had to be perfect. I could never do anything good enough. Mother was a big, scary person to me as I grew up. My thoughts didn't matter, so I could never talk her out of anything. She ended up divorcing Dad after 41 years of marriage.

"When I was 13 and she was in her fifties, she was going through menopause and had episodes of severe depression. She eventually went into the hospital for the depression, where they gave her electric shock treatments that did her some damage. When she came home, she was a changed person. She couldn't even cut her own meat. She lay on the couch for several years, severely depressed. With Mom incapacitated, my sister and I had to take over the family and keep it going.

"Then, one day while she was in a manic period, she fell asleep while driving, crashed into a tree, and broke both her ankles. Following that, she had abdominal surgery and then broke her hip. Eventually, she died in a rehabilitation center.

"I didn't go to my mom's funeral. I didn't have the money to travel the long distance from where I was living then, but I really didn't want to go. I had mixed feelings about my mom. She was harsh, mean, and manipulative sometimes. I had no doubt that she loved me, but I didn't get expressions of love. I was criticized and attacked a lot. I didn't like her constant yelling at me. To this day, when I get upset I can't hear what people are saying because it was so traumatic being yelled at and criticized all the time. In fact, I was nervous about coming to the session today. The thought of encountering my mother was frightening. I kept thinking, 'Will she attack me? Will she criticize me?' I hope I have a good encounter with her and not a frightening one.

"Intellectually, I have forgiven her, but emotionally, I have resentments about the constant criticism she gave out. But all the good things I have—my character, drive, motivation, ability to feel for people and get along with people—all the good life skills, I learned from my mother. "

After Connie finished telling me about her mother, we began the Guided Afterlife Connection protocol. We started with the memory she rated with the highest number on the 10-point Subject Units of Distress Scale (SUDS). She said it was a 10+++++. It was when her mom came back from the hospital after the electric shocks and everything had changed. Connie and her sister had to take over the family.

When she opened her eyes after the first procedure, Connie said, "I am irritated. I am mad. I didn't have any control over what happened to me with my mother. Now my roof is leaking, my furnace doesn't work. I'm angry." Connie was sighing and breathing deeply, releasing pent up energy that she had been carrying. "I am mad. I don't know what to do. I have no control. There's nothing I can do about it."

During the second procedure, the afterlife connection began. When Connie opened her eyes, she said, "I saw Dennis, my boyfriend who died in February, waving at me." She was sighing and releasing energy. "Everyone I love vanishes. They just leave me. You know, I don't think I ever remember missing my mother, but right now, I miss my mother!" she said emphatically.

The afterlife connection continued during the next procedure. "I saw an image of a young woman with long, brown hair. It was my mother, but she was more like my friend now. She was saying, 'Come on, let's go play. Let's go do something fun.'" Connie was crying, releasing old negative energy. "She wanted me to join her. 'Come on, come on,' she was saying, being playful and daring. I said to her, 'I can't go over there.'"

After another procedure, Connie said, "My mother is the girl that was there. She was saying 'Come on.' I went with her. We were the same age, young, running toward a lake. We jumped into the lake, laughing. I said, 'What is your name? Is that really you?' She said, 'I'm Eula.' That was her real name. She went by Fern. 'I'm Eula. See, we're like playful, fun sisters.'

"The water of the lake we were in was different. It wasn't cold. It was just the right temperature. Everything is different where she is. I said to her, 'I want to go back and be with you.' She said, 'Not yet,' and she splashed me playfully. I asked her, 'What do I do with the rest of my life?' Mom said, 'Do anything you want to.' I was like in an altered state. I asked, 'What do I do?' Mom said to me, 'You can't control it beforehand. You just have to do it.'"

When she finished telling me what she experienced, I said to Connie, "Go back to the memory that you had to take over everything when your mom came home from the hospital. It was a 10+++++. Where is it now?" Connie said, "It's a 3." I asked, "What about the memory that it was traumatic being yelled at and criticized all the time." It had been a 10+++ at the beginning of the session. Connie answered, "I don't feel anything in this state. It's a 5."

As Connie went through another procedure, the afterlife connection resumed. Afterward, she said, "I asked Mom about our childhood. She apologized, then said 'It's nothing. It's in your head. It's the bigger picture that's important. Drop the old thoughts in that water. It is special water, and it will disintegrate those thoughts.'

"Mom said to me, 'See what you can do here,' and she jumped and grabbed onto a beam of light and climbed over it onto a star like she was in the Cirque du Soleil, laughing. She was jumping around stars and onto moonbeams. 'See what I can do,' she said. Everything is petty down on the Earth." I said, 'That doesn't help me deal with the petty things on Earth.' Mom said, 'Do what you want. Make more of an effort to do what you want to do. Don't be bound by "shoulds." Cling to your spiritual practice, and that will help you. Take risks. Go for what you want. You're taking things too serious. The Earthly life is not worth that.'

"I said, 'But I don't know what I want.' She said, 'Try things until you find out what you want.' I asked her, 'Will you help me if I ask for your help?' 'Yes,' she said, 'I will help you.' She was on an elevated ring, doing tricks, like in the Cirque du Soleil. It looked like so much fun. I said, 'I would love to do that, but I can't.' She said, 'Throw those thoughts in the lake.'"

The fact that Connie didn't go to her mother's funeral really bothered her, so I said, "Ask your mom, 'Do you forgive me for not going to the funeral?' I led her through another procedure. When she opened her eyes, she said, "I asked for her forgiveness. She said she was OK with it. She forgave me. Then she said to me, 'I love you. I'm here for you. This life is insignificant. You can do what you want, and if you do, you're going to have more fun. You can't really make a wrong decision.' Rochelle, I agonize over making the right decision. Mom just said, 'Why, why do you worry about decisions? They're so insignificant.'"

After another procedure, Connie closed her eyes and asked her husband in spirit, Dennis, "Do you have anything to say to me today?" She described his response: "He said, 'My passing was preplanned. We arranged it before we came into this life. It was all meant to be.' Then he said to me, 'I miss you, and I'm sorry it was so hard for you. I love you. It was all prearranged, but my body knew. Do you remember my heart palpitations and fainting three days before I passed away? I knew something was going to happen.'"

When Connie opened her eyes after a final procedure, she said, "I asked Mom and Dennis, 'Is it over for today, our session?' Dennis kissed me. He held me for a little bit. When it was time to go, it was like a big vacuum sucking him back. And my mother was still doing the Cirque du Soleil thing. 'I'll save a ring for you,' she said. 'See you later.'"

With that, the session ended.

Tina's Grandmother Speaks to Her in German from the Afterlife

Tina had a successful Guided Afterlife Connection with her husband, Joe, and came back for a second session to connect with her grandmother. This is Tina's description during the Guided Afterlife Connection.

"I was in a room, but it faded to black. Someone grabbed my hand from the right side. I think it was my husband, Joe. He was taking me to a room where my grandma may be. We went through a door and emerged into a garden room. I saw Grandma to my left, saying 'Mein Kind.' That means 'My kid.' My grandma and I walked a short distance and sat together on a bench. I said, 'Can I ask you questions in English?' She said, 'Natuerlich. Naturally, naturally.' I asked her if my grandfather was there. She said he was, in the distance. I asked if he knew I was there, and she said, 'Yes!'

"Grandma began stroking my hair, and I burst out crying. Grandma said, 'Don't be sad. We will all be together again.' She then gestured to show me that Joe was standing in the background. I went to him and we kissed and hugged. The three of us sat down together. Grandma said, 'Be happy we are all together. It's nice to sit together. It's been a long time, and wonderful to have Joe sit with us, Mein Kind.'

"She said to me, 'You are doing okay, but you must go forward. She then spoke in German, starting with 'Mein liebling,' meaning 'My love.' The translation of the rest was, 'My life was mine. Joe had his. You have your life. We have to all move forward.' She was showing me my people in the distance, saying 'See. They are all doing something!'

"My grandmother then said that her mother and father were there, and added, 'We are all moving forward. We do everything together, like we did before. We have our jobs to do. There is always work to do.'

"'Mein Kind,' she said, continuing in German. This is the translation: 'You have to live every day to the fullest.' I asked her, 'What about the work I'm doing with Rochelle in afterlife connections?' She said in German, 'You can only go so far with the afterlife. Everything is not to be seen. It's good to do this work, but you can't go as far as you'd like.

Otherwise, you would be in the afterlife. The work does help people, but when you go too far, you end up there.'

"Joe was sitting close by. I acknowledged him for a minute.

"Then my grandma said, 'All is good. All is clear. It's nice we could get together.' Grandma and I were hugging. 'You don't have to be sorry for anything,' she said in German. 'Das war schoen,' she said, meaning 'This was nice!' Then she said, 'I love you and Joe loves you. We look out for each other.' She ended with 'Bis dann,' meaning 'until later.'"

Merna's Unexpected Visitor Heals Her Guilt

Merna came to Rochelle for a Guided Afterlife Connection to connect with a close friend of hers who had passed. However, the appointment turned into a psychotherapy session. Merna had unresolved feelings from her childhood. Due to some unfortunate circumstances, she had been separated from her mother and placed into a foster home when she was four years old. Merna had feelings of misplaced guilt, believing that she had been "sent away" because of some failing or character flaw in her. For many years, she had engaged in psychotherapy to try to alleviate the disturbing feelings, with some relief, but she still suffered from her conviction that her mother didn't care about her and had no attachment to her.

At the beginning of the session, Merna described the close friend she wanted to connect with. When she had finished, Rochelle began the Guided Afterlife Connections procedure. During the procedure, Merna was surprised when her biological mother, who was not the target for the connection, came to her. Merna was astonished by the visitation. Merna's mother said to her, "I loved you. I always loved you. I loved you when I was carrying you during the pregnancy. I still love you."

Merna was then guided to the realization that just as she had a secure attachment to her biological mother prior to birth through the umbilical cord, she was still attached to her mother in a loving way and always would be. Afterward, she said the visitation and the message were, "quite healing, and I must say unexpected. This insight brought release for me."

Her birth mother entered the Guided Afterlife Connection intentionally to help Merna heal the guilt and remove the feeling that some weakness or flaw in her that kept her mother from loving her had resulted in her mother's abandoning her.

Fran Has a Connection with Her Son

"I saw him, and I knew he was gone," Jeanette said to Rochelle during her session. Her son, Brandon, had passed unexpectedly in his sleep at age 11. Jeanette rated the disturbing effect of that memory as a 10++++ on the 0 to 10 disturbance rating scale, so Rochelle used that memory for the beginning of the Guided Afterlife Connection procedure. Rochelle performed the procedure and Jeanette closed her eyes. After a few seconds, with her eyes still closed, Jeanette said "I see a beautiful area of water, with a vibrant rainbow and a waterfall off to the side. I can see a part of a hand and arm." She was breathing deeply, releasing energy. She then said she saw her son, Brandon. "Oh my gosh, you're here," Jeanette thought to herself. "Is this real?"

After another set of eye movements, she said, "I see my brother in back of Brandon. He passed 22 months before

Brandon. They're jumping in the waterfall. I jump in and I'm sinking and sinking in the water, with my hair going straight up. I come up out of the water and gasp. I shake my hair off. Brandon says 'Fred!' I didn't know what he meant at the time. I was in bliss, in their world, not like it is in a reading when they're coming into my world.

Rochelle led Jeanette through another procedure. She described what she was experiencing: "Brandon is hugging me and squeezing me. My brother is standing there with his arms folded and a smirk, like he said 'Didn't you think I would take care of him?' It's raining a warm rain. They're laughing and we're running to the left. 'Come on, you have to get an umbrella,' Brandon says. We go through a gray puckered thing, like lips puckered to kiss, and through a curtain. We enter what seems like a field, with beautiful high grass, yellow flowers, and daisies. It's just beautiful.

"We stop and we're lying in the grass. My brother isn't there. We're looking up at the sky. Brandon is holding my hand. 'Mommy, Mommy,' he says, 'I know this is hard for you.' I can hear his voice so clear. I'm touching his hand. Our hands are clasped and we're talking. We're so happy. There's no sound but Brandon's whispering. 'I miss you,' Brandon says to me. Then he says, 'We're going to make a world of difference.' I touch his nose with my finger. It's as real and solid as if I were touching my own nose. He says, 'There are things you don't understand, but trust me, you will.' We are lying together. I can feel his cheek against mine. I say, 'None of this makes any sense, though.' Brandon says, 'It will. Ask Daddy about red and the truck.'"

Jeanette is crying softly. After another set of eye movements, she continued. "We are in the sand now. It just changed suddenly. I say to Brandon, 'What happened?' He says, 'We can do that here! Cool, huh!' He has the biggest smile! 'Mom, watch the waves. See how they roll out slowly and roll back in. They always roll back. Remember, if the tide goes out, it always has to go back in, regardless of what happens. It always has to come back in.' He's showing me the back and forth motion. I say, 'Explain it to me.' Brandon says, 'Mom, the tide goes out. It always comes back in. When it is out, we know it will come back in.'"

Jeanette is crying, releasing energy. Jeanette is a talented medium; Brandon refers to that in what he says next. She continues: "Brandon is saying, 'Mom, I want you to see something.' We roll over onto our stomachs so we can see the shore and our feet are toward the water. 'I want to show you something,' Brandon says. I look ahead and I see all these children, all the children I have connected with in my medium work connecting parents with their children. Brandon is pointing and saying some of their names. Lois, Lennie, James, Simon, Luke, Brad, Nathan, Linda, Jeannie; there are so many kids. All of the little kids are in front. There's Trisha, Allen, Bart, Laura, and Kris. Melanie is there on the far left. They're all smiling. I say to myself, 'This can't be why it all happened.'

"Arnie is sitting next to Brandon. Arnie passed the same day, at the same time as Brandon. I'm squishing Brandon's face, saying 'I just love you.' Arnie, Brandon, and I are sitting there. I can see every grain of sand and feel it too. I ask for a sign this is all real, and Arnie asks me to tell his mother to get the photograph out of the wallet.

"Now Brandon is making fun of me, smiling, like 'You need a sign? I already told you Dad's secret word!' I said, 'Brandon, tell me something else I don't know.' He says 'Ask Rochelle about the doctor's appointment she had on Wednesday.'" When Jeanette opened her eyes, she said to Rochelle, "Did you have a doctor's appointment on

Wednesday?" Rochelle responded, "Yes! I did have a doctor's appointment on Wednesday."

Rochelle led Jeanette through another procedure. She spoke with her eyes still closed: "I'm hugging Brandon and Arnie. I'm giving Arnie a kiss on the forehead from his mom, and I'm telling him his mom loves him." Jeanette is smiling broadly. "I'm just hugging Brandon. We are still at the beach. It's like the kids are all there." Jeanette stretches out her arm to the left, pointing. "I'm holding Brandon's face in my hands. I tell him, 'You will always be my precious baby.' He and Arnie are laughing. Brandon says, 'You act as if I'm going away.' I said 'Do you have to go or stay?' He turns to the kids standing there and says, 'You and I made a difference.' He's saying he's helped make the connections with these children and their parents.

"We are lying back down again on the sand. He says, 'I was bored,' and he shrugs his shoulders. He would always say he was just bored. I think he's saying he passed because he was bored. I asked, 'Are you bored now?' He points to all the kids and says, 'Mom, how could I be bored?'"

Rochelle then said, "Ask him if there's anything he wants to say before we close." She led Jeanette through the procedure. When Jeanette opened her eyes, she said, "Brandon said to me, 'The picture doesn't always look like the photograph.' I said to him, 'What does that mean for me?' He said, 'Sometimes things are not always what they seem. Like the crystal bluebird.'"

Rochelle led Jeanette through another procedure. "Brandon and Arnie are standing up. Brandon says, 'You act as though I'm leaving again, but I'm just going with them,' and he's pointing to the kids. The kids are dressed in different clothes. Some have jeans on, some have hospital johnnies, and some have on their regular clothes. They are all whole and perfect, with no blood or wounds. They're all smiling. Melanie is saying, 'Don't forget me. Don't forget me.' They are like a choir, with the younger ones in front." Jeanette paused. "They are gone now." She opened her eyes.

"Brandon and I were interlocked. I could feel the skin on his cheek the same as when he was physically here. I could feel his soft cheeks."

Rochelle said, "Bring up the memory we started with, when you saw him lying there and knew he was gone. It was a 10++++. Where is it now? Jeanette said, "It's a zero. It's like it didn't happen." Rochelle said, "How do you feel?" Jeanette said, "I feel like I did a reading on myself. Wow!"

Postscript

Tom, Jeanette's husband, had his Guided Afterlife Connection session first. While Jeanette was having hers, he walked 10 miles to ground himself after the remarkable session he had. He took pictures. In one of them was a fence with a bird on the fence that looked like a crystal bird. Jeanette and Tom were trying to figure out if the bird was real or crystal when Jeanette remembered that Brandon had referred to a crystal bird in her session. He said, "The picture doesn't always look like the photograph" and " Sometimes things are not always what they seem. Like the crystal bluebird." They also discovered that the crystal bluebird is a symbol of being close to Heaven.

Brandon had said to tell his father "red" and "truck" when they got together after the sessions. It turned out that Mike had seen Brandon holding a large red heart, and shortly thereafter, sitting in a monster truck in the sky.

Mike said that in his Guided Afterlife Connection, he saw an image of Jeanette standing on the ground, holding her hand up really high toward the sky. Brandon was reaching his hand down and their hands connected. At the beginning of her Guided Afterlife Connection, Jeanette was seeing a vibrant rainbow, waterfall, and a part of a hand and arm. The connection to Brandon followed immediately.

When Jeanette first asked for a sign the connection was all real, Arnie asked her to tell his mother to get the photograph out of the wallet. When Jeanette returned home, she contacted Arnie's mother to tell her what happened. Arnie's mother said she was involved in putting together a two-year anniversary editorial about Arnie. She had been searching through photos for a picture of him to use with it and finally found the perfect picture. It was in a wallet. Arnie had told Jeanette to give the message to his mother so she would know he is fine and never far from her.

Validations of the Experiences

Often, sessions include validations of the experiences. Something happens that can be explained only by the realization that the loved one is coming through. Or the client learns something he or she couldn't know about that is later validated. Examples of validating sessions follow.

Christine Receives a Validation from Her Husband

Christine's original Guided Afterlife Connection experience is in the book, *Guided Afterlife Connections*. She connected with her husband, Joe, living in the next plane of life, and had the wonderful experience of hugging and kissing him. After her first session, she came to Rochelle to talk about a dream she had about Joe. Rochelle said that they could examine the dream through a shorter Guided Afterlife

Session targeting it. What happened during the short, targeted session was remarkable.

Rochelle took Christine through the audio and visual bilateral stimulation of the Guided Afterlife Connection protocol for the short session. She connected with Joe and they had a conversation. Toward the end of the session, Christine asked him point blank, "How do I know this is really you?" Joe immediately replied, "I have turned off the music." At that moment, the music coming through the earphones stopped.

Christine opened her eyes and told Rochelle what had happened. Christine and Rochelle checked the CD player; it was running fine, with the indicator showing that the player was going through the music selection. But there was no sound. Rochelle put the headset up to her ear and turned up the volume all the way. There was no sound. Finally, she turned off the CD unit and started it again. It worked fine.

Throughout the Guided Afterlife Connections session, the music and sounds play through the headset. There has never been an instance in which the music suddenly stopped, for any reason. And it doesn't seem physically possible for the CD player to be running, apparently playing the music, yet there is no sound, even when the volume is turned up all the way.

Joe answered Christine's question, giving her, and us, a validation of the reality of this wonderful experience.

Christine Has Another Validation from Joe

Christine wanted to have another Guided Afterlife Connection with Rochelle to connect with her husband, Joe. Christine spoke to Rochelle about it, but there was no time for a session. During the conversation, Christine explained that after her last Guided Afterlife Connection, she had several dreams about Joe. In the latest one, at the end of her dream, Joe opened a door, peeking in telling her he loved her. Rochelle said that when they had time for another session, they would use that dream as the beginning target for the session. Rochelle also said she had some questions she wanted Christine to ask Joe.

Finally, two weeks later, Rochelle and Christine had time for the session they had been wanting to have. Christine connected with Joe, and he showed her beautiful places, including a beach with boulders on it, and butterflies. They walked down a spiral rock stairway to the bottom, where there was a bench. Joe asked Christine to sit on the bench. He looked at her and said "Now, what about the questions?"

Rochelle and Christine were both very surprised that Joe would ask that. Christine had not remembered that two weeks prior, Rochelle had mentioned having some questions for Joe to answer. Rochelle and Christine had not spoken about questions before this session. Joe brought up the questions completely out of the blue. Joe then answered Rochelle's questions, at one point answering concerns she had by saying, "Don't underestimate the power of the power!"

Carole Receives a Validation from Her Friend's Son in Spirit

Carole, whose daughter, Kate, had been killed in a car accident, received a validation of the experience through the actions of her friend Linda's son, Martine, who also was in spirit. This is the account from the book, *Guided Afterlife Connections*: "After another set of eye movements, Carole closed her eyes again. 'Now I see Martine, Linda's son. He passed away eight months ago. He's sitting on his couch looking at me, with one leg up and his arms dangling in a funny pose, smiling. But I can still see Kate. Martine's flashing in and out. Now there are two things going on. Kate's outside and Martine's inside. He has his leg up with his arms in that funny position. I can see Kate's dress, but not the bottom. It keeps going to Martine sitting on the couch being silly. I don't understand this.'

After the session, Carole wrote Rochelle an email describing a remarkable validation of her afterlife connection. She wrote that as she and Linda, Martine's mother, were riding home, she told Linda that she had seen Martine in her Guided Afterlife Connection. Carole showed Linda the comical pose he was in, with his leg up and arms dangling. Linda's eyes opened wide. She said when Martine was clowning around, he would make what they called his "monkey pose," with his leg up and arms dangling. It was exactly what Carole saw, without knowing that Martine did that.

The pose was a distinctive message from Martine to let his mom, Linda, know that he was fine, happy, and clowning as he always did.

Links to More Cases and Information

Links to more cases, the study of Guided Afterlife Connections and reduction of grief, and explanations about the procedure are online at http://ascsi.org/conference/resources.htm.

The Soul Phone

Gary E. Schwartz, Ph.D.

Gary E. Schwartz, Ph.D. is a Professor of Psychology, Medicine, Neurology, Psychiatry, and Surgery, and Director of the Laboratory for Advances in Consciousness and Health, at the University of Arizona. He is also the Chairman of Eternea (www.eternea.org). He received his Ph.D. from Harvard University in 1971 and served as an Assistant Professor of Psychology at Harvard before moving to Yale University in 1976. There he was a Professor of Psychology and Psychiatry, Director of the Yale Psychophysiology Center, and co-Director of the Yale Behavioral Medicine Clinic before moving to the University of Arizona in 1988. He has published more than 450 scientific papers and chapters, including six papers in the journal *Science*, and co-edited 11 academic books. He is a Fellow of the American Psychological Association, the American Psychological Society, the Academy of Behavioral Medicine Research, and the Society of Behavioral Medicine. His research integrating body, mind, and spirit has been featured in numerous documentaries and television shows, including the documentary *The Life After Death Project* (2013), produced and directed by Paul Davids. His books for the general public include *The Afterlife Experiments, The G.O.D. Experiments, The Energy Healing Experiments,* and *The Sacred Promise.*

For more about Gary, visit drgaryschwartz.com.

The Soul Phone

Summarized from *The Sacred Promise: How science is discovering spirit's collaboration with us in our daily lives*

by Gary E. Schwartz, Ph.D.

My research and experience with people living in spirit have taught me that they are able to manipulate things on the Earth plane to let us know they are present. They turn lights off and on, rap on walls, move objects and otherwise get our attention by doing something that shows unmistakably they're with us. I surmised that if we could create a device that would take very little spirit effort for them to make an event happen, the people living in spirit could communicate with us by repeating the event in a pattern.

The telegraph is an example of communicating through a pattern of events. The telegraph operator presses and releases a key to make short and long bursts of electricity travel through copper wires over thousands of miles. The bursts of electricity cause a key on the receiver's end to make short and long sounds that match the sounds the sender made. The sender and the receiver both know the combination of short and long sounds that stand for letters, so the sender can communicate a message to the receiver with simple bursts of electricity.

I wanted to make a telegraph for spirit. To do so, I thought that I would make the task of sending bursts of something easiest by having them send bursts of tiny particles of light called photons into a device that would detect the photons. Photons are smaller than atoms, so it should take very little effort.

To find out whether people in spirit could communicate by sending bursts of photons into a device, I created a prototype of what someday may become the Soul Phone. Its primary component is a photon detector called a silicon photomultiplier system that counts the photons going through it. The type of photomultiplier system I used is a PCDMini. I hooked up the PCDMini to a computer showing a graph I could watch. If a burst of photons were detected by the PCDMini, the burst would appear as a spike on the graph. I could find out whether people in spirit could make photon bursts detected via the PCDMini by watching for the spikes. Then we might eventually create an electronic keyboard, where each letter had its own sensor (or small array of sensors). The bursts of photons would be transformed into electronic text.

In the Soul Phone, the PCDMini is in a sealed box that is encased in another sealed box to keep normal room light from coming into the photomultiplier tube. I tested the Soul Phone without asking anyone in spirit to be involved to see how it would work with no spirit effort by turning it on for five-minute trials. Even though the PCDMini was in a box within a box, there was a little leakage of light into the PCDMini, so there were approximately four bursts of photons that leaked into the boxes (or were created by noise in the detector). They made little spikes on the graph displayed on the computer monitor. The heights were around 25 units on the graph, meaning 25 photons had been detected by the PCDMini, so I knew what to expect if no person in spirit was sending photons to the PCDMini: around two bursts of 25 photons in five minutes, or four bursts of 25 photons in 10 minutes.

Testing the Soul Phone

The Soul Phone was ready to be tested to see whether someone in spirit could communicate using bursts of photons. To test the Soul Phone, I invited some experimental partners now living in spirit with whom I had worked successfully before. For the test, they would cooperate in attempting to send bursts of photons to the PCDMini. I would then prompt them to see if they could create the bursts upon my request. That would show they could communicate using the Soul Phone. For every five-minute spirit trial, we collected five-minute control (baseline) trials.

The first person from the other side I asked to participate was Susy Smith. Susy was a capable lay scientist when on the Earth plane who penned some 30 books about parapsychology and the afterlife. She continued research activities when she passed into spirit, cooperating with me from the other side in research projects. I had asked a medium to interview Susy about whether she observed what I was doing on the physical plane and what would happen to me in the near future. Susy cooperated perfectly, even telling me portentously that I should check the tires on my car. It turned out that a few hours later I walked into the parking lot of my laboratory to find one of my tires had gone flat. As a result, I established that she was aware of what I was doing in my daily life, could predict what would happen to me in the near future, and would be a cooperative partner in research from the other side.

Later, I was wishing that a family whose loved one had transitioned off the Earth plane could know their loved one was fine on the other side. Within a short time, Susy brought the family's loved one in spirit to a medium. The medium received a message that she conveyed to me, and I gave it to the woman's family. Susy had brought a woman from the other side to a medium to convey a message to the woman's family that the family needed to hear. Susy was serving as an afterlife or spirit experimenter.

As a result, I enlisted Susy's help from the other side to test the Soul Phone.

The second person in spirit I asked to help was Marcia Eklund, my mother-in-law now in spirit, who also had cooperated in activities from the other side. When my wife, Rhonda, Marcia's daughter, needed to find copies of documents, she asked Marcia for her help in locating them. As she described it, "Immediately, the thought came to me, as words being spoken to me in my head, 'Go into the closet in my office and look behind Dad's folded flag on the floor.'" She did as Marcia directed and found the papers behind the flag. Marcia had responded by giving her daughter what she asked for.

As a result, I asked Marcia to cooperate from the other side in testing the Soul Phone.

The third individual I asked to participate is not a person; she's an alleged angel. Her name is Angel Sophia. Mediums claim she is one of my guardian angels. In previous research, Angel Sophia helped us test whether the presence of an angel would affect the biophotons given off by plants. "Biophotons" are light particles all living things give off, although different living things give off different amounts and patterns of biophotons. Plant material gives off biophotons.

We wanted to determine whether Sophia's presence would affect plants' emitted biophotons. Angel Sophia agreed, through a medium, to participate. In our experiment, we placed plant material in a darkened room. We focused a camera capable of recording the biophotons given off by plant material on our sample.

She performed perfectly. Before she entered the room, we took baseline video to show the biophotons given off by the plant material in a normal circumstance with no angel presence. We then asked Angel Sophia to enter the room as we continued recording the video. After a while, we asked her to leave the room. We continued the video recording to see whether there was a difference when we asked her to leave.

I then analyzed the video using an image analysis technique called a two dimensional Fast Fourier Transformation. What I found was that there were no unusual patterns in the Fast Fourier Transformation analysis before Angel Sophia entered the room, but there were ripples or wavelike structures in the video when we asked Angel Sophia to enter the room. The ripples then disappeared when we asked her to leave the room. I had found a way to detect the presence of a purported angel.

Angel Sophia turned out to be a very cooperative partner in the research, so I invited her, through a medium, to be part of the Soul Phone research.

The fourth person I invited was someone in spirit who also had cooperated in earlier research. In that study, we were attempting to see whether Susy Smith could bring a person I specified to a medium during a scheduled meeting with the medium. I chose Harry Houdini, the legendary magician, who was especially renowned for escaping from being bound and immersed headfirst into water. Houdini had participated in other spirit activities, so I knew he had an interest in advancing our knowledge of the afterlife and communication.

When I first encountered "HHH" (Hypothesized Harry Houdini) in spirit, I wanted to see if a person in spirit would come through when requested to do so. That would demonstrate that HHH heard my request and was willing and able to fulfill it. I met with the medium who was to do the experimental reading, but told the medium nothing about whom I expected to come through so it wouldn't bias the medium and the reading.

During the reading, the medium was perplexed. Someone was coming through, but the medium couldn't understand the impressions he was getting. The medium said things like (1) "now I see him, now I don't," (2) "he could hold his breath for a very long period of time," (3) "he was connected to New York," and (4) "his name was not his real name." All fit HHH perfectly: he would appear and disappear on stage, held his breath a long time while immersed in water during his escape stunt, was from New York, and was actually christened Erik Weisz; Harry Houdini was a stage name.

The First Test with Susy and Marcia

The test of the prototype Soul Phone was an attempt to see whether the PCDMini could detect photon bursts caused by someone in spirit so it could eventually be used as a kind of spirit typewriter. I referred to the effort of those in spirit as "Spirit Intentions" or "SI" because they would just intend for the photons to come through the PCDMini in bursts, and if they were capable, that would happen.

I set up the experiment to measure the number and strength of the photon bursts the PCDMini detected within five-minute periods. We invited Susy and Marcia to participate as a team in this part of the experiment. We began the test by asking Susy and Marcia to stay away from the PCDMini while we recorded the photon bursts in five of these five-minute measurements. This became the baseline, showing us what the results would be if no people in spirit were trying to make photons go through the PCDMini.

We followed with another set of five measurements lasting five minutes apiece during which we asked Susy and Marcia to try to make photons enter the PCDMini in bursts. These were the Spirit Intention trials.

We then did a second set of these measurements, but this time we had 10, five-minute period measurements when we asked Susy and Marcia to stay away from the PCDMini, 10 when we asked Susy and Marcia to try to make the photon bursts occur, and a final set of 10 measurements in which we asked Susy and Marcia to stay away from the PCDMini again.

Finally, we conducted a third set of tests just as we had the first set. We asked Susy and Marcia to stay away from the PCDMini while we took five measurements, each five minutes long. We followed those by asking them to try to make photons enter the PCDMini in five measurements of five minutes apiece. We ended with a final set of five measurements in which we asked Susy and Marcia not to approach the PCDMini.

That gave us three sets of data to look at. Since I am not a medium, my only gauge of whether Susy and Marcia showed up would be positive test results as measured by the PCDMini. The mediums who have read both Susy and Marcia assured me that they were showing up as requested.

Before we interpreted the data, we added another measurement that would take care of a valid question that someone could ask: "If we obtained positive results, couldn't they be due to my mind influencing the PCDMini in some way?"

To address this question, I added 10 measurements in which I attempted to use my mind to increase the photon bursts. I included another 10 measurements in which I didn't attempt to influence the photon bursts as a baseline or control.

The results of these experiments were very revealing. The baseline number of photon bursts detected by the PCDMini when Susy and Marcia were not trying to send photon bursts to the PCDMini averaged a little under five bursts in five minutes. When Susy and Marcia were asked to try to influence the number of photons coming into the PCDMini, the average number of bursts increased to 7.5 bursts in the five-minute periods, a 150% increase in photon bursts.

The data from my attempts to use my mind to send photons to the PCDMini showed a baseline average of around five bursts per five-minute period, the same as during Susy and Marcia's baseline trials, and a little under five bursts per five-minute period when I focused on having photons go into the PCDMini. I failed miserably. My efforts had no effect, meaning it is unlikely that my mind was influencing the results of the trials.

Second Test, with Angel Sophia and HHH

The next question was, could other beings in Spirit do the same thing, or were Susy and Marcia special cases because they had a strong motivation to connect with their loved ones in the physical realm and had done so for years?

To find out, I invited Angel Sophia and HHH to participate. I started with 10 baseline measurements, each five minutes in length, asking Angel Sophia and HHH to stay away from the PCDMini. Then I asked Angel Sophia to try to send bursts of photons through the PCDMini in four measurements of five minutes apiece.

Finally, I involved HHH in a set of trials. For him, I arranged eight total measurements. Four were baseline, five-minute measurements, during which I asked him to stay away from the PCDMini. Interspersed among those four baseline measurements were four measurements in which I asked him to try to influence the number of photons going into the PCDMini.

The results of all of these careful measurements were also very informative. The baseline number of photon bursts when Angel Sophia and HHH were not influencing the PCDMini was around three bursts on average during the five-minute interval. However, during the measurements when Angel Sophia and HHH were asked to make photon bursts register on the PCDMini, there were around six bursts per measurement on average for each of them, with Angel Sophia's a little higher, but not statistically significant. That meant Angel Sophia and HHH had approximately 220% increases in photon bursts over the baseline measurements when they intended to have photons enter the PCDMini, and they were working individually, not as a team as Susy and Marcia had been working.

In this research, we learned that those in spirit will come and participate in research when asked to do so, and that they can influence the prototype Soul Phone in order to interact with the researcher.

During this segment of the research, something very interesting happened. I began to wonder whether HHH was actually participating in the research. I was explaining the research to Jerry Cohen, CEO of Canyon Ranch, where we have conducted a number of research studies. I explained that the photon bursts registered by the PCDMini were normally in the range of 25 to 30 photons that appeared on the graph as spikes 25 to 30 units high.

During the conversation, Jerry said, "If Harry is that good, can he hit a home run? Can he make larger spikes than just 25 or 30 unit bursts?" I told Jerry that every now and then, we might see a larger spike—50 or even 75 units high. But I had never asked them to try to make larger ones, or smaller ones, for that matter.

As I drove home, I recalled the movie *Field of Dreams*. I remembered the comment that a secret sitter once made about psychic-medium Mary Occhino. He said, "Mary not only hit the ball out of the park. She hit it out of New York City."

I wondered, could HHH hit a home run, on command, and could he hit it out of the park, if not the city of Tucson?

I arrived at home, and looked at the TV monitor in my study. I had been leaving the computer and video running when I went out to give those in spirit "Free Play," when they could experiment themselves with the PCDMini. To my amazement, the sporadic bursts on the screen were tiny—less than one-fifth their normal size. Normally when I looked at the graph, the 25 unit-high bursts reached up to the full height of the graph so 25 units appeared on the Y-axis near the top of the graph. Why did they now look so tiny? Had the software automatically adjusted the Y-axis scale because a larger burst had been recorded and the software had to change the units' sizes on the Y access to allow for a higher unit number showing the spike?

When I looked at the Y-axis, I saw that the scale was not reading 0 to 25 units; it was reading 0 to 175! The graph had adjusted itself so it could show the full height of larger spikes on the screen, resulting in the normal 25 unit high spikes appearing shorter. In other words, the new 0 to 175 range meant that at least one burst had occurred that was possibly as large as 175 photons. Remember, virtually all the bursts in the pitch-black box within a box were only 25 units high or less. A burst of 175 photons would be 700% greater than a typical burst of 25 photons.

I thought to myself "Wow . . . I need to check this out."

I replayed the time-lapse video and discovered that a 173-unit burst had occurred just around the time that I was driving into my garage. I wondered, could this be an intentional response by HHH? If something happens once, it could be a chance event, an artifact, something unimportant. But if this phenomenon was real, somehow attached to HHH, he should be able to duplicate it.

I decided to restart the Free Play period and watch what was unfolding. The time-lapse camera was taking snapshots of the screens. As I was watching the screen, I asked HHH in my mind, "Can you make a large spike?"

What happened next I witnessed with my own two eyes. There was a huge spike on the PCDMini output screen. It was approximately 173 photon units high, or the same 700% increase as recorded earlier!

In watching hundreds of hours of outputs, I rarely saw bursts above 50 to 75. I was now seeing a 173-unit burst, and it occurred shortly after I had asked HHH if he could make a big one!

Was this just a coincidence? Could it be something more? I did not know. Unfortunately, I had to give a lecture at Canyon Ranch that evening, so I left the system running in "Play Time." When I returned, I noticed that the Y-axis was back to normal: 25 units high. I was really tired, but wanted to watch a little more. I decided to ask HHH if he could make another "big one." This time I invited my wife, Rhonda, to be present.

To my and Rhonda's utter amazement, another huge 173-unit burst appeared on the screen. I was reviewing the past history, typing it in, when a third one occurred. HHH was responding with vigor and power over the photons being sent to the PCDMini.

A Third Test: "Yes" and "No" Answers

After the experiment with Angel Sophia and HHH, I decided to conduct another experiment. I began to wonder, could the PCDMini be used by those in spirit to give "Yes" and "No" answers to questions? I designed the third experiment with HHH acting as the spirit Intender. In this experiment, I placed instructions on the monitor for HHH to read and respond to. The graph showing the bursts of photons was in a separate area of the screen. The monitor would display a B if HHH was to establish a baseline measurement. Hopefully, he would see the B and leave the PCDMini alone. The monitor might show a "Yes" or a "No" also. I didn't instruct HHH about what I expected to happen with the photons and PCDMini when "Yes" or "No" appeared on the screen. I left that up to him. I assumed he would work out his own code using photons and the PCDMini for a "Yes" and a "No."

The measurements were five minutes long, as in the earlier experiments. The order in which "B," "Yes," and "No" appeared on the screen was **B** during a five-minute measurement, **Yes** during the next five-minute measurement, and **No** during the third five-minute measurement. For the next measurements, the order was **B No Yes**, **B Yes No**, and **B No Yes**. The change in the order of the Yes and No trials was to counterbalance the attempts.

I asked HHH to make one kind of burst when he saw "Yes" and another kind when he saw "No," but the kind of bursts was up to HHH.

I conducted the trials and began analyzing the data. I found that, in fact, HHH had been sending bursts of photons through the PCDMini when "Yes" and "No" were on the screen, at the rate of between three and five bursts in five minutes, but the number of bursts remained at the low, baseline level of around two bursts in five minutes when B was on the screen.

I also noticed something peculiar. The bursts of photons coming into the PCDMini when "Yes" was on the screen were occurring during the first 150 seconds of the five-minute period, meaning the first half of the period. The bursts of photons when "No" was on the screen were occurring during the second 150 seconds, or second half of the period. That was consistent whether "Yes" was the first word on the screen and "No" was the second or whether the words were reversed. HHH had created a code for "Yes" and "No" that clearly distinguished the two.

The Next Test of the Soul Phone

I decided to perform another experiment not yet completed at this time that would ask someone in spirit to indicate "Yes" or "No" responses using more sensitive equipment. For this experiment, I have set up two boxes with a PCDMini in each box. One box is labeled "Yes." The other is labeled "No." Graphs for each of the PCDMini instruments show on the monitor so I can see what is happening with each of them at the same time.

The question is, will the person in spirit be able to send photons through the "Yes" PCDMini when asked to do so, and through the "No" PCDMini when asked to choose that alternative?

We won't know until "they" try.

The Soul Phone shows great promise for developing a device that will enable us to communicate fluently with people living on the next plane of life. I will be following through with the research to develop such a device.

Aiding Lost Souls

Bruce Moen

Bruce Moen is an author and international lecturer on exploring the afterlife and performing "retrievals." In a retrieval, someone from this side of life goes to the afterlife to help people who are "stuck" after their passing from the Earth plane and unable or unwilling to go on to the next level of their lives. Bruce's work is based on the Monroe Institute's Lifeline procedure.

Bruce is an engineering consultant with his own firm. You can read more about him on his website at afterlife-knowledge.com.

His description of his retrieval work follows.

Aiding Lost Souls

by Bruce Moen

Since my own perceptual skill development and evidence gathering was for the most part a result of attending Robert Monroe's six-day Lifeline program, some of the elements of that program were used in the development of my system. Specifically, the concept of "retrieval" is used as a way of making contact and interacting with those who have died. Retrieval assumes that when some people die, for some reason they get "stuck" before reaching a more appropriate place for them to exist beyond physical reality. While all the various reasons some people get stuck after death are not fully understood, my system makes the assumption that this is possible. It also assumes that in some perhaps rare occurrences, interaction between a physically living human and the stuck individual can quickly resolve whatever issues are causing the person to be stuck. And that once these issues are resolved, the stuck person can easily be assisted in moving to a more appropriate place to exist within our afterlife.

Now, in my mid-60s, I have had the opportunity to teach this system of afterlife exploration to thousands of people in countries around the globe. I'd like to share a few of those stories here to give you the flavor of what's possible. These examples are in the early stages of our participants' learning to use the system of contact and communication within the area of consciousness we call the afterlife. The focus here is on developing the perceptual skills necessary for such exploration rather than obtaining verifiable information.

In these first retrieval examples, you'll see references to a "helper." The helper is a nonphysical being who provides assistance to the retriever with navigational guidance and in the actual retrieval of the stuck person. Some of the reasons individuals become stuck are brought out, and their resolution and the subsequent retrieval are described.

Jamie and the Clown

This example is taken from the experience of a novice during a two-hour, introductory version of my workshop presented some years ago at a Mind, Body, Spirit conference in Sydney, Australia.

After only two hours of training, a woman I'll call Betty described her experience during her first retrieval exercises to the entire group. Betty began by saying that she had no previous experience with retrievals and didn't know quite what to expect. When she asked for a helper to come, a clown in full costume walked out of the surrounding darkness into the scene with her. She described the clown as having a big red nose, wearing big boots and pants with polka dots, and having a comically painted face.

When she asked the clown, her helper, to guide her to someone needing retrieval, she explained that the clown turned and began to walk away into the surrounding blackness. She imagined herself following along. When they ·stopped, a hospital room began to materialize around her. She said the visual imagery was quite clear and that she could see a hospital curtain drawn around a hospital bed. She described a little boy she called Jamie who was sitting in the hospital bed looking somewhat confused. As Betty approached the boy and introduced herself, Jamie explained what had happened. He said that at first he had gotten sick and that as he got sicker he was no longer able to go outside to play with his friends. When he became sicker, he could no longer go to school. Now he had become so sick he was in the hospital and confused by what had happened.

From her discussion with Jamie, Betty understood that both of Jamie's parents, especially his mother, were distraught at his impending death. Each time Jamie's mother was in the room with him, she implored Jamie not to die by saying, "Jamie, don't leave me, stay here with me Jamie." Jamie then pointed around the room at all the medical equipment and told Betty that the last time he had seen his parents they were with the doctor. The doctor had switched off all the machines and drawn the curtain around his bed. Then the doctor and his parents left the room. He told Betty he didn't know what to do now. He had stayed there in his hospital room just like his mother had told him to, but neither his mother nor his father had returned to the room. At that point the clown helper stepped toward Jamie's hospital bed.

Betty said that she expected the boy would be happy to see the clown but he wasn't. In fact, he appeared to be afraid of the clown. Seeing Jamie's fear, the clown gave a big theatrical bow and tipped his hat to reveal a baby chick chirping and walking around on top of his bald head. Jamie happily slid down off the bed and took the clown's outstretched hand. They turned together, walking toward the door.

Betty followed them out the door and down the hallway toward an elevator. When Jamie and the clown stepped into the elevator, Betty followed, standing behind them. Betty said that when the elevator doors closed, she expected the elevator to go up (presumably toward heaven) and was taken aback when it instead started moving down. When the elevator doors opened, Betty said she saw a huge grassy field, like a park. There were dogs, cats, goats, and ducks walking around the park and lots of other children at play.

A little dog walked up to the elevator door and looked up at Jamie. The dog seemed to recognize Jamie and

Jamie seem to recognize the dog. Jamie left the elevator smiling and laughing as he chased after that little dog.

Comment by Bruce:

In Jamie's case it appears that his retrieval was necessary because he had become confused by his mother's strong insistence that he stay there with her and then her disappearance. In all likelihood, he did not realize he had died and so continued to stay in his hospital bed waiting for her return.

Civil War Slave Girl

On my website, there is a forum called Retrievals Only at http://afterlife-knowledge.com/cgi-bin/yabb/YaBB.cgi?board=retrievals. On this forum, people who perform retrievals share and discuss their experiences with other retrievers. At this writing, there are 22 pages of posts to this forum. Ginny, who attended my two-day workshop several years ago, continues to practice the art of retrieval as an act of service to those who become stuck after death. She is an accomplished retriever who has developed a remarkable level of perceptual skills. This retrieval account is just one of many of Ginny's retrievals. This retrieval account is taken directly from her post to the Retrievals Only forum.

Ginny's Forum Post

The helper and I arrived into what I could tell was Focus 23. It was dark, the kind of dark you get when all lights are off at midnight, but I could make out what appeared to be a narrow hallway with doors and windows, which seemed odd, but I put that on a back burner for later. I sensed the helper to my right move away so I focused my attention on the immediate situation.

I could feel the little girl's fear before I could see her or even locate where she was. I got that she was around four or five years old, and she was shaking because she was afraid of being discovered. Not knowing how she would take my sudden appearance, I decided to focus on her and send her as much love as I could. In a few seconds, I could see her in a doorway several yards away. The somewhat puzzled expression on her face confirmed the PUL (Pure Unconditional Love) was working to open her awareness. When she dared to peek around the door trim, looking in my direction, I received her name from the helper and whispered to her. It was like blowing a kiss, except the exhalation of breath was love energy and the kiss was her name, Prissa.

She watched me carefully as I knelt in front of her. For some reason, her face remained in shadow. She was wearing a white cotton dress that was a bit dirty and worn. She had curly black hair cascading down her back. I noticed several rings on her fingers and ooo'd and ahh'd at their beauty, which helped her relax a little. She balled her hands into fists and tried to hide the rings at first, but then decided I must have been safe because she held her pudgy fingers out for my inspection. Some of the rings looked as if they were made for an adult. She responded to my interest in the rings quickly, letting me know they belonged to her mother. I told her I liked her name and she confirmed that I got it right. It was Prissa, not Priscilla. Then she said, Prissa Magnolia. I smiled and suggested we get going to be with her mother.

I picked her up in my arms and we started moving slowly away, following the helper. Prissa kept announcing her name, wondering why I hadn't questioned it. I wasn't sure if her middle or last name was Magnolia, or if she was from a place called Magnolia. When I felt she was communicating that both were correct, I decided it was one more thing about the retrieval I'd ask the helper about at a later time. I then hugged her close and started repeating to her, "You're free now, Prissa. You're free now." I could feel my emotion threatening to take over and I pushed it away for the sake of the retrieval. She remained calm, watching with a sense of wonder as we left the darkened area for clouds and blue sky.

We were entering Focus 27, and I could see that a small crowd had gathered. A black woman, dressed in a long dress with apron, stepped forward, saw Prissa, and tried to muffle a scream as she started running for us. Her daughter was in her arms in a second and they disappeared into the gathered family. I watched with contentment until I got the signal from the helper that it was time for answers; best to leave.

We were then back at the spot in Focus 23 where Prissa had lived in such paralyzing fear. As I stared into the dark hallway, I got a download that I found interesting. The hallway was really a part of a system of servants' tunnels that paralleled the regular rooms in the spacious, two-storied home. Some of the doorways functioned as entranceways to and from the rooms in the house. Even what appeared to be windows had a purpose. They were all camouflaged or hidden from the unsuspecting eye. Only the owners and slaves knew how to negotiate the halls and stairways.

Prissa was wearing her mother's rings to hopefully save them from soldiers who were looting and burning homes. She had lived in Magnolia, Georgia, during Sherman's March to the Sea campaign, in the Civil War, and died in an upstairs servants' hallway from smoke and fire. No one knew she was hidden in the home as it was burned to the ground.

Thanks for reading and much love,

Ginny

Simon's Retrieval and Emotion

by "Outsidecreative"
(forum name of the person who posted this account on the "Retrievals Only" forum)

Outsidecreative's Forum Post

Big thanks to everyone here, in teaching me to drop looking for verification and trust in the process and the reasons we do this—simple compassion.

Here's a description of a retrieval I did only minutes ago to prove that you can't make up emotion (unless you're a good actor, and I'm not).

It took a while to tune into my guide, but when I did, he led me to the left, and we were in a hospital corridor. It seemed fairly modern, last 20 or so years, I guess. Then we were standing in front of a door.

At this point my guide disappeared. I opened the door to the hospital room and felt an intense wave of sadness wash over me. Information poured in so fast I instantly knew the situation.

Tears welled up (physically) as I felt so much compassion. I saw a man in his 20s or 30s sitting against the wall on the floor with his arms around his knees. I knew he was very frightened, scared to death of dying. He was wearing striped PJ's and looking so scared.

I instantly sent him some PUL.

His name was Simon. I tried to feel for information instead of asking him. I felt he'd been in a car accident, been in the hospital a few days and then died. Unfortunately he was so scared of dying that once he realized he was still alive, it freaked him out; he was too scared to go any further. So he was staying in the hospital room paralyzed with fear.

I think the PUL lightened his energy field as well as reassuring him that the afterlife isn't so scary after all, because the ceiling of the hospital room became white light. At this point, I introduced him to my guide, who had come in through the door dressed in a business suit. I realized he was Simon's brother, who had passed on years earlier.

Simon was so glad to see someone familiar that he hugged him instantly. Then the understanding of his situation deepened. His brother said, "C'mon let's go and see Grandma and Grandpa."

I followed them out the door and watched a wonderful reunion in a beautiful, sunlit garden with a grassed area, butterflies, and people milling about. There was a great feeling of joyousness. I feel this was a deliberate creation by helpers to make the scene as calming and happy as possible for Simon.

Simon was still in his PJ's looking around in wonder. He asked about getting in contact with his parents. He was told he would be able to see them soon, after a little rest.

He looked back to me, said thanks, and said that once he learned to visit Earth again, he would drop by to say hi. I said thanks, and I would look forward to it as I'm still learning.

The emotion I felt during this, was eerily close to when I had a past life regression. That indicated to me that I wasn't making it up.

Thank you to everyone for reminding me to trust.

Coma Patient

This next retrieval account is provided by Steve D. who hosts and attends my workshops at the Temple Mound Spiritual Wellness Center in Tarpon Springs, Florida (website at: http://www.templemound.com/) .

Not all retrievals are of deceased individuals. Sometimes, as in this account, the individual retrieved is in a coma. Steve is a well-practiced, skilled retriever who continued to practice the art of retrieval after receiving training in one of my workshops.

Steve D.'s Forum Post

This particular retrieval is unusual in the fact that it was performed without a helper and without setting an intent. In fact, I was in a meditation with another intent altogether. While in a meditative state having a vision along the lines of my stated intent at the time, I was interrupted and taken to another vision altogether.

I found myself standing in front of a women whom I did not recognize, but I was immediately made aware of her identity. She was Karen, the older sister of a friend of mine. I had casually met Karen once, several years earlier. I had heard that almost two months previous, Karen had developed bacterial meningitis while on vacation, had slipped into a coma, and was still in a coma at the time of my meditation.

I became excited as soon as I saw her. Although I had had no training in retrievals and had performed none, I had read several books on the subject, so I felt I might be able to communicate with her and actually help her recovery. I immediately wanted to tell her that she did not belong on the other side, and she needed to come back to her physical

body. I seemed to have been stopped in mid-thought; I felt
or was told that I could not make that broad statement
because it was not mine to decide where she belonged or did
not belong. Only by her free will could she make that
decision.

So, I simply made her aware of the fact that she had a
physical body in another place, and that there were many
people in that place who loved her and would miss her if she
chose to stay where she was. I also told her that she needed
to make a decision. She could not remain in both places. She
had to choose between remaining in the place she was in
now and returning to the life she came from.

Karen was confused. She was not aware that there
was any other aspect of herself other than the person
speaking to me. She didn't realize she had a physical part
lying in a coma somewhere. She thought that where she was
was the only place she could be. I could see (or feel) by her
expression that what I told her was beginning to register as
true, and she started to rapidly fade as I began returning to
my previous meditation. I knew I needed some proof for
myself to verify that the contact with Karen was real, so I
quickly concentrated my attention back on her and projected
the thought that I needed some kind of evidence.

I had barely finished the thought and I was shown
her bare feet with a meticulous pedicure and what I thought
at the time was a toe ring with some sort of insect on it,
possibly a butterfly or ladybug. I tried to get further
information, since I thought it would be uncomfortable to
ask my friend about her sister's feet, but she faded as quickly
as she appeared and I was back in my meditation exactly
where I left off.

When I contacted my friend the following day, she
excitedly told me she had received wonderful news from her

brother in-law, that her sister, without explanation, had come out of her coma the previous evening. As I asked her about her sister's condition, I was able to awkwardly bring up the subject of a possible pedicure that her sister may have had and whether she had any foot jewelry. She seemed puzzled by the question, but said "Yes" to both. The last thing her sister had done the day she was rushed to the hospital emergency room was to have a pedicure, and though she did not have any toe rings, she does have a cluster of moles on her toe that looks like a butterfly.

Karen has since recovered fully but continues to have no recollection of anything while in the coma.

Truck in the Ravine

Steve D. posted another retrieval on his Temple Mound Spiritual Wellness Center website.

Steve D's Second Forum Post

I had a helper appear to me after another retrieval attempt and take me to the scene of a man buried under heavy wreckage. He was barely visible, with only a small portion of his face showing from under heavy wooden timbers and dense foliage. He seemed very surprised that I was able to find him. As a matter of fact, he became stuck in this belief because of his overwhelming feeling that he would never be found because of where he was. He kept repeating that he could not believe I had found him.

He was dressed in a blue denim jacket with a leather collar and a plaid shirt. I asked him his name and he told me it was Michael Britton. He said he was 46 years old, the year was 1958, and the place I found him in was Plainfield, Illinois. He kept repeating that I had to let his wife Belinda and his two sons know where he was and that he was OK. He insisted that I promise him I would do that.

Then he explained what had happened. He had gone out hunting in his blue pickup truck. He had to cross a ravine in the woods by going over an old timber railroad trestle that had been abandoned long ago. He had done so often before. All the track leading up to it had been removed and the forest obscured most of the old railroad bed. This time, as he attempted to cross the bridge the timbers gave way and he plummeted to the bottom of the ravine with the bridge timbers and much of the surrounding branches and vines falling on top of him.

I told him I had brought some help that would be able to get him out. There were several helpers that showed up, though many of them seemed to be just thought forms filling in the picture with needed workers. As we pulled him out, I guided him to a helper, telling the man that this gentleman would help him to safety. The man leaned on the helper's shoulder, and they began to walk out of the forest. They came to a large clearing that turned out to be the park. He seemed very disoriented, since he was many miles into the forest and knew he had never seen a park there before. But now, just a dozen or so yards away from his hunting spot, they happened upon a city park.

As they entered the park, they saw sitting on a wooden park bench along the walk a woman wearing a small, white hat, a blue and white dress, and white gloves. She was knitting. I actually chuckled because it seemed so staged. He immediately recognized this woman as his deceased mother, Lucy, and in a questioning tone said, "Mom?" It was then that the scene faded from me.

I came to know that his name was Michael Britton. The report verified that at the time of the accident, he was wearing a blue denim jacket with a leather collar, and his accident occurred in Plainfield, Illinois, in 1958. He was very concerned about his wife and two sons. He wanted to make sure someone contacted them to let them know where he was and that he was OK. He still seemed concerned that no one would know where he was.

World War II Dogfight

These next three accounts, again by Steve D., are interesting because they involve three separate attempts to retrieve the same deceased individual.

Steve D's Dogfight Forum Post

I went to bed with the intention of doing a soul retrieval before I fell asleep. I drifted off, but awoke to a vision of a WWII dogfight scene. This was happening over the water, but along the shoreline of what I felt was a Pacific island. I was first watching from behind a gun emplacement on a pier or possibly a boat tied up to the pier. The gunner was shooting at the plane or planes. There appeared to be one plane against 3-5 opposing planes.

As I got my bearings and realized what was going on, my awareness shifted to the single pilot, and I immediately was made aware through his thoughts that he was being fired on by his own forces and had already lost his wingman, who was a close friend, as they were flying in from another base. He was unable to communicate on the radio for some unknown reason but was aware that these were his own planes.

He had become enraged by the mistake and was determined to shoot down every one of the opposing aircraft regardless of their being friendlies. I became confused by the number of players present and could not determine who was the subject of the rescue. As I tried to analyze the events, the scene quickly faded. I felt as if I had failed and tried to return but could not.

Steve D's Return to the Dogfight in Another Forum Post

During an attempt to perform another soul retrieval, I unconsciously ended up back at the WWII dogfight retrieval scenario. I was immediately at the cockpit of the lone pilot and now realized he was my retrieval target. I first tried to appear to him as his friend who was just shot down, but could not get his attention and believed that he just thought it was his imagination. I then thought I could speak to him on the radio as a way of playing into his reality, but that failed to get his attention as well. I sensed that he believed the radio to be off, so in his reality it was. It seemed that he was so caught up in the intensity and anger of the moment that nothing could draw his attention away from shooting down the other planes. Retrieval attempt number two also was a failure.

Steve D's Third Forum Post on the Dogfight

After the two previous, failed attempts at retrieving a pilot from a World War II Pacific dogfight scenario, I was determined to go in and get him this time without fail. I armed myself with a new technique I had not yet tried. I would go in, and rather than try to smoothly fit into the scene created by the deceased's belief system, I would do something so extraordinary, and set up a diversion so unique, that I could not help but get his attention.

With this, I entered my meditative state and set up my intentions to perform this retrieval once again. I very shortly made contact with a helper named Jeremy, who wore a long white robe and had long brown hair and a beard. I was thinking that the "Jesus look" was a little over the top. I looked at him and smiled with a small chuckle and said, "Really"? Jeremy smiled back and said, "A lot of us on this side like to go with this look," and laughed. He told me not to be so serious with the retrieval and to just have some fun with it. There are no failures or wrong ways to do them.

As I came upon the pilot again I came to know his name was Charles Danforth and that he held the rank of captain. I saw him in the same scene, intently at the controls of his plane, trying to avoid the other planes that significantly outnumbered him. On this retrieval attempt, I decided to stop the progression of time, and froze his plane as if suspended by a string in midair. As he sat there in shock and disbelief, I parachuted down onto the right side wing of his plane. I very casually released the chute and walked up to the cockpit canopy and knocked on the glass. His reaction was priceless, and it made me half laugh and smile (Jeremy told me to have some fun with it and I intended to). I signaled for him to open the canopy and I addressed him by name and said, "Captain Danforth, open up. I have an urgent message from the CO (Commanding Officer)." He very slowly and somewhat hesitantly opened the canopy, and I handed him a very official looking envelope. Still in a state of disbelief, not quite sure that he was actually holding anything, he opened the envelope and read the message. It simply read, YOU'VE BEEN KILLED. RETURN TO BASE. He turned his head to me, and I nodded, affirming the message was true. The expression on his face alluded to the disbelief that he was actually dead. I told him to look at the condition of his shot up plane, and pointed to a fairly large hole in his chest.

As he began to register what had happened, the helper, Jeremy, parachuted down on the left side wing, and as he released his chute, he walked up to the other side of the cockpit and extended his hand. I told Captain Danforth that this gentleman would escort him to his new squadron where his wingman, whom I instantly knew was Captain Barney Dunn, would be waiting for him. He let Jeremy help him out of his seat though he seemed to float out easily. They walked to the end of the wing where a white marble-looking staircase now appeared. As they began walking up the stairs, I scurried after them to follow them to the park, but the staircase disappeared behind them and they faded into the clouds.

I did some research, and besides learning the pilot's name, I also learned that he died in 1943 in an area around the Truk Islands and he flew a single-seat plane called the "Warhawk."

Verifiable Evidence These Are Encounters with Real People

In workshops around the world, participants have been able to successfully gather information that validates and verifies that the person encountered is a real individual who lived somewhere and passed away. It is quite common for 50% to 80% of the participants in any workshop to receive at least one piece of solidly verifiable information. In some of these cases, both the volume and accuracy of the information is impressive. What follows are just a few of many such examples.

You Can Get in Your Car Now

Jacquom's Retrieval Experience

A workshop in Germany I (Bruce) conducted was attended by approximately 30 participants, about half of whom were psychotherapists. We were debriefing the exercise called Getting a Special Message. In this exercise, each of the 30 participants is asked to write on small, identical slips of paper the name of a person they personally know who is deceased. These slips of paper are then folded twice and placed in a basket. Then, one by one, each participant draws one of the slips of paper from the basket. Each participant now has in his or her possession a slip of paper with the name of the person known to be deceased. Since the slips of paper are all identical and chosen at random they have no way of knowing who this deceased person is, nor do they know which of their fellow participants provided that name. Once all the slips of paper have been drawn, the exercise begins.

The exercise is similar to a guided meditation. Participants are seated in chairs with their eyes closed and are following my verbal instruction. After following instructions intended to help participants relax, and a few other instructions, they are ready to begin the guided imagery portion of the exercise. This guided imagery portion might be an imaginary walk in a forest, a walk along the beach, or some other imaginary journey intended to stimulate their imagination for use as a means of perception in the exercise. Then the exercise to make contact and communicate with the deceased person whose name they've drawn begins.

My instructions guide participants into an imaginary meeting with the deceased person. During this meeting participants are asked to gather certain information from that person. This information includes things like the person's physical appearance, manner of dress, age, manner of death, habits, basic personality and several other such details. The deceased person is also asked to show, or tell about, a physical lifetime scene he or she was in, together with the participant who provided their name, that both would remember. The deceased person is also asked to show, tell or give something as proof that this contact and communication with them is real. Near the end of the exercise, the deceased person is asked for a special, meaningful message to be given to the person who provided their name.

After the completion of the exercise and making very detailed written notes of their experience during the exercise, one by one each participant shares that experience with the entire group. The name of the deceased person is not disclosed to the group until all the information is shared. The participant who provided that name then identifies himself or herself and gives feedback regarding the accuracy of the information that has just been shared.

During the debriefing of this exercise at that workshop in Germany, Jacquom prefaced his sharing of the details of his experience with what I found to be a rather odd statement. Jacquom was one of the psychotherapists in the group who felt that what I was teaching led people to believe that the fantasy stories they were making up during the exercises are real experiences. In his prefacing statement before describing his experience, Jacquom said, "If any of the information I received during this exercise is verified, I'm going to get up from my chair, go out to my car, drive myself to the nearest psychiatric facility, and check myself in."

After sharing some mundane details like age, manner of dress, manner of death, and so on, Jacquom shared the physical lifetime scene that both the deceased and the person who provided his name were in together, as he was shown by the deceased person. In that scene, Jacquom had seen a small round table crowded with cigarette butt filled ashtrays, several empty coffee cups, and a chessboard. He said it felt like a small sidewalk café in a city on the southern coast of France. There were two men sitting on opposite sides of the table casually chatting and playing chess.

In response to Jacquom's asking the deceased to show him, tell him, or give him something as proof that this contact and communication is real, the deceased man said that he and the man who had provided his name often played chess, and that before his death, the deceased man had given the participant a chess set as a gift. The deceased man also said that one of the white nights in this chess set had one of his ears broken off.

It was at this point that one of the other participants, a man named Richard, spoke. Richard's first words were, "You can get in your car now." Richard continued by saying that every piece of the mundane details Jacquom had given were accurate. Richard explained that his friend had died a couple of years earlier. He remembered the specific sidewalk café scene in which he and his friend were playing chess. He also disclosed that his friend had given him a chess set as a gift before he died, and that, indeed, one of the white nights was missing one of its ears.

Comment by Bruce:

Jacquom was immediately so disoriented and befuddled that he could not share any more of his experience, so we never did get to hear the deceased man's special message for Richard.

The Truck Driver in Arizona

Sometimes verification of the knowledge gathered during the "getting special messages" exercise comes in a very peculiar way. In a workshop in Payson, Arizona, after a participant described her experience during the "getting special messages" exercise, not a single bit of information could be verified.

After her experience during the exercise, a woman I'll call Joanne, described encountering a man dressed in Western attire who was showing off his 18-wheeler semi-truck. She described the metallic red color of the truck, the name of the company, the name of the driver painted on the driver's side door, the trailer, its color, and the company name painted on its sides. She described this man's physical appearance, hair color and style, eye color, mustache style, cowboy hat, and colorfully patterned cowboy boots.

As she tried to begin a conversation with the man, he seemed to be avoiding her. Each time she approached, he would walk away going around the truck. She described his behavior as very odd. She spent perhaps five minutes during the exercise attempting to start a conversation with the man, but was able to bring back only information she had seen during her experience. Absolutely none of these details were verified by the person who provided the deceased person's name for the exercise, whose slip of paper Joanne had drawn.

About one month later, Joanne was up late one night, bored and channel surfing on cable TV, when she saw an image of the man she had attempted to communicate in the exercise. He was on her television screen. The TV program was an old rerun of an episode from a series called *Unsolved Mysteries*. Watching that episode, she saw a home movie of that same man looking exactly as she had seen him during the exercise. In the home movie, the man was giving a tour around his metallic red, 18-wheeler tractor-trailer rig. The same company and driver names Joanne had identified in her "getting special messages" exercise were painted on the driver's side door. The name painted on the driver side door of the truck turned out to be the name of the truck driver in the video.

While watching the *Unsolved Mysteries* episode, she learned that this man had disappeared years earlier while driving his truck on a mountain road less than 60 miles from where the workshop was held. It had been reported that he was seen driving erratically and dangerously by others who were driving along the same road. Some of those other drivers drove to Flagstaff, Arizona, to report this to the authorities who sent a highway patrol car to investigate. When a state trooper found the truck, it had been driven off the road into the surrounding forest. The driver's side door was open and it appeared that the driver had left the truck's engine running when he left the scene. Neither the driver nor his body was ever found.

Steve's Submarine

Steve attended a workshop in Sydney, Australia and more than a month later shared this description of his experience during his workshop self-guided exercise. Perhaps you will recall some of the details of the Russian submarine Steve describes.

Steve's Description of His Experience

My second story is more recent. A Russian submarine sank near Norway in the Arctic Sea in August 2000. A day or so after it sank, the story was on the news and I decided to go looking for it to see if anybody was still alive. I started to do my exercises and focused on finding them. I found myself moving through blackness toward a submarine on the sea floor. It was leaning on its right side and the whole front was full of water. In that front area was a strong impression of crew who had already died. At the rear there were many survivors all crammed on the very upper deck.

A few days passed after I did my exercise, and the news reported that the submarine was leaning to one side, which was making it very difficult for a rescue. The news also reported that if there were any survivors they would be on the rear upper deck right where I saw them. I don't know very much about submarines, but this seemed to verify what I saw in my experience. Some people would call it coincidence, but in my experience there seem to be fewer and fewer coincidences.

They Hear You

Suzanne Giesemann, M.A.

Hay House author Suzanne Giesemann is a retired U.S. Navy Commander with a master's degree in Public Administration who served as a Commanding Officer and as aide-de-camp to the Chairman of the Joint Chiefs of Staff on 9/11. The author of 10 books, today former-Commander Giesemann is an evidential medium and spiritual teacher. She addresses questions about the purpose of life, the nature of reality, and attuning to higher consciousness, including connecting with loved ones who have passed on. Her books, workshops, and presentations focus on bringing hope, healing, and comfort. Suzanne backs up her teachings with verifiable evidence received during hundreds of one-on-one sessions with clients and personal experience with higher levels of consciousness.

In a recent test by researcher Gary E. Schwartz, Ph.D., her medium reading was 93.5% accurate, an unusually high score. Using another analysis, her score was 100%.

For more about Suzanne, visit LoveAtTheCenter.com.

They Hear You

Excerpt from the book *Messages of Hope*,
by Suzanne Giesemann

When I greeted Joanne Olsen at my door, my first thought was, *This isn't someone who would normally go to a medium.* Many who come to see me are nervous, but excited. To me, this woman felt unsure and out of her element. I found myself wondering, *Why is she here?*

I invited Joanne to make herself comfortable in my study. She still appeared nervous, so I did my best to put her at ease as I described how the reading would proceed. When I finished my introductory remarks, I held Joanne's hands to tune in to her energy, and then said a prayer. We both sat back; I closed my eyes and invited her loved ones to gather around me.

Joanne's mother and father came in with enough force to leave me lightheaded, but the details were sketchy at the beginning. Her parents' energy was so linked that I mistakenly attributed most of the initial evidence to her mother. After repeatedly getting "no's" from Joanne, we figured out that the evidence I was bringing through actually belonged to her father.

As I more accurately described the couple's personalities, I couldn't help but think that these two souls felt almost familiar to me. Either that, or my readings were starting to sound disturbingly similar. It seemed as if I were bringing through more than the usual number of closely bonded couples from the northeast. The woman came through to me as particularly frail at the end of her long life, and she showed me problems walking. Other facts about their lives seemed to mirror recent readings I'd given, and I began to question myself. Were the details I was getting so common that everyone sounded alike?

Thankfully, I also heard and sensed things I'd never brought through from the spirit world, such as the correct information that Joanne's mother had been adopted and had a difficult childhood. Joanne confirmed my statements that her father enjoyed *National Geographic* magazines and had a penchant for counting pennies.

I'd been holding the link with her parents for half an hour when her father gave me the clearest impression of the entire reading. "What I sense with him," I said, "was that he was a good worker, dedicated to the job, and I'm hearing 'banker's hours, like 9 to 5.'"

"Banker!" she exclaimed. "You got it!"

"Thank you, Dad!" I said aloud, but inside my mind was spinning. I'd learned that once the spirit world gets through to you with a good piece of evidence, they'll use it again if the same thing comes up in a subsequent reading. When I'd heard "9 to 5, like a banker" with Connie England two months earlier, that had been one of my best hits to date, but now I couldn't help but wonder, *How many bankers are out there?*

The two spirits' energy receded after that *wow* moment, so I wrapped up the reading by recapping the highlights. I reiterated a thank you I'd received from her mother for Joanne's care at the end, and the message that her mother and father were happy and together on the other side.

"Was there anyone else you'd hoped to hear from today?" I asked.

"Yes," Joanne replied, looking a bit unnerved. "I was hoping to hear from my husband."

I jerked in surprise and did a quick review of the sensations I felt during our time together. I had sensed no other male presence other than her father.

"How long ago did he pass?" I asked, now feeling as if I'd failed, in spite of the strong evidence from her parents.

"Last March."

I sighed and shook my head. Her husband hadn't even been gone a year. While I could tell that Joanne was pleased to have evidence of her parents' presence, I felt sure she would have much rather heard from her husband.

"Let's see if I can tune in to him," I offered. I closed my eyes and waited, but I felt nothing other than the lingering energy of her parents.

My dismay increased when Joanne told me that Homer, her husband of 22 years, had been the love of her life. The energy in the room felt far heavier now than minutes earlier.

"I'm sorry," I said, "but there's no way to control who comes through and who doesn't. I know it has nothing to do with how much a spirit wants to be present. It's most likely a matter of not being able to match his vibrational frequency with mine."

Joanne seemed resigned to not hearing from her soul mate, but now she made a special request. "I was told that you type up the transcripts of your readings, and I'd like to get one, if I could."

I did my best not to let my face reveal my thoughts. *Who told her that?* I wondered. I'd stopped transcribing each reading several weeks earlier due to the extra time involved. Putting the proceedings in print was a good way to keep track of how my mediumship was improving, and clients enjoyed getting the transcript, but it often took me more time to type them than to do the actual reading.

My to-do list never seemed to let up, but I didn't see how I could say no to Joanne. "I'll try to get to that sometime today," I said. "Do you have an email address I can send it to?"

"It's all right here," she said, and handed me a 3 x 5 card with several lines of handwriting on it.

I took the card and laid it on the credenza next to our chairs. I stood and opened the door to the hallway. Joanne didn't follow me. Instead, she picked the card up and held it out to me again.

"I think you're supposed to read this."

I gave her a puzzled look as I took the card. I scanned the first few lines, but failed to see why it was so important for me to read her name, snail mail, and email address. Then it was as if a light went on in the darkened room as I read the bottom line: *Connie England's sister.*

I looked up at Joanne and tilted my head. "You have to be kidding me."

She didn't seem to understand my reaction.

Then I got it: Yes, Connie England had set me up again. After the reading in which I brought through Connie's parents with such excellent evidence, she had sent me her sister without telling me who my client was. Now I realized that Joanne was sister number three, and it appeared that Connie had set up Joanne as well.

Now I understood Joanne's reticence when she first arrived. I was right: Joanne wasn't the type who would normally go to a medium. Connie had obviously wanted to see if I would get the same evidence from her parents on a third try. Now I also understood why the reading had felt so similar to others. It was the third time I'd had this spirit couple in my study. There was only one banker out there trying to get through to his daughters, and he'd done a darned good job of it.

I stepped into the hallway. "Ty!" I called out. "Connie did it to me again! This is *another* one of her sisters."

He crossed to us from the kitchen and laughed. "That explains it."

"Explains what?"

Ty described how he'd taken the dogs outside just before Joanne arrived. A car went around the cul-de-sac at the end of our street and dropped Joanne off at our house as he and the dogs walked down the street. He noticed how the woman at the wheel had shielded her eyes as she drove past—an act he found peculiar, considering the thick cloud cover that morning.

Now we both knew who the shady character was: Connie, trying to avoid detection.

I couldn't help but laugh. She took my work as seriously as I did, and she knew that by my not being aware that Joanne was her sister, any evidence I brought through would be all the more meaningful.

I looked through the panes on the front door, and sure enough, there she sat at the wheel of her white SUV, now parked in plain view at the curb. I opened the door and marched toward the car with Joanne at my heels. Connie looked up and gave me a guilty grin as I waggled my finger at her. "I can't believe you did this to me again!"

She lowered her head and looked up at me through her lashes. "Do you forgive me?"

"Yes, I forgive you, because I sensed your parents again clear as day, but please tell me this is the last of your sisters."

She assured me there were no others. I then excitedly told her about the evidence I'd gotten during this most recent encounter, including the identical phrase about her father's banker's hours. "There's no doubt it was the same two people," I said. "I'll type up the transcript right away so you can compare all three."

"I didn't tell Joanne anything about the other two readings," Connie said.

We briefly shared some of the more evidential details with Joanne, who still seemed a bit shell-shocked from her experience with me.

"I'm so sorry about your husband," I said again. "Maybe this reading was all about letting you three sisters hear from your parents." I gave Joanne a hug and told her that we could try another time to connect with Homer.

I waved as they drove away, then walked into the house. I was grateful for Connie's gift, but unsettled at my inability to bring through the one person Joanne had wanted to hear from. I knew first-hand the intense longing to find evidence that our loved ones are still around. I'd found that comfort when my stepdaughter Susan had come through so evidentially at my first reading, but I'd been unable to give that gift to Joanne.

I thought about Joanne's reading several times over the next few weeks, especially when I ran into Connie and Joanne at a presentation on mediumship. I ended my speech with the suggestion that those in the audience talk to their loved ones with the assurance that their words would be heard.

Afterwards the two sisters came up to greet me. Connie and I hugged and chatted for a moment, but Joanne merely gripped my hand in both of hers. Her eyes said "Thank you," but she seemed unable to speak.

When I questioned Connie later about Joanne's emotional reaction, she explained, "It was your mention of our loved ones hearing us that got to her. Joanne talks to Homer all the time, but she never senses his presence."

I nodded in understanding. It was difficult enough to go through a loss, but even harder without any signs from the other side for reassurance. Joanne had nothing to go on but faith that what I said was true.

Two nights after running into Connie and Joanne, I awoke from a dream for no apparent reason and looked at the clock. It was 3 A.M. I attempted to go back to sleep, but the dream lingered, niggling at the back of my mind. I rolled onto my back and tried to identify the figure who had played a starring role in the dream. Then suddenly I knew: It was Homer, Joanne's husband.

Still in that hypnogogic state between sleep and full wakefulness, I felt a now-familiar sensation: a presence. I realized with a shiver of excitement that I hadn't just been dreaming about Homer. He was there now. He had used my dream as a way of knocking on the door of my subconscious mind. Now that he'd gotten my attention, a sense of urgency made it clear to me that Homer wanted to get through to his wife.

Okay, I thought, and sent him my own clear message back: *If you're going to wake me up in the middle of the night, you'd better give me something really good.*

I closed my eyes, and just as I do in a reading, I cleared my mind and waited for Homer to put something there.

Necklace.

It was as clear as if he'd spoken it aloud. Then, as an added bonus, he added, *Fingering a necklace.*

I realized I needed to record the words on paper, lest I forget them by morning. Aware that my movements would rouse Ty from his sleep, I rolled onto my left side and quietly slid open the top drawer of my nightstand. Just the day before I'd rummaged through that drawer in search of some scratch paper. The only paper I'd seen was a spiral notebook filled with scribbles. I couldn't risk writing over something and leaving myself with an illegible mess.

Unwilling to turn on the light and disturb Ty, I plunged my hand into the drawer and smiled in surprise at the serendipitous sensation of soft canvas under my fingers. I hadn't noticed my old travel tote there the day before, but now I recognized it by feel. Inside its canvas cover was a full pad of blank paper. My fingers blindly located a pen with equal ease, and I was in business.

"Necklace—fingering a necklace," I wrote in the dark. Grateful to the spirit world for the months of practice they'd given me at writing with my eyes closed, I silently asked Homer for more evidence. He demonstrated his eagerness by giving me one unusual tidbit after another:

"Member of a fraternal org," I wrote. "Either police or Elks."

Then, for some reason, I wrote the next word in all caps: "ROSES—especially the scent of roses."

I tried to write neatly, giving plenty of room between the phrases so as not to lose what would surely be precious gems for Joanne. I flipped the pages with deliberate care, aware that my movements and the scratching of the pen might awaken Ty. Thankfully, he remained silent. I didn't want anything to interrupt this very special exchange.

I needn't have worried. Homer wasn't going anywhere. In fact, he now seemed downright insistent. *I hear her!* he said, and I underlined the word "hear" in just the way he emphasized it to me, followed by his very emphatic, *You have to get through to her!*

Don't worry, I thought back to him. *There's no way she's not going to hear about this.*

Homer followed up his message with a few solo words, sent about thirty seconds apart—just long enough for me to write each down on its own line:

"Hammer."

"Hunting."

"Fishing."

During a face-to-face reading, I always ask for confirmation after each piece of evidence I pass along. Joanne wasn't there to confirm if what I was getting was correct, but I didn't need the feedback. I felt the truth in my heart.

Now on my third page, I wrote a partial phrase as Homer gave it to me. I waited for more, but he seemed to have said what he came to say.

I rolled onto my back and sent a message of my own to Homer: *Thank you so very much for coming, but would you let me go back to sleep now?*

I heard nothing else and drifted off in minutes.

The next morning, I sat on the edge of the bed and read with great excitement the notes I'd written. I knew the spirit world was real, but this was the first time a spirit had come to me in this way. Unlike in a reading, it had taken no effort or request on my part to bring Homer through. The clock told me it was too early to call anyone, so I busied myself getting ready for the day. As soon as it was late enough to place a call without being rude, I dialed Connie England's number.

"Is Joanne still visiting you?" I asked, holding my breath.

"No," Connie replied. "She's back with our sister, Margaret."

I felt a tinge of disappointment. I'd wanted to deliver Homer's message in person, along with the hug that I felt sure he wanted her to have.

I filled Connie in on my nighttime visit. She said nothing in response to my mention of the necklace and the fraternal organization, forcing me to continue reading her my notes. When I brought up the roses, she took in a breath.

"Oh!" she said, "Roses were Homer's 'thing'!"

I went over the rest of the list, ending with the final phrase Homer had given me. For some reason I'd enclosed it in quotation marks: *Etched in stone.*

"Do you know what that's about?" I asked. "Do you know if there's something special on his gravestone or some other reason why he'd give me that?"

Connie remained guarded. "You'll have to ask Joanne about that."

A bit nonplussed at her lack of feedback, I hung up and dialed the number she gave me to Margaret's home. No one answered. I didn't want to state the purpose of my call on an answering machine, so I left a simple message, saying, "Please ask Joanne to call me as soon as she gets in. It's very important."

Finally, she returned my call. Hearing her voice, I took a deep breath and picked up the notes that by now I'd committed to memory. I smiled in anticipation. Unlike when Susan had visited me during my morning meditation, this wasn't a case of having to prove myself and what I'd heard. Homer had been so clear, so *present*, that it was simply a matter of delivering his loving message.

"You may find this a bit shocking," I said to Joanne, "but Homer paid me a visit in the middle of the night."

Her swift intake of breath revealed her astonishment, but it also hinted at the same hungry hope I'd experienced after losing our Susan: *Are they really not gone forever?*

The line remained silent, and I savored the moment. I knew that nothing could replace the human touch, but in a way, I was about to give Joanne her husband back.

One by one I shared the notes from the pages in my hand. One by one Joanne confirmed them all.

The necklace Homer spoke of was a crucifix that Joanne had given him on the day they were married. It hung on a gold chain that he wore every day during their 22 years together. Joanne informed me that she'd been wearing it since the day he crossed over and that she fingered it all the time, just as Homer had said. "In fact," she told me, "I'm fingering it right now."

She confirmed that yes, Homer had, indeed, been a member of a fraternal organization, but it was the Odd Fellows. When I told her about the roses, it became clear why I'd written the word in capital letters. They truly were his "thing," as Connie said. Joanne described the great pride he'd taken in growing a wide variety of roses around their yard, pruning them, and bringing them to her as a special gift. The note about especially remembering the scent of roses reminded Joanne of a time when she'd been feeling particularly down while driving her car. Her cigarette smoke filled the confined space, until the air was suddenly and inexplicably filled with the scent of roses.

The hammer, Joanne informed me, was in reference to Homer's life's work in construction as a builder. Yes, he hunted, and yes, he fished.

Those details, while meaningful and appreciated, paled in importance when I shared Homer's most critical message: *I hear her.*

I gave Joanne a moment to digest this, then asked her about the final phrase he'd given me. "Why would he talk about something being 'etched in stone?' Is there something meaningful written on his gravestone?" I asked.

Joanne's voice was filled with wonder when she said, "He wasn't just a builder, he was a master *stonemason*."

Even though I knew the spirit world is all around us and not off in some faraway place, I still raised my eyes skyward and whispered a heartfelt thank you to Homer and to God for this precious gift. I still don't know why Homer hadn't been able to get through to me when Joanne came for her reading, but he made up for it in a way that neither of us would ever forget.

"How can I possibly thank you?" Joanne asked with palpable emotion. I shook my head on the other end of the phone and told her there was no need for thanks. I was simply the messenger—overcome with gratitude at how the spirit world had used me to reunite these two soul mates, and awed at the persistence of a loving husband who wanted so badly to let his wife know that he was still around.

Look upon the window.
See the shiny glass
Just like that through which you go
When to our world you pass.

It's like a one-way mirror—
That which you look through.
You look but cannot see us
But we certainly see you.

We're with you when you call us.
We gaze upon your face.
But know that while we like this,
Your touch it can't replace.

We miss your hugs and kisses,
The feel of your soft skin.
But all else remains the same for us,
Most of all the love within.

Call us when you want us 'round.
We're with you in a flash—
Brushing by your shoulder
Like the flutter of a lash.

One day you'll know our world up close.
For now you see it not,
Yet you go there in your dreams at night
And by morn you have forgot.

But remnants of us do remain
In your thoughts when you awake.
This gift we leave you in your mind,
A part of us that you can take.

So gaze around you through the glass
That so thinly does divide us.
And know that when you think of us
Much joy you do provide us.

Automatic Writing

Irma Slage

Irma Slage is a psychic medium who has shared her abilities for over 30 years through her automatic writing, private and public readings and lectures, clearing negative energy from real estate, hypnosis workshops, group events, and helping law enforcement. She uses automatic writing as a tool to teach communication from the spirit world. She gives messages and comfort to those on Earth. Irma can see deceased individuals and hear their voices as if they were in the physical world.

Irma is the author of *Phases of Life After Death—Written in Automatic Writing*, an inspirational account by spirits who answer the questions about life after death written in automatic writing through Irma. Irma also authored the book, *Psychic Encounters—A Guide to Having Your Own Spirit Contact*, which tells about ways of having psychic communication.

She has been featured on NBC television, and led viewers on a psychic tour of the Winchester Mystery House in San Jose, California. She has also appeared on many radio and television stations and major national and local newspapers.

Irma uses her gift to help paranormal researchers investigating ghost hauntings. She is also enlisted by people who need her help to clear their houses of unwanted spirits.

You can read more about Irma on her website at irmaslage.com.

Automatic Writing

Excerpt from the books *Phases of Life after Death — Written in Automatic Writing,* and *Psychic Encounters — A Guide to Having Your Own Spirit Contact*

by Irma Slage

When my mother Sophie died of a sudden heart attack in her Philadelphia, Pennsylvania, home, my own life seemed to end as well. My mom. Always there for me. Always a supportive friend. Always so gentle and so strong. Always so firm, yet considerate and thoughtful and forgiving.

While sitting in my living room, alone in my darkness, I suddenly felt the need to pick up a pen, then paper. I started to write the capital letter "G." It was curved in a very round, artistic, distinctly creative way. We each have our own way of writing the letters. This was definitely not the way I would form the capital letter "G."

I went to my mother's house to help my dad the following weekend. I was cleaning my dad's kitchen when my eyes were drawn to a corkboard my mother had hanging on the wall for phone messages. It was near the phone, not far from the kitchen sink where I was standing. For some unknown reason I had put the paper with the capital letter

"G" I had written in my pants pocket. I pulled it out and matched it to the writing on the corkboard. The "G" on the board and the "G" on the paper in my hand were written exactly the same.

Excitement filled my shaking body as I called to my husband, who was in the next room.

"Ted!"

He came running as if from the tone of my voice something was terribly wrong.

"What is it?"

"Look at this." I tried to control the excitement in my voice. "The 'G' I showed you last night and the 'G' written on this paper, by my mother are exactly the same."

He took a closer look at the writing on the paper in my hand and then at the paper on the wall.

"They are the same."

"Look at the way the "G" is sort of rounded at the top, but then squares off.

He looked again.

"They are the same."

While I was almost jumping with excitement, my husband appeared shaken, a little less color in his face, and a great deal of concern for our sanity.

"What do you think of that?" I asked.

"I don't know. It is the same, that's for sure," he said reluctantly.

"It must be my mother trying to tell me she can use my hand to form letters.

"It seems so."

My husband was a skeptic back then and didn't want to believe that my mom was contacting me. I believe it frightened him.

"When we get home, I'll try again."

Later that night, I got a piece of paper and pencil, sat down on a comfortable chair at my kitchen table, paper in front of me, pencil in hand, and immediately the pen began to move. I watched in astonishment.

"Hi, Irma. I'm glad you understood the message from the capital letter 'G.'"

"That was you writing with my hand?"

"Yes," the pencil wrote.

There was no doubt that the person was my mother. I don't know how I knew; I just felt it.

"Are you all right?"

"Yes, everyone here is loved. It is so beautiful. Don't worry about your dad. He will be fine. It makes me sad to see him walking around that big house by himself."

Tears came to my eyes. I was very worried about my dad, dependent on my mother for so many years. They just celebrated their fortieth wedding anniversary.

"He'll be fine," my mom wrote again.

We communicated for another few minutes.

"Mom, is there something you can tell me that will prove that this is really you?"

The pencil wrote, "I took care of the dolls you had as a child. I bought them new shoes and socks. I washed their dresses. Take them home with you. Don't leave them in your dad's house."

"I will," I promised, speaking out loud.

I sat back in my chair. I felt so relaxed, as though I had taken a nap.

I stared at the writing on the paper. The handwriting was not mine. My handwriting is much smaller and bolder. The writing on the paper was shaky and irregular, and all of the words ran together. I had to make notes so I could remember some of my questions and fit them to the answers.

I didn't know it at the time, but writing through the pencil in this way is called automatic writing. Since then, I've read many books on it. Many people can do it and are not aware of their ability.

My father had Alzheimer's, and on his bad days on Earth when he appeared not to know what he was doing, his spirit body was sitting in my house enjoying my family, and talking to me. On those days when he appeared to be coherent on Earth, he was mostly in his body.

My father's spirit continued to communicate through my automatic writing while he was still on the Earth plane with Alzheimer's. The one thing he wrote with my hand many times when he would visit me in his spirit form was how unhappy he was to go back to his body on Earth and that he wanted to stay in the spirit world. He was so sad for years, and then one day he came to me and he was smiling. I could tell he was happy, but he didn't say why. Within a month he broke his hip and after a successful operation, died suddenly. He came to see me after he died, a very happy and relieved man, filled with the wonder of his new life.

In my book, written through automatic writing, a man wrote through my hand telling me much the same thing as my dad. He expressed it word by word. He wrote,

> My following feelings are mine alone. I was
> never in my body during the times it appeared.
> I had no memory or thoughts. I was not there. I
> was here watching people trying to control
> their tears and frustration. Then, when I finally
> left for the last time, when my time to stay in
> the world had come to an end, I knew it in
> advance and was very happy. I can't tell you

how happy I was to be leaving that body for
good.

He further went on to say through the automatic
writing,

> My life here continues in a helpful way to
> those who need me. For as I see a person going
> through what I did with Alzheimer's, I tell him
> to hold on because the end is near and the end
> is always here in a place where we can
> continue.

Our loved ones always hear us when we think of
them, no matter how much time goes by. It brings to mind a
young mother I helped on Earth. She lost her husband when
he was flying in a small aircraft and it crashed.

"Oh well," she said, "It's been so many years he
probably doesn't think of me anymore."

Her husband then spoke to me through automatic
writing and I gave her messages from him that meant
something to both of them. It was descriptions of things
between them that I wouldn't know anything about. It
showed her that our loved ones are never far from us.

Through automatic writing many of the people I
write with who have died at an older age prefer to be about
thirty years old in the spirit world, or any age that makes
them feel comfortable. The first time I saw my elderly great
aunt after death, she appeared to be in her late 20s and I
didn't recognize her, but still, somehow I knew who she was.

Most of us know someone who has taken his or her
own life. I didn't until 1977. Until then, people on Earth had
told me that because these people took their own lives, they
were in a terrible place so they would pay for doing such an
awful thing. Here's what I've seen for myself.

His name was Lou, a neighbor who was five years younger than I was. He had marriage problems that he could not handle, and he hanged himself. I was sitting at my kitchen table crying after hearing this news, when I looked up toward my kitchen light fixture on the ceiling. Lou was looking down at me. He was a very bright light. He wanted me to stop crying because of him. With my pen on paper, he wrote that if I had died first and had come back and saw him crying, I would feel terrible; that's how he feels.

I stopped crying and stood up closer to where he was. My sadness stopped and in its place was one of the greatest joys I ever felt. I asked him if he was okay, because I heard that people dying as he did were in a terrible place.

He continued to write that he was in a beautiful place surrounded by love and not to worry about him.

There are times when spirits can use their energy to move physical things on Earth, including a pen to paper. I've heard these stories from people I have helped and they know the person who is moving the object. Generally, it is close to the person's funeral, or when a problem comes up that concerns them or someone they love, or even to let us know they are with us. They may push a picture to the floor, or make a light go on and off. In my case, I've had doors slam shut and open in my house. I felt my mom's arms around me as she hugged me after she died. And when I put her wedding ring on my right ring finger, I felt a jolt of electricity as she put the ring on my finger with me.

My husband, Ted, felt a special connection with a friend of ours after he left Earth. When I showed him my technique to have him use automatic writing, the person who wrote through my husband's hand was Owen.

It was years before this when I heard that my friend Owen was in the hospital. The first thing I did was talk to him through my mind. I can talk to anyone, living or deceased, including pets.

Shortly after his surgery, I asked Owen if I could help and what he would want most. He told me he wanted to go home. I then worked through my guide to get him well enough to go home. It was wonderful to know that he got his wish and was doing well. That was short lived, because soon after, he was taken back to the hospital with complications.

His health went up and down, and during this time I was in constant mental communication with him, making sure that he got plenty of help from the spirit world and that he knew I was trying to get him home once more.

In talking things over with some friends of ours, everyone knew that, in all probability, Owen would not make it through this illness. I felt Owen next to me at that moment and knew that he was counting on me to help get him out of the hospital once more. I asked all the people who have power on the other side, and one day as I sat typing, I heard a very nice voice in my mind say, "You don't know what is best for the people you are trying to help. Please know that you can't change anything this time."

The spirits were very nice but firm on this. I knew then that Owen was not going to make it, and I also knew that I was not to ask anything else of them.

A couple of days later, I was putting something on a low bench that is in my bedroom. As I bent over, I felt as though I had stopped in midair, body forward, and I had the feeling that time had ceased. As I stood up, I knew that a male spirit was behind me. I looked at the clock and it was 6:40 p.m. Later that evening, I received an email from his wife, Arlene, saying that Owen had died that night at 6:40. I felt elated that he had come to see me shortly after passing and that he knew I had tried to help and didn't feel that I had failed him. That would not have been Owen anyway. He was someone I was lucky to know.

Years later, I asked the other side for help as we struggled through a problem. The response came from Owen to Ted and me using automatic writing. He wrote that all will be well, and that he is with us.

While our life continues on Earth, as well as after we die, I felt that being one with each other is the most important concept of the books I wrote. We certainly felt one with Owen; he understood our problem and reached out to help.

Stories showing that we are all one in my first book, *Phases of Life After Death — Written in Automatic Writing*, are written by the spirits of men, women, and children of all ages, races, and religions. They came from different countries and backgrounds.

They may have been rich or poor. They may have been powerful people, or average people while on Earth. All of them have one thing in common: the memories and emotions of the life they just left.

In writing these stories using automatic writing, and as I transcribe these stories, I feel that all of the writers are trying to help us by giving us insight into their world as we continue our life on Earth. They want us to read their stories and keep them in mind as we experience our lives here.

Some of these people will give you memories that will stay with you for a long time, such as the young soldier who was in the Vietnam War. I will remember his story always, because I saw his face in front of me while he was using my hand to write. He was a tall black man in his early 20s with kind eyes. While in Vietnam, he was part of a combat team that was completely wiped out. His description of watching his family as they got the news of his disappearance brought tears to my eyes.

Here are excerpts of his words as he had me write them on paper:

> I was a military man, complete with a rifle and a lot of other arranged equipment. I am not certain of the passing of time but when I left my body, it did not seem as though a lot of time had transpired from the time I felt the pain in my shoulder. Other deceased soldiers were there with me, and one by one we were shown the way to a different spot. We drifted in different directions. One of the spots I was taken to was my mother's living room. There was a military man standing in the middle of the room dressed in his proper attire who came to give my mom my medal and tell her of my disappearance. The people who were in that room were the ones who mattered to me, and a few others, and they would find peace through each other.

Some of the people who spoke through my automatic writing in my book will be like people you know from personal experiences.

A man who had abused alcohol wrote through my hand that when he was on Earth he felt that his life was not worth anything. He found after his death that it wasn't true. The one person who needed him, his brother, learned most from him after he died. These are his words written through automatic writing:

> My brother was in the hospital trying to conquer alcohol. He was crying and grabbed

my picture, holding it in his hands, and all in
that room, including me, hovering beside his
right shoulder, knew he wouldn't leave the
facility again without winning his fight with
alcohol. My picture never left his hands or his
pocket in his pants. In death, I became his
inspiration to get well.

And some of these people will take you through their
own lives that may mirror your own. They are teachers.
They will guide you as you read, just as they guided my
hand and my heart as they wrote these stories.

They want you to remember them, and not to forget
why we are on Earth and what our lives mean to each other.

We all have a continuation of life after the initial
leaving of our bodies. Automatic writing gave me the
opportunity to communicate with those people we can learn
so much from.

That includes pets. Anyone who is close to their pet
will tell you that communication between pet and owner is a
very special bond. I give messages to people from their pets
whether they are on Earth or have passed on. Messages
about pets are also included in my book using automatic
writing. This is one example of what was written as my
hand was guided:

My cat was taken away from me by death. No
matter what happens to us, when a person or
animal seems lost to us, that is not the way it is.
The way it is is that we are connected to
everyone. That's how we are still together. On
the side I am on now, I just focus my mind on a
person's name or an animal's name, and I have
their locality.

Our life with people is interwoven. It is the same with our pets.

We are constantly communicating with the spirit world through our subconscious. Using automatic writing is one of those resources to bring those messages to our conscience mind.

An example of confirmation came when we first moved to the area where I live in California. A lot of information comes to me in the first five minutes of waking in the morning. We had just moved to a new city, and I felt I had to go to Castro Valley, California. I asked my husband how close Castro Valley was because I had never heard of it until that moment. I also got the names of streets to visit using automatic writing. I went on the Internet to find out how to drive to those streets. This is my interpretation of the reason this information came through and of what happened next.

Ted and I got in the car, and while Ted drove along the streets written on the paper I held, I did more automatic writing, asking the young spirit girl from whom I was getting the messages why we were going to where she was directing us. She wrote that I would find out soon. When we arrived at the street she had specified, we emerged from the car, not knowing what we were to see, and walked around. We noticed an in-ground water tank. Not seeing too much else, we got in the car and drove down another one of the streets she mentioned. I knew that street was significant to the young spirit with us, but I didn't know why, so I again wondered why we were there.

The next instruction from the deceased girl was to go to a nearby park. We parked and walked to a section of the park with small hills and valleys that had nothing on it. We stood there enjoying the view and thinking how nice it was.

My husband and I enjoyed the beautiful summer day, but still did not understand why we were sent to these places in Castro Valley. I found out the next day when I went online.

I opened an email from Cheri, who told me about her young daughter, Valerie, who had recently died of cancer. The email was pretty long, and at the end she mentioned in that they used to live in Castro Valley. I wrote Cheri back telling her the complete story of where we went and what we saw in Castro Valley and that we did not understand why we were there until her email. She wrote back and said that not many people who live in Castro Valley know about that water tank, which told her that we had walked around the area. The street we drove was the street where her family, including her deceased daughter, Valerie, lived while growing up. The park was shown to me because her daughter loved the hills and valleys that are there and the peacefulness that her daughter felt while looking at them.

Valerie's aunt wrote to me after buying my book. Using automatic writing, I wrote a letter to Valerie's aunt. The letter was signed, "Scarlett." I didn't know why until I received her aunt's email shortly after with the following explanation:

> I was filled with excitement to realize the identity of the Scarlett about whom you wrote. Valerie was fascinated with the movie, "Gone With the Wind," and had collected all the memorabilia, which Cheri has saved. What a validation. Who else would call herself Scarlett?" A Scarlett and Rhett Butler dancing figurine was given to Valerie by my mother-in-law many years ago, knowing her love for the

movie. Cheri also reminded me of the Valerie-Scarlett connection.

Valerie, the young spirit girl who sent me to Castro Valley, found a way to let all of us know that she was with us. I used automatic writing to give her mother and her aunt messages from her, and those messages continue today. The spirit world is always helping us with many things.

Sometimes when people come to see me for a psychic reading, I give them a letter to take home with them using automatic writing. In a sitting with a woman, I gave her a letter to take to her sister who couldn't make the reading. I signed the letter, "Take it easy, Pal."

I didn't know why it was signed that way at the time, but I received an email later from the woman's sister telling me that her deceased father used to always say those same words when she left his house: "Take it easy, Pal."

You Can Use Automatic Writing

Automatic writing comes in many forms. It may come in drawings, numbers, or letters. You may be shown something in your mind like a picture; you may hear something in your mind like words; or you may feel an emotion. It may be none of these or all of these. Whatever it is, just write it down as you see it, hear it, or feel it.

While keeping our minds as clear as possible, our hand writes whatever comes across. I always start automatic writing by concentrating on writing a letter of the alphabet. From there, things take different paths for different people.

One example happened to a woman named Rhonda. When she put the pen to paper, she wrote the letter "M." The picture she formed in her mind was of her deceased mother, whose name was Marie. The picture was of her mother at a young age, in the house where she grew up. It gave her the emotions of love, comfort, and feeling calm. She reported feeling treasured, peaceful, and not alone. She had been thinking of her mother for the past week because Rhonda's husband had just passed and she wanted her mother's comfort.

Another message through automatic writing came from her deceased husband. The message was "Love, time, live, happiness, and enjoy."

Rhonda felt it was from her husband and felt the message meant he will always love her and wanted her to find happiness and enjoy life.

When Alice came to do automatic writing, she had been thinking of her Uncle Dee who had passed away recently. The message she got through automatic writing was, "The bump is on the stairs. It has to do with something big."

Alice explained that her great, great Aunt Florence lived in a Victorian house in Monterey. Alice and her husband visited the front of the house a few years ago with a copy of the original picture that they gave to the current tenant. There were grey cement steps that were steep going up to the front door. Alice's great Uncle Dee had been there many times, as well as Alice. The house had been in their family for generations.

Alice felt that the bump on the stairs had to do with the conflict in the family through many generations.

She also said that while writing the message, she felt relaxed and open, and although it was two generations back, she felt as though all took place in the present.

Alice spoke to her spirit guide through automatic writing. Her guide described himself as an older male. She saw blue rays shooting out of his hands toward her as a healing. He wrote the names of colors on the paper for her to feel. He described them as orange, blue, and yellow. He also wrote, "Have fun. Soon. Good-bye."

In asking her how she felt during her automatic writing session, Alice described herself as feeling, "sad, like crying, when he said good-bye."

Her feeling was that the colors were energy levels for her to live by and that she had a physical healing. The next day, Alice said that she had a physical condition that was greatly improved.

When Pam came to me, I brought her down to a very relaxed physical state. I told her to write a letter in the alphabet that meant something to her. The letter that came on the paper was "A." Pam said it stood for "alligator." For some reason that word came to her with thoughts about her female cousin named Willie who died years before. When they were kids, they spent a lot of time together, including overnights. They would play cards and have fun. While sharing a bed, if a pillow went off the bed, her cousin would tell Pam that she was not allowed to get it because alligators were there. To this day she can't get her pillow if it falls off of her bed in the middle of the night.

When Albert came to do automatic writing, the message that came through was, "This is from David S. your friend. I am glad you know who I am. I am doing well. I hope to see you on this side someday. I am sorry that we didn't contact each other before." The picture in Albert's mind was of David 45 years ago when they were in high school together. He was happy to see David's face. The letter from him meant a lot.

Frank didn't have anyone in mind to speak to when he came to do automatic writing. The pen began to write, "My name is Alan. I am here to help you with your kids.

Stay true to yourself. Enjoy life. Don't worry." Alan had died years before. Frank was worried about his kids and knew Alan had kids also that he had problems with.

An example of speaking with someone through automatic writing came from Jessie. Jessie was sad when he came to see me and needed someone to help him know that it was okay to be happy. His Uncle Simon had just passed to the other side. Jessie's pen went to his paper and it began to write, "This is Simon. We are all going to have fun today. Be upbeat and happy about everything and have a happy day. Listen to music, sing your favorite song, and dance to make you happy and forget." His Uncle Simon knew that Jessie enjoyed music and it made him happy to get that message.

When we are children, psychic occurrences seem natural. We don't give things like this a second thought. We don't know how different and special it is. As we grow older, we realize how important communication from the spirit world is, and it is nice to know that our loved ones are not far from us. Automatic writing is one way to give us the opportunity that opens up a new world.

Healing through
Direct Connections

Mark Ireland

Mark Ireland is the author of *Soul Shift: Finding Where the Dead Go*, a moving account of his personal quest for answers about life after death he embarked on after the loss of his youngest son. Mark is the son of Dr. Richard Ireland, a renowned mid-twentieth-century psychic-medium. Mark is co-founder of an international organization to assist bereaved parents called "Helping Parents Heal" and author of *Messages from the Afterlife*.

Mark's website is at markirelandauthor.com.

Direct connections

Excerpted from *Soul Shift: Finding Where the Dead Go*, and *Messages from the Afterlife: A Bereaved Father's Journey in the World of Spirit Visitations, Psychic-Mediums, and Synchronicity* by Mark Ireland

Although the books I've written to date have focused primarily on spirit communication facilitated through mediums, my family, friends, and I have also experienced some extraordinary direct connections. For me it is the aggregate evidence from all these forms of contact that provides great comfort and confirmation that my loved ones (and yours) carry on after physical death—with their personalities intact. I would like to share some of these direct connection experiences with you from my two books: *Soul Shift: Finding Where the Dead Go,* and *Messages from the Afterlife: A Bereaved Father's Journey in the World of Spirit Visitations, Psychic-Mediums, and Synchronicity.*

I realize that some readers may not know me, so I would like to provide a brief introduction. I am the son of Richard Ireland, a renowned twentieth-century psychic who founded an inter-denominational church called *The University of Life,* where he demonstrated his psychic and mediumistic abilities to validate the reality of "the Gifts of the Spirit." He also ventured into the secular world to open minds, counseling celebrities such as Mae West, Glenn Ford, and Amanda Blake, and was acquainted with the Eisenhower family.

Although my father had phenomenal abilities, I was not really interested in following in his footsteps, nor was I particularly inclined to enter this field. But that all changed with the unexpected and gut-wrenching passing of my youngest son, Brandon, in 2004. This triggered me to embark on a personal search, resulting in my engagement in afterlife research, a renewed desire to carry on my father's legacy, the pursuit of a speaking and writing career, and the co-founding of "Helping Parents Heal."

To date I have participated in mediumship research studies, serving as a test sitter in experiments conducted by the University of Arizona and the University of Virginia. I have also been involved with my own consciousness-survival investigations, assisted by respected scientists such as Tricia Robertson of the Scottish Society for Psychical Research and Dr. Don Watson, a neuroscientist. My approach has been to take complex information and distill it into something clear and relatable to the layperson.

In 2011, I published a book written by my father in 1973 titled *Your Psychic Potential: A Guide to Psychic Development*. It was never released during his lifetime. In the summer of 2004, a man acquainted with my father handed me the complete manuscript for the first time. This was a book I'd never seen. The man explained that he'd been holding it for twelve years, since my father's death in 1992. I asked why he decided to give the book to me at this time and he responded, "I don't know, I just feel like I'm supposed to do this."

Approximately two weeks later, I had a reading with medium Allison Dubois. While referencing communication from my father, Allison said, "He's signing a book and trying to hand it over to you — like it's his book he's handing over [to you]. Do you understand that?" Yes, I understood.

With this background information in place, I will move on to personal stories of direct connection, beginning with one of the very first experiences I had after Brandon died.

Just a few days after Brandon's passing, I sat meditating quietly in a darkened room. In the past, I had experienced feelings that proved to be accurate, but rarely anything graphic. Now I saw an image of Brandon's face, which I felt was surrounded by something indescribable, but which gave the sensation of warmth and joy. I can best describe this feeling as a simultaneous melding of different sensory input. After the vision of Brandon's face, I saw a symbol: a cross with an oval loop at the top. I was not familiar with this image, so I later searched on the Internet. The cross proved to be an "ankh," an ancient Egyptian symbol that predates the cross of the crucifixion. The lower portion of the symbol represents physical life, while the oval loop portion at the top symbolizes eternal life. I took this visionary message as a symbolic way to confirm that Brandon was indeed alive and well.[1]

These experiences were not limited to me, but came to my family members and friends as well. My son Steven also began meditating after Brandon died. About a week into the process and two weeks after the passing, Steven had a vivid dream that both he and I believe was an astral experience.

Astrals, commonly referred to as "Out-of-Body Experiences," are different from everyday dreams. During astrals, our senses are astonishingly lucid, and surroundings seem exceptionally real. While in this state, our physical body remains asleep while our soul or "spiritual body" apparently travels in other realms or "planes."

While sleeping, Steven heard music emanating from our living room. Walking toward that room, he saw Brandon playing the bass guitar. He immediately ran to his brother and gave him a hug. He later noted that the embrace was so real he actually felt the threads of fabric on Brandon's shirt.

Steven then asked his brother, "What's it like?"

Brandon replied, "At first it was so weird, but now it feels incredible. Why don't you come visit me more often?"

The scene was amazing for its ordinariness and obvious supernatural aspects, and it also suggested that Brandon had entered a different zone of space-time because it seemed too soon to ask this poignant question.

After the encounter with his brother, while still physically asleep, Steven hovered above his body and observed the time on a clock in his room. As he awoke,

Steven opened his eyes and looked at the clock, finding that the time was exactly the same as the time he had just seen in his "dream" without the aid of his physical senses . . . his grandfather's son, for sure. So, it seems that the incident with the clock was a validation.

While lying in bed on Saturday, February 17, 2004, I was thinking about Brandon and strongly sensed his presence. In my mind I thought, "Brandon, I know that you are here—please just give me a sign." Within a millisecond, I heard a very loud rap in the bedroom and, since the sound originated from the room's interior, it was clear that no external force could have caused it.

A few nights later, in my dream, I saw a young version of Brandon playing in the back of a minivan that we used to own. For some odd reason, I couldn't seem to stay in a dream state and started to wake up. As this occurred, I noticed a pronounced rattling coming from the area around our sliding glass door. I then realized that the chain used to open the vertical blinds was banging. There was no draft in the room at the time, nor was there any physical explanation for this phenomenon.[2]

About two weeks after Brandon's passing, I made contact with James Linton and Eadie Ostlund. These two people had been following Brandon's group on the mountain on the day he died and they were the first to arrive on the scene in an effort to provide assistance.

The couple noted that they'd been hiking in the McDowell Mountains that day with friends and followed Brandon's group for about three hours. Eadie was strangely drawn to Brandon and his friends and felt the need to stay near the boys. Eadie recalled experiencing mixed emotions, ranging from delight upon seeing the teenagers laughing and joking, to an inexplicable sense of anxiety. She did not understand these feelings, yet they persisted all day. What was it, I wondered, that drew Eadie to Brandon's group? Was she an unwitting aide in a cosmic process, beyond her immediate surface awareness? Brandon and his friends moved at a fast clip, creating separation from James and Eadie's group. As Eadie noted, "We saw the boys throughout the day, on a pace that was typically about twenty to thirty minutes ahead of us. I continued to keep an eye out for them and remembered that one boy's red shirt was particularly easy to spot. [Stuart Garney was wearing the red shirt.] Mike, one of the men in our group, wanted to venture around the back of the mountain through a wash, but I was reluctant because I wanted to stay close to the boys. I just kept thinking about the possibility of an emergency. "For about an hour, I had this anxious feeling and wanted to get to the top in order to see the other group again."

As James and Eadie reached the summit, they saw one of the boys waving for help in the distance. As Eadie shared, "When we made it to the top I saw a boy waving his arms, jumping up and down. [This proved to be Stuart.] At first I thought he was saying 'hello' but soon realized that he was calling for help. At this point I knew something was seriously wrong and immediately called 911. Mike ran ahead to meet the boys, while I stayed put in an effort to retain my cell phone signal. Despite these efforts, my call dropped about halfway through the conversation and I was forced to call back two more times. The person I spoke to failed to grasp the extreme urgency of the situation, as I had to repeatedly stress our need for immediate help. Jim, Laurie, and I started moving toward the boys, following Mike's path. Mike arrived at the spot where Stu and Brandon were located about ten to fifteen minutes after leaving our group.

Upon his arrival, Mike yelled back, 'He's not breathing — call 911 again to send a chopper!' At this point I knew that someone in their group had died."

When Jim, Eadie, and Laurie approached the group of boys, they saw Brandon lying on his back, pale white. It was obvious to the adults that he had already passed away, but they didn't know how to share this with the boys, who seemed to be in a state of confusion and perhaps denial.

Stuart Garney, Brandon's best friend, and another friend, Chris, had been working vigilantly, performing CPR for over thirty minutes in an effort to resuscitate him. Eadie encouraged the boys to head back down the mountain and most of them did, but Stuart refused to leave Brandon's side. The EMTs arrived soon thereafter and tried to revive Brandon, but it was too late.

Eadie continued, noting, "I remembered feeling bad for the family, knowing that the parents would soon hear from the authorities about their son. I also remember feeling terrible for those young men and what they had to go through that day, losing their friend and not being able to save him. I had this feeling of guilt inside for not paying attention to my sense of anxiety and worry. Could we have intervened and helped prevent this or at least provided CPR sooner?"

James said that the area where they found Brandon's body seemed hallowed, and that he sensed his spirit "hovering above." I then shared my uncle's earlier affirmation, where he noted that my father had met Brandon upon his passing.

In response James said, "Not only was your father there with Brandon, but a host of angels as well." Continuing, James noted, "As I stepped away from Brandon and allowed the EMTs to work on him, I first sensed him hovering. I didn't see a person in the flesh per se, but had a vision in my mind's eye, where the sky opened up and a host of angels was there to welcome him."

James and Eadie sensed a positive spiritual energy all around them. James shared, "To me, the feeling was almost like being on camera; you know that a lot of people are watching but you can't see them. I knew something tragic was happening, yet I felt as if there was an invisible arm around each of us, letting us know 'It's going to be all right.' In fact, I was drawn to a boy [Stuart] whom I hugged. I then remember saying, 'It's going to be all right, it's going to be all right' even though I knew he [Brandon] was gone. I felt calm and comfort in the midst of chaos. Stu had noted seeing multiple points of strange lights in front of him as he hiked back down the mountain. When I asked him to describe these lights, he said that they were like "auras" or "small colorful orbs." Other friends at the base of the mountain, including Stephen Varns, also noted seeing some "strange twinkling lights" in the area where Brandon died.

Six months after Brandon's passing, my wife and I took a vacation cruise with our son Steven and the boys' friend Stuart Garney. On the evening we returned home, my wife, Susie, while sitting at the foot of our bed, felt Brandon's presence and then saw him to the right as a "shadowy figure," discernable through her peripheral vision. She felt a sense of warmth and comfort.

On the following morning, we received a call from our new musician friend James Linton, who had been alone all week while Eadie visited relatives in Michigan. During this period, James spent most of his time composing and recording music, and strongly sensed the presence or energy of another. He felt pushed to modify a particular song, which would later become "The Other Side." As James sat down he saw a "shadowy figure" out of his peripheral vision in much the same manner as Susie had, and also (later in his songwriting session) flashes of white light—in fact, multiple points of rapidly moving light that produced something akin to "a vapor trail."

James had experienced accurate precognitive dreams before, but nothing like this. Wondering if he was losing his mind, he kept trying to regroup and snap out of this mental state, but there was no escaping this odd sensation. After accepting the apparent reality of what was taking place, he finally gave in. At this point, James found himself asking the following question out loud: "Okay, Brandon, what do you want me to do?" After this bold affirmation, everything started to flow.

James was guided to modify two main parts of the song, the bass line and lyrics. James' initial bass track was basic by design to feature the guitar. Additionally, he did not own a bass guitar so I had loaned him Brandon's instrument, which presented another complication. Since James is left-handed and Brandon was right-handed, James had to play the bass upside down. Initially, this seemed to be a limiting factor. As he began to revise the bass track, however, something very unusual took place. James started playing an entirely new and more complex line and said, "It felt as if someone else took over while I was playing." The new track resembled Brandon's style of playing.

After finishing the bass track, James felt instructed to "listen to the music without the words." His original lyrics and music were now completely different—this was entirely new material. The new lyrics, which came to James rapidly, were captured and recorded almost immediately.

After finishing the project, James told us that "The Other Side" was the best song he'd ever written, but that he didn't write it. James explained that the song was a gift from Brandon to us, his family.[3]

In late fall of 2005, my son Steven and a friend had independent experiences that seemed to correlate to one another, followed a short time later by the most enjoyable and exhilarating connection experience I've ever had.

On September 28, 2005, my son Steven had an intensely vivid dream involving his brother that we both assumed was astral projection or out of-body experience. The event was so real and tangible that Steven woke up depressed upon realizing that his brother Brandon was not physically with him. On his drive to work that morning, Steven noted feeling his brother's presence just as if he were riding along in the car next to him. The visitation was bittersweet for Steven, comforting on one hand, yet painful on the other.

Later that morning Steven received a phone call from a friend, David Friedman. David, who had been close with both Steven and Brandon, described a similar dream encounter, which occurred on the same night as Steven's episode. Before this event David had not experienced a single dream involving Brandon since his passing—a period of one year and nine months. In recalling his encounter, David described a conversation in which he asked Brandon to share his thoughts about dying at such a young age. In response, Brandon told David that he had "no regrets" and shared his perspective that "death is part of life." Brandon went on to explain that he now enjoys tremendous freedom, which allows him to be wherever he wishes with just a thought. David was then able to experience a sampling of Brandon's world, sensing a lack of restrictions as he "sailed over mountaintops with an indescribable feeling of joy and freedom."

In the afterlife, perhaps there is no need for "real mountains" in order to facilitate such an adventure—maybe one just has to think it to live it. When you consider how we perceive such things—through senses that are subject to distortion, merely relaying interpretations of what seems to be out there—who is to say which experience is more real? Then again, the next realm could conceivably be just as real and solid as this one. It seems a matter of the arrangement or architecture of energy.

Ultimately, the tandem nature of Steven's and David's encounters point to something outside chance, beyond coincidence, especially knowing that this was David's first such "dream" involving Brandon, and both boys' experiences took place the same night.

Two months later, I experienced my own profound episode involving Brandon. Just before going to sleep one night, I made a prayer request for a visit from my son and asked to be able to remember everything afterward. This appeal was answered beyond my wildest hopes. I experienced one of the most profound and enjoyable occurrences in my life —a visit with my son.

The first thing I must say is that the experience was incredibly lucid, feeling every bit as vivid as a personal interaction with someone while wide awake. In fact, I truly thought I was awake and knew with certainty that the encounter was absolutely real. The two of us were alone in a stark room that was "self-illuminated" in white light. There was no furniture or light fixture of any kind; it was just an empty white room with three walls. It was amazing to note that where the fourth wall should have been existed was a deep void, which I assumed to be the rest of the universe. . . infinity. It appeared that our small room was but an island or sanctuary, a place for the two of us to meet in the midst of all eternity. Despite the surrealistic nature of our surroundings, it truly seemed that we were both in physical form, fully awake and totally conscious, as mentioned before. Brandon sat in a wall cutout, about counter height, suspended about three to four feet above the ground with his legs dangling but not touching the floor. Dressed in his standard garb, Brandon appeared in a tee shirt and jeans and wore his favorite skater-style sneakers.

Excitedly, I looked at my son and said, "Brandon, you're back, I can't believe it!" I then looked around for someone else to tell, calling out for Steven, Susie, and Stu Garney, but none were nearby. I then told Brandon, "I've missed you so much since you died," and he responded with a statement that puzzled me greatly, saying, "I didn't die, my father died."

I pondered Brandon's statement for days, wondering why he would refer to me, his father, in this manner. Then I thought about whether he might have been referring to God or someone else with him now who might represent a father persona. After repeated attempts to decipher the meaning of Brandon's statement, it came to me intuitively. Two nights later I was explaining my experience to Stu, when the meaning came in a flash.

Brandon was simply trying to tell me that there is, in fact, no death. There is but a transition from this physical realm to the next one, like walking through a doorway, perhaps akin to the missing wall in the white room. So in this respect, Brandon "did not die." In saying that his "father died," Brandon was referring to the pain I suffered in "losing" him, which made me feel as if a part of me had died. In hindsight, I believe that the message was delivered in a veiled way so that I would be forced to contemplate the deeper meaning and ponder the significance of his statement.

But it could also have been simply that meanings are different in that other world and this was the only way in which he could speak, or more precisely, the only way in which I could understand what he was saying because he wasn't actually speaking in the embodied sense (mouth, tongue, and pharynx). In fact, this "disconnect" ultimately served as a point of greater validation to me. Had this episode merely been the creation of my mind, seeking to provide a sense of comfort, a different and more predictable set of circumstances surely would have resulted. In such a scenario, I would have expected my son to say exactly what I'd hoped for in a literal way I would have understood. I would have also been satisfied to hear and see him in a manner far less vivid that what I actually experienced. Instead, I encountered something beyond anything I could have requested or had even imagined possible. I was like one of Plato's cave dwellers suddenly come into the light.

As a footnote, I also came to view the statement about my "dying" in an added way. I understood that a spiritual rebirth had taken place in me, which might never have occurred if not for this painful catalyst.[4]

I later experienced two impactful dreams involving Brandon in the same week. Each of these events occurred at the end of my sleep, while lying in what was likely a deep REM state. While these episodes were not as vivid as an "astral" experience I had in 2005, which was as clear and tangible as waking reality—in which I believe I went "out of body"—they still bore the stamp of an authentic encounter with my son.

Brandon was younger in these dreams—about ten years old rather than eighteen as he was at the time of his passing. And while these particular experiences were not as lucid as the earlier event, my interaction with Brandon felt completely real and I could sense the love between us. Our talk was relaxed, and Brandon demonstrated the dry sense of humor I'd grown to love. We even hugged.

If the spiritual realm is an alternate dimension of reality, it seems reasonable to think that communication between such divergent spheres would be challenging. I also suspect that the type of manifestation may correlate to our emotional readiness for such a meeting. Further, the validity of the encounter should not be measured solely on the basis of the visual clarity, but equally, or perhaps even more, on the feeling of connection. Assuming that this sort of contact is telepathic in nature, perhaps the mind receives the equivalent of raw data and converts it into a meaningful message or experience, with consideration for our degree of understanding. When you think about it, such a premise is not so different from waking-state "reality," where our eyes and ears pass along information to our brain, which interprets the "sights" and "sounds" comprising a significant portion of a personal experience.

In the few days following these experiences with Brandon, I asked myself if they were real encounters or just comforting dreams. It wasn't until another dream a few days later that my question was answered for me.

Just before waking one morning, I dreamed that I was holding an open container of milk that smelled sour. This odor lingered even after I awoke. I wondered if the milk really had gone bad—the carton was less than a week old. I walked into the kitchen, reached into the refrigerator, and grabbed the carton. The milk was sour. It became clear that I should trust the information I received, whether dreaming or awake.[5]

In the summer of 2006 I took part in a healing workshop facilitated by my father's friend and former assistant minister, Lin Martin—a man I respected greatly.

During the workshop, I was instructed to complete a "chakra balancing" exercise with a woman named Lyndsey. In this process, one person lies down while the other stands over them and administers healing. Through visualization and intuitive feel, the healer seeks to balance energy evenly among the body's seven chakras. (The concept of the chakra is tied to Eastern/Hindu philosophy and refers to seven energy centers where the physical body is said to be linked to the soul, spiritual body, or higher self, depending on your terminology preference.)

When I finished administering Lyndsey's healing, she started crying. I must have had a puzzled expression on my face because she looked up and was compelled to explain what had taken place. Lyndsey said that Larkin, her deceased husband, had visited her during the exercise. She sensed his presence very strongly and felt his large face next to hers but was frustrated that she couldn't hear him. Then, telepathically, she attempted to tell Larkin, "I can't hear you, try something else." A short time later, while my hands were above her second chakra, located near the lower abdomen, Lyndsey suddenly heard Larkin for the first time since his death. Later, in our group debrief, Lyndsey told everyone that this was the most compelling and exhilarating event she had experienced in the four years that had transpired since receiving a startlingly specific and pertinent message from a complete stranger at Larkin's funeral service. In this case, Lyndsey divulged that her husband had apologized for an unresolved issue during the healing and also told her, "You are so precious." Lyndsey responded to Larkin with a sense

of deep forgiveness and felt as if a major burden had been
lifted.

Next it was my turn to experience a chakra balancing.
I climbed onto the table, stretched out, and relaxed, hoping
to achieve a meditative state. While lying there well into the
exercise I started thinking, "This is nice, but nothing much is
happening." The very next moment I received a mental
impression that seemed to reflect my father's energy and
sense of humor, conveying the message, "You're not done
yet. We've got something else in store for you."

The next thing I knew, the Eastern meditation music
being played seemed to morph into "How Great Thou Art,"
one of my dad's favorites and also a selection at Brandon's
service. Moments later my body was flooded with what felt
like a strong electrical current running from my head to my
toes. This sensation was different from anything I'd ever
experienced. I felt as if I were connected to two ends of a
high-tension wire—one attached to my feet and the other
attached to my head. Along with this electrical sensation, I
felt a strong spiritual presence, which I assumed to be my
father and possibly Brandon. It felt as if they had poured
themselves into me for this brief period, which seemed to
last about fifteen seconds.

Just as I was coming out of this state of consciousness,
I felt someone touch my nose quite firmly. I initially
suspected that Lyndsey did this to stir me, but when I
opened my eyes I found her hands nowhere near my face. I
then asked if she had touched my nose. She hadn't and there
was no one else near us. This process impacted me deeply,
and I surprised myself by breaking down when it
concluded. What ran through me felt so loving, joyful, and
lighthearted that I was brought to tears. It's very hard to

capture the essence of these feelings in words, other than to say it was a hallowed experience.[6]

Not long after this experience, another interesting connection took place involving this workshop group.

In early December 2006, I received an email from the medium Jamie Clark, who shared the message, "Brandon says 'Merry Christmas.' He wants you to know that he is going to give you a present." Jamie then asked me to let him know when I received the gift. Christmas came and went and nothing unusual seemed to come my way that would fit the description of a gift from my deceased son. Then a few days after Christmas something rather remarkable happened that seemed to match up with Jamie's prediction.

I was attending one of Lin Martin's seminars on December 30, 2006, when another participant named Wendy Hill told me that she had a gift for me. When she handed me the present I noticed that the wrapping paper bore the word "Believe!" Wendy explained that she had been inspired to craft a hand-made wind chime for me, featuring a silver metal frame and stained glass inserts. She noted that the gift was ready before Christmas and she planned to give it to me then, but she missed the prior session due to illness.

I thanked Wendy for the kind gesture, but expressed my confusion over what had stirred her to do this. I couldn't see why I'd been singled out for such a gift when there were many other deserving people in our group. Wendy then told me that she'd been inspired and felt strongly compelled to craft this gift for me. She initially assumed that the inspiration was coming from my sister Robin, who had recently succumbed to cancer, but something else didn't seem to fit with that idea. Wendy explained that she had begun working on a specific piece when "a strong male energy" told her to try again with the design she had selected initially. Resistant to the unsolicited directive, Wendy continued to work with the piece she'd already picked, but the metal frame somehow broke in the process. She soldered the damaged spot but it immediately broke again. Resolute, Wendy soldered the spot one more time, yet it broke again! She had never experienced anything like this in many years of working with these materials. Submitting to the request she was feeling, Wendy said, "I give up—what is it that you want me to do?"

At this point, Wendy felt guided to start working on a different piece. She had been "told" that she must place a green bead in the center. This seemed to provide a clue as to who was doing the nudging; Brandon's favorite color was green, and the color had come to symbolize our son to us in many ways. Wendy also felt a sense of insistence that pushed her to wrap the item, although she initially intended to provide the gift unwrapped. Wendy's experience of being guided in this way sounded remarkably similar to the account provided by James Linton in relation to the composition and recording of the song "The Other Side."[7]

Endnotes

[1] Ireland, M. (2008). *Soul Shift*. Berkley, CA: Frog Books. pages 50-51.

[2] *Soul Shift*, pages 51-52.

[3] *Soul Shift*, pages 56-62.

[4] *Soul Shift*, pages 188-190.

[5] Ireland, M. (2008). *Messages from the Afterlife*. Berkley, CA: North Atlantic Books. pages 135-136.

[6] *Messages from the Afterlife*, pages 141-142.

[7] *Messages from the Afterlife*, pages 142-143.

Pendulum
Communication

Carol Morgan

Carol Morgan is a happily married mother of two sons, Joey and Mikey. Her oldest son, Mikey, passed into Spirit in 2007 at the age of 20. He was killed in a jeep roll-over accident in the Colorado mountains at the beginning of his junior year of college. Awakened by the doorbell in the early hours the following morning by a policeman, paramedic, and minister, chills went down Carol's spine. Their worst nightmare had happened. Carol and her husband Mike had physically lost one of their precious sons. Joey's brother and hero was no longer with him. The devastation and deep heartache that followed were unbearable. How could they ever survive without him? A huge part of their family was gone.

The heartache and fear extended to Mikey's friends who were present at the accident. However, there was never any blame or anger toward anyone. The Morgan family felt deep love and concern for them. They did all they could to help these friends get through this tragedy as well. Everyone

181

was hurting and everyone made much effort to comfort one another.

Two years after Mikey's passing, Carol was one of seven mothers in the United States chosen by the Dying To Live Again Foundation to participate in a Mother-Child Reunion Retreat in Sun Valley, Idaho. The retreat was to focus on communication with their children who had passed into the afterlife. This foundation was started by Sally Baldwin, a spiritual medium. At this retreat, Sally told Carol she had the ability to communicate with her son. Sally taught Carol how to communicate with Mikey using a pendulum. Without mediumistic abilities or any prior knowledge or skill, Carol has practiced her pendulum communication techniques so vigorously over the past four years that Carol and Mikey are now in regular contact. They work together to answer questions on Afterlifeforums.com and elsewhere, and provide detailed afterlife education for people from all over the world.

Here is her story.

Carol and Mike Morgan lived a regular life in Minnesota raising their two sons, Mikey and Joey. Carol worked part-time as a physical therapist at the local hospital, and tried hard to attend all the different activities her boys were involved in. Carol and Mike belonged to the Catholic Church and raised their sons with this belief system.

For years before Mikey's passing, the Morgan family would go to Colorado for skiing and snowboarding vacations. As they drove up Interstate 70 to Copper Mountain, it was tradition to play a John Denver CD and sing "Rocky Mountain High" at the top of their lungs! Mikey always said that his friends would probably make fun of him if they knew how much he liked John Denver music.

Mikey's love for snowboarding and the mountains brought him to Colorado for college.

Mikey loved life and was very involved in activities. He had a smile that would light up any room. His beautiful auburn hair curled out from underneath the Minnesota Twins baseball cap he always wore. Mikey was in the business school at Colorado State University, focusing on marketing.

He loved to listen to music and had great interest in the messages that songs give. He pursued this interest and ended up working as a DJ at the popular restaurant and bar near campus. Mikey worked hard at this job, eventually getting to be the main DJ on the big college nights. Though his song selection had to focus on the most popular tunes of the time, he had a few favorites that he played at every event he could. Bob Sinclair had written two songs that Mikey felt had some great lyrics with a strong message. "Love Generation" and "World Hold On" talked about the importance of love, peace, and unity. "Love Generation" was Mikey's favorite song at the time of his passing. This song became his trademark, and he pushed it out there for everyone to hear as much as he could. "Be the love generation, peace and love to everyone you meet . . . look to the rainbows and you will see, the sun will shine to eternity!" Little did Carol know that Mikey was laying the foundation for a bigger plan and message that was about to unfold.

Mikey passed into Spirit on September 22, 2007.

Almost immediately following the accident, Mikey began to give signs of his survival to Carol, his dad, and younger brother. As people found out what happened, they came to the Morgan house to help give comfort. One of the neighbors turned on the radio and John Denver was playing.

Mike was outside crying for Mikey when he looked up to
see the flag on the flag pole flapping in the wind, but there
was no wind! Joey called Mikey's phone number with his
cell phone and within a minute their house phone rang.
When they picked up the phone, no one was on the line.
This occurred at almost 11 p.m. Joey knew Mikey had called
him back!

Friends and other family members were noticing
signs and having dreams with messages as well. Hearts
showed up on bowls coming out of the dishwasher and in
the bottoms of coffee cups. The kitchen light would go on
and off by itself when someone talked about Mikey. Mikey
hated the sound of a vacuum cleaner. Vacuum cleaners of
friends and family were burning out the first week after
Mikey's passing. He still hated the sound!

The most significant sign for Carol occurred three
days after the accident, again two days later, and then again
when she was in stores as time went on. After Carol found
out about the accident that caused Mikey's passing, one of
Mikey's friends called from Colorado. Carol asked him to
please send home Mikey's treasured baseball cap. She felt if
she could not have Mikey, at least she could have and hold
his beloved cap. His friend said he had the cap and would
send it to Minnesota with some of Mikey's clothes.

After planning the funeral and arriving home to a
kitchen full of people, Carol noticed a box on the counter
that was delivered to the house while they were gone. She
opened the box to find the Minnesota Twins baseball cap
sitting on top of some of Mikey's clothes. Carol grabbed the
cap, holding it and smelling it. She took it into the bay
window area with Mike and Joey following her. The sky
suddenly opened up on this heavy overcast day, with sun
rays beaming in strongly into the kitchen. The warmth was

tremendous, with a strong feeling of Mikey's presence. Carol called out to everyone, "I can feel him! I can feel Mikey! He's here! I know it!" As she said this, a John Denver song was playing in the background.

When the song finished, the sun went behind the clouds and the feeling of Mikey's presence was gone. Carol began to weep with heartache. A strong feeling of concern filled the room. One of Carol's friends said to her, "Did you hear that song? It was "My Sweet Lady" by John Denver. Mikey was using that song to talk to you." Carol could not remember the lyrics, so she got out the CD and played the song. The words described how she felt perfectly, and Mikey was making it clear that he was as close as he could be.

Two days later, Carol was sitting at the kitchen table with Mike and Joey, getting pictures ready for the video Mikey's friends were putting together for the funeral. They were listening to music on the CD player, trying to calm themselves. The player was full of discs with the music on full shuffle. The doorbell rang and Mike got up to answer the door. When he got there, all that was outside the door was a box, with no return address. As Mike stood holding the box, Carol suddenly noticed the song that was starting to play: "My Sweet Lady" by John Denver. Carol told Mike to hurry and open the box. She became frantic about it as the song played. When Mike opened the box, inside was Mikey's original Minnesota Twins baseball cap, all worn out. The cap they had already received was the new one Mikey had gotten as a gift for his birthday that year. He apparently never threw the old baseball cap away. Carol knew that hearing "My Sweet Lady" at the moment she opened the box with Mikey's treasured original cap was her son communicating with her! It had happened each time the hats arrived.

This song played over the PA system when Carol walked into Walgreens; it played when she went to Joann's Store to buy decorations for Mikey's gravesite; it followed her for two years. The lyrics of this song were so powerful, it was as though the song had been written for Carol. The words perfectly described her tears and heartache as she grieved for Mikey, but she needed to understand that their lives were now joined and entwined. Truly, their time was just beginning.

Carol was having dreams of Mikey that were so real she could feel him. He would talk to her and tell her he was not really gone. "I can hear you, Mom, when you talk to me!" Carol also felt she could hear Mikey's voice at times during the day. But she put that off as wishful thinking and that it was probably her imagination.

Carol attended meetings with Compassionate Friends, a grief support group for parents who have lost children. During one session, she met Mitch Carmody. He was presenting on Whispers of Love, which was about signs from our loved ones who have passed into the afterlife. Carol was thrilled about this presentation; it confirmed to her that what was happening was real. It was not a coincidence like some folks told her.

Mitch asked if anyone in the audience had a sign to share. Carol talked about two signs she received from Mikey. After the presentation, Mitch asked Carol if he could publish one of her stories in his column in the *Living With Loss* magazine. Carol agreed, and one of her stories was published. A few months later when the magazines arrived, Mitch called Carol to tell her she could pick up some extra copies at his house. When Carol arrived at Mitch's house to get the magazines, he looked at her and said, "I just received an e-mail from Sally Baldwin from The Dying to Live Again foundation. She is picking a small group of mothers from all over the United States for an all-expense paid trip to Sun Valley, Idaho, for a Mother-Child Reunion Retreat based on communication with signs and dreams. Carol, I am tingling all over! You need to apply for this! You have had so much going on with signs and dreams." Mitch gave Carol Sally's email address. When Carol got home, she contacted Sally and told her about all her experiences.

A few days later, Sally contacted Carol and asked her to fill out the application for the retreat. Many mothers applied. Within a couple of weeks, Carol was told she was accepted. The retreat was in October 2009. Being raised Catholic, Carol suddenly felt hesitant. She was excited but also worried because of what she had been taught by the church. She decided to talk to her elderly cousin, a practicing Catholic nun who had been loving and helpful to Carol since Mikey's passing, to ask her what she thought. Her cousin was a strong believer in signs and dreams as communication and believed some mediums truly have the gift to communicate directly with our loved ones. Her cousin told Carol she needed to attend the retreat. She felt that what was happening to Carol was real, and she was picked for a reason.

This gave Carol the confidence she needed. She attended the retreat.

The retreat was at a beautiful resort in the mountains of Sun Valley. Carol met the retreat staff, including Sally Baldwin, her husband Steve, grief counselors, Reiki and healing touch practitioners, a massage therapist, and other loving supporters. All the mothers met together on the first day. Sally explained the format for the retreat. She first focused on signs and dreams as communication.

The second day, Sally did private readings for each of the mothers. During this session, Sally told Carol she had the ability to communicate with Mikey. Sally said that Mikey was of a high energy and had great ability. Sally told Carol that Mikey was persistent in getting his mother to this retreat and that he had communicated with her. She said the fact that Carol never held blame or anger to anyone involved in the accident, including God, was just not the norm. She said to Carol, "Because of your loving connection with your son and the fact you hold no blame or anger, you have the ability to communicate with Mikey. I will show you how to communicate using a pendulum."

In the days that followed, Sally taught the seven mothers who attended the retreat how to use a pendulum for communication. She gave each a pendulum and a colored disk that had the alphabet and numbers 0 through 9 on the outer edge. The mothers sat at a large table, each working with a pendulum and disk. Sally had the mothers ask for God's loving guidance as they learned to communicate with their children.

The mothers were asked to decide how the pendulum would move for the answer "yes" and for the answer "no" from their children. Carol asked Mikey how he would move the pendulum for her. Mikey moved the pendulum clockwise when Carol said "yes', and counter-clockwise for the word "no." This was a miracle for Carol! She could see the energy change the movement of the pendulum with each question.

Sally then told the mothers to center the pendulum on the disk and ask their child to spell a message. For Carol, the pendulum started to swing up toward the letter L. When she lifted the pendulum over this letter, Mikey moved the pendulum in a clockwise motion confirming "yes" to this first letter. Carol then centered the pendulum again on the disk and it started to swing up to the letter O. When Carol moved the pendulum over this letter, again Mikey circled it clockwise confirming "yes" to the second letter. This pattern continued until Mikey spelled "LOVE." When Carol asked him if this word was correct, he swung the pendulum strongly in a clockwise motion confirming "yes."

Tears began to roll down Carol's cheeks. She could hardly believe it. She was actually communicating with Mikey! She could see what he was saying! Sally had the mothers practice by asking their children simple questions and working on getting the answers with the pendulum and disk. Again and again, Carol received messages from Mikey. It was truly an emotional experience.

When Carol returned home, she was excited and fearful. Who would believe this? Her husband supported her; he too was amazed by the whole thing. She was cautious about whom she would share this with in the beginning. Carol practiced every day. She would ask for God's protection and would ask Mikey questions. He would answer them by spelling out each word on the disk. It was obvious to Carol that it was her son as he talked just as he did when he was on Earth.

One day as Carol practiced, the pendulum started to swing wildly at an angle, a direction it had never moved before. When Carol asked Mikey what that meant, he said that is how he will move the pendulum when he is laughing. Soon the pendulum became much more animated with Mikey's humor!

As long as Carol continued to develop her pendulum communication in this way, her messages were consistently brought forward with integrity and love.

As Carol improved her skill, she began to experiment. She substituted coupons and a newspaper for the alphabet disk and had Mikey spell things with the pendulum. He did it successfully. She put a key on a string and had Mikey move it in different directions. He did it. He could even do it with a full set of keys! Carol began to notice how precise the movement was becoming. Mikey was moving anything on a string, including a necklace. What she used did not matter.

Over time, Carol began to realize she was hearing Mikey telepathically as the pendulum moved. As she continued to practice, Mikey would give her the first letter of the word and Carol would say the word she heard. Mikey would confirm by a "yes or no" movement of the pendulum whether she was correct. This made their communication much faster. If Carol made a mistake, Mikey would correct her and give her the letters until she had the right word. This continued to improve over time until Carol could hear up to a sentence of information from Mikey. She would then say the sentence and Mikey would confirm with "yes" if it was correct. If necessary, he would make changes to messages by spelling the corrections with the pendulum on the disk.

Carol began to practice her telepathic communication as she drove to and from work, asking Mikey questions out loud and then listening to the answers. When she arrived at home from work, she would confirm how accurate she was with the pendulum. Her ability continued to improve with practice, and the pendulum always gave Carol the validation she needed with the messages received. The pendulum is now a critical communication tool for Carol.

Mikey's communication started out quite simple for Carol. He would tell her how much he loved her and his family. Mikey said that life is eternal and the "Heavenly dimensions" are all around us. Mikey told Carol she would see him again and that their hug in the afterlife would be 100 times better than a hug on Earth! Death on Earth is only a temporary physical separation; we are still very connected with our loved ones. They do come to our important Earthly events and watch over us. They can see and hear us, especially as they draw close to this dimension. Mikey talked about the signs and dreams he gave her, confirming they were real communication. He talked about their dogs in the afterlife, and how Chelsea, the golden retriever, still loved to play fetch with her ball. Mikey described the beautiful colors, scenery, and music he experienced. He said he was still snowboarding and was really good!

Mikey told Carol he was wearing his baseball cap and that he looks exactly the same as the last time she saw him. He feels and looks solid. He just does not have his Earthly internal organs. Mikey told Carol they generally take on an appearance with their energy of when they looked good while on Earth. Communication is telepathic in the afterlife dimensions. Vision is 360 degrees.

Gradually, Mikey progressed with the knowledge he was giving Carol. He told her that they had a plan before they came to Earth to teach through the veil about the afterlife. That it is all about LOVE. Mikey said he needed to leave when he did to fulfill this plan.

Being raised Catholic and having absolutely no knowledge of afterlife concepts, Carol was overwhelmed with the information Mikey was giving her. Through the pendulum, Mikey communicated to Carol using vocabulary she was not familiar with. He talked about the many vibrational dimensions in the afterlife, that these dimensions are based on love, and that everything is energy. Whatever dimension we are experiencing will feel real and solid to us.

Mikey told Carol that the afterlife dimensions are more real and solid than the Earth dimension! The higher a soul's loving vibration is, the more magnificent the loving dimension that is achieved. With that comes progression in spiritual ability. The souls in higher vibrational aspects or dimensions can move lower, but lower cannot go higher. This is what gives us the desire to increase our loving vibration and progress spiritually.

Mikey told Carol that the basis of all things is love; we come to Earth for life lessons to grow spiritually and raise our loving vibration; we may come several times. Mikey said we generally travel in soul groups and work on our life lessons together. We have spirit guides who try to keep us on course. However, free will can alter things along the way. Mikey feels the Earth is our toughest school because of the many influences that exist here!

Mikey describes God as the unity of absolute, pure love, which is infinite. It is the collective, loving force: the "Love Team" we are all part of. He said God is beyond anything the human mind can comprehend. Mikey told Carol that God is not a man who sits on a big throne and judges people. God does not strike us down. There is no eternal damnation. There is always loving guidance to help souls progress if they choose. God = LOVE. The more loving we are, the more God-like we are. It is truly a unity of loving souls! Mikey said life is really all about love, kindness, forgiveness, and not judging others.

Mikey said there is no concept of time in the afterlife dimensions. Those constraints apply only here. He told Carol they travel through the various afterlife dimensions by altering their vibration. They can walk, travel in a "vehicle," or move instantly by thought. They visit loved ones, enjoy music and other activities, and continue to work on their spiritual growth.

Mikey told Carol they are aware when a loved one is about to return home. As we transition out of our bodies, our dear loved ones come to guide us back to the afterlife dimensions. There may be some confusion initially, but our loved ones do help us greatly. We are embraced in love and light! Mikey says the celebrations are glorious!

Mikey says that the technology advancements on Earth are guided and channeled to individuals. Scientists in the afterlife dimensions continue to work on progression and improvements of various technologies here. Mikey says that many movies and songs have been influenced by those in the afterlife dimensions as well.

It has been quite the journey for Carol. She knows Mikey led her to meet Sally Baldwin to learn she had the ability to communicate with him in the afterlife dimension. Mikey also guided Carol to meet Roberta Grimes, who gave her the opportunity to use the knowledge from Mikey to help others have a better understanding of the afterlife. Together, Carol and Roberta work on Afterlifeforums.com, answering questions from people all over the world. Carol moves forward with the mission of helping others with afterlife concepts, and having people understand that our loving connections with those who have passed never end!

They can communicate with us!

Dream Connections
with the Afterlife

Rosemary Ellen Guiley

Rosemary Ellen Guiley is a leading expert in the paranormal, metaphysical, and spiritual fields, and is the author of more than 50 books, including the *Pocket Dream Guide and Dictionary*, *Dream Messages from the Afterlife*, and five other books on dreams. She has been a lay facilitator of dreamwork since the early 1990s, helping people explore their dreams in one-on-one and group settings.

Rosemary has been featured in documentaries, docudramas, and television shows on The History Channel, The SyFy Channel, The Discovery Channel, Animal Planet, A&E, Destination America, NBC's Sightings, and a number of other broadcast media.

She also conducts workshops on developing intuitive and psychic ability. She is a former board member of the International Association for the Study of Dreams. Rosemary is a frequent guest on *Coast to Coast AM*, where she often discusses dreams. Her website is visionaryliving.com.

Dream Visits from the Dead

Excerpted from *Dream Messages from the Afterlife*
by Rosemary Ellen Guiley

Two weeks after his forty-ninth birthday, Bob
suffered a heart attack at four one morning and died. His
death, completely unexpected, was a severe shock to his
wife, Anne. Soon after Bob's passing, Anne had the most
profound dream she had ever experienced:

> We were holding each other and I felt
> something running down my leg. I looked and
> it was blood. Bob tried to help me wipe it away
> and I realized I had no skin at all. I was just
> raw meat. He tried to gently stroke me to help
> me stop bleeding. I knew that he was trying to
> tell me he was there for me, and although I felt
> totally raw, exposed and unprepared for his
> death, that he would help me.

The dream graphically expressed the intensity of
Anne's grief: total rawness and exposure, and a bleeding
away of vitality. Years later, she still experienced waves of
emotion just recounting the dream. Yet despite its painful
imagery, the dream contained a healing balm as well:

> To have my lover gently stroking my raw body
> to help sooth me, in retrospect, was a message
> about the work I was about to begin toward
> my spiritual rebirth. His death freed me from
> physical concerns, and the knowledge that we

don't die has changed my life. Who needs skin to connect? We don't!

Bob's death led Anne on a spiritual journey in which she awakened her natural gifts of intuition, psychic ability and healing. The comfort she felt in the dream gave her the courage and energy to undertake the journey.

Dream meetings with people who have died are seldom sad, but bring comfort, relief and joy instead. They have a transformative, healing power that is felt on both sides of the veil. Many dreams of the dead are so intense and realistic that people often wonder if they had a dream or a real experience.

Most of our dreams featuring the dead are symbolic, and when they occur soon after a person has died, are a natural part of the mourning process. In grief counseling, such dreams might be treated as wish fulfillments and emotional releases, such as for the last conversation we never had, or the ways we miss someone. The dead also appear as ordinary dream symbols, representing something about the dreamer or waking life. For example, a deceased father in a dream might represent an authority figure.

Many other dreams of the dead are distinctly different, however. They are true and real encounters with the dead in an alternate reality, the dreamscape. Under certain circumstances, we have genuine reunions with the dead.

Dreams take us beyond the limits of the physical world during sleep. The ability of dreams to bridge the worlds of the living and the dead has been acknowledged since ancient times. Plato referred to dreams as the "between" place, a meeting ground that exists beyond waking reality.

These special dreams with the dead are purposeful, to impart important information and heal wounds and grief. We may even help the dead complete their transitions to the afterlife.

I had a meeting dream after the death of my father, who was upset about unfinished business and was delaying his transition. I had always been close to him and was devastated when he died of a ruptured aneurysm. At the time of his passing, he was active in his passion: amateur astronomy. His calendar was filled with upcoming events.

Eighteen months prior to death, Dad suffered a burst abdominal aneurysm and was rushed to the hospital. Doctors said he would not survive the emergency surgery, but he did. He was diagnosed with a second aneurysm threat in his chest, one that was inoperable due to its location and his weakened condition.

Dad resumed as much of his activities as he could, although he was in chronic pain. Eventually he suffered the second aneurysm, and died on the operating table. I had the feeling that Dad felt somewhat cheated: he had struggled through a painful recovery, only to have life snatched away.

About two weeks after his death, I had this intense and realistic dream meeting with him. The air was charged with a heavy, electrical energy, and everything had sharp, intense colors and tangible forms that I could feel. I recorded this in my dream diary:

> I am at my parents' house, sitting in a chair in the living room. Mom is home, somewhere in the house, but I do not see her; I just know she is there. Across from me, sitting in his favorite easy chair, is Dad. I know he's dead, and he knows he's dead, and that I know it, too. I also

know that I am the only one who can see him.
The room is lit with a peculiar bright light, and
there is strange electricity in the air. I feel
rather strange.

I say, "Dad, what are you doing here? You're
dead! You can't stay here. You've got to move
on."

Dad smiles and shakes his head. He explains to
me that he has things he still has to do here. I
argue with him: He's dead and he must not
stay.

The scene suddenly shifts. I am no longer in
my parents' house, but am watching Dad
disappear into the distance. He is walking into
a large building. Somehow I know it is a
factory, or something like it—a place where
work is done. Dad is going to work.

I had no doubt that I'd had a real encounter with my
father, and that it concerned his need to fully leave the Earth
plane. Upon awakening, I could not recall the exact content
of our conversation, but it had seemed to be quite detailed,
and our meeting had the feeling of lasting a long time. In
life, Dad could be stubborn. I could well imagine his
irritation that death inconveniently interrupted his
upcoming plans and activities. The symbolism of being in
the *living room* of the house was not lost on me.

Evidently I prevailed upon Dad, since the final dream
scene was one of transition. Dad going "to work" in a
"factory" seemed apt symbolism. Throughout his life, Dad
was a continual student, interested in learning about many
things, especially the nature of the cosmos. Astronomy

provided many hours of pleasure to him. He had projects going all the time, making things, building things, investigating things. He was recognized in amateur astronomy, with an observatory named after him: The Pettinger-Guiley Observatory in Puyallup, Washington, operated by the Tacoma Astronomical Society. I knew that in the afterlife, Dad would not be one to prop his feet up, but would want to plunge into a new line of work.

I did not have the feeling that Dad was stuck and unable to move on himself. Rather, he needed a nudge, and the dream happened in order to provide the opportunity for one. Interestingly, my mother, who had quite a bit of psychic ability, told me that she had felt Dad's strong presence in the house for about two weeks after his death. He often sat in his favorite easy chair in the living room. Then suddenly the energy was gone, and she knew he had made a complete transition to the afterlife. She had no knowledge of my dream when she told me about her impressions.

Types of dream visits from the dead

Most dream visits from the dead occur in several types:

Farewell

The dying person comes to say goodbye. There may be telepathic communication or only a silent image of the person that fades away. The next day, the dreamer discovers that the person died the night before or in the early morning hours.

Patti had a dream in which her younger brother, Bill, appeared to her in ripped clothing streaked with blood. He said he had to go somewhere. The next morning, Patti learned that Bill had been killed the previous night in an auto accident. He had come to say good-bye.

Reassurance

The dead most often visit to give messages that they are all right and the living should not worry or grieve. If someone has died in old age or in illness, they are likely to appear restored to youth, health and vitality.

Linda suffered from severe grief after the death of her grandfather, especially as her wedding day approached. She was visited by him in a dream:

> It was one of the strangest dreams I have ever had to this day. One wall of the bedroom looked like a movie screen, and it was showing me a movie of my grandfather when I was a very small child. He was at the lake in his bathing trunks, holding the raft for one of us to get on. He called to me, and as I looked at him, he told me, "Linda, don't worry, I am all right and I am happy." I laid back down. When I woke up in the morning, I was finally able to accept his death.

> I believe to this day that my grandfather came to me in my dream to let me know that he was finally okay, and that I had nothing to worry about.

Life guidance

The dead return to give important advice, warnings, solutions to problems and creative ideas, or to bestow blessings of love and forgiveness. There may be an involved conversation. The dreamer may not remember all the details upon awakening, but will nonetheless "know" what is to be done.

For Rose Anne K., a favorite uncle appeared in a lucid dream years after his passing in order to give her a warning:

> I had always loved him best and missed him dearly. When he appeared to me in a dream, I was beside myself with joy. It was so real, not like a dream, but as though I were awake and in my living room. He told me he had something very important to say but very little time. "You must be very careful this year, you are in danger." I reached out my hand and touched his cheek. I could feel him and I ached to embrace him, but he pulled away and walked out of the room.

> He was right. I hesitate to elaborate, but suffice it to say vigilance made the difference.

Unfinished business

The dead may inform the living of the location of unknown important papers, such as estate documents and other information necessary to settle their estate. Some have significant personal requests they would like to see fulfilled.

In 1321, Dante Alighieri died, leaving the final pages of his masterpiece, *Divine Comedy*, hidden away in an unknown location. Family members searched in vain. Dante appeared in a dream to his son to reveal the hiding place, which was behind a wall in a house where Dante once lived. Why he placed the last pages there is a mystery, but without the dream, *Divine Comedy* may have been an incomplete work.

Helping the dead

In some cases of sudden death, the dead need help making their transition to the afterlife. They may appear in a dream as though they were lost or waiting for something to happen, and the dreamer may be able to guide them to their crossover point.

Three months after Richard C.'s sister died in a car accident, he had a dream in which he found her wandering about lost and confused, not realizing she was dead. With the aid of a spirit helper, he guided her to a crossover point where she was greeted by deceased family members. He awakened certain that he had actually met his sister and helped her.

Dreams that foretell death

Precognitive dreams warning of impending death have been documented since ancient times. People dream of the deaths of others but rarely of their own passing. The dead are often the messengers of another person's impending passing.

Precognitive death dreams have been recorded since ancient times. In 44 BC, Calpurnia, the wife of Roman Emperor Julius Caesar, had a dream in which senators stabbed a statue of her husband, and the statue bled bright red blood. It was an uncanny dream, for later the following day, the emperor's enemies in the Senate, who had been conspiring against him for some time, actually stabbed Caesar to death in front of the Theater of Pompey in Rome.

The most famous precognitive death dream on record was experienced by President Abraham Lincoln, who foresaw his own death. Ten days before his assassination on April 14, 1865, Lincoln had a dream in which he saw a

catafalque in the East Room of the White House, and was
told that the president was dead, the victim of assassination.

Dreams of the dying and deathbed visions

Dreams and dream-like visions of the afterlife occur
to individuals who are nearing death. Terminally ill patients
may begin experiencing vivid contact with the dead and
previews of the afterlife up to several weeks before they
pass. Sometimes caregivers and family and friends
participate in the experiences as well, by sharing visions and
having their own corroborating dreams.

Deathbed visions include scenes of Heaven, usually a
park or garden (see below); the appearances of family
members and friends who are dead; appearances of angels
and other spiritual beings; and sounds of heavenly music
and singing. "Deathbed apparitions," as the visiting dead
are called, begin arriving up to several weeks before a
person's passing. Rarely does anyone but the dying person
see them. Their visits become more frequent and longer as
the time of death approaches.

Previews of the afterlife

Dreams take us to the edge of the afterlife, to places of
transition and glimpses of what lies beyond. We have
meetings with the dead and spiritual guides and helpers
who explain the afterlife to us. These extraordinary dreams
occur throughout life, often as part of spiritual awakenings
and major transitions in life.

The most common afterlife settings viewed in dreams
are beautiful gardens and parks similar to Earth, but more
vibrant. Robert A. Monroe, the pioneer of out-of-body
traveling in the hypnagogic states of consciousness (falling

asleep), often visited a place he called "The Park," and said it was a first place of transition for newly-dead souls.

In some dreams, the dead explain to the dreamer what the afterlife is like, usually a place where thought instantly creates reality, and where they are restored to health and vigor.

Characteristics of afterlife dreams

Dream encounters with the dead are like waking experiences. Sometimes there is an "awakening" that is part of the dream experience. Dream visits are often lucid, in which the dreamer is sharply aware of being in a dream, yet one that is intensely realistic. Colors may be unusually bright and the atmosphere may have a heavy or electrical feel to it.

The dead may look as they did when they were alive, and still seem very much alive. There may be an unusual, glowing light around them or in the general environment of the dream. The dreamer may have physical contact with the dead that feels lifelike. Communication is not verbal, however, but telepathic.

The meeting places are often familiar, such as home, but may also be in a neutral place such as a park or garden, or an unknown location. The dreamer may have a sensation of traveling out of body at great speed at the onset of the dream, or, the dream may start with the meeting itself. The dead may state that they cannot stay long, and the dreamer cannot go with them when they have to leave.

The dream may involve other people who are living, but the focus of the dream will be between the dreamer and the dead person. There may also be spiritual beings present, such as angels. The dreamer experiences intense emotion during the dream and upon awakening.

Dream visits from the dead have tremendous healing and transformation power. Often, the dreamers are able to overcome their grief and feel confident in the survival and well-being of their loved ones. A dream visit may even change a person's beliefs about the afterlife. For example, a visit that does not conform to religious teachings may bring an expansion of thinking.

The mechanisms of afterlife dreams

Dream visits with the dead operate under conditions and perhaps even "rules" that we do not fully understand. Not everyone who dies makes a return in a dramatic dream. Some make more than one appearance. What's more, the choice of recipient is sometimes puzzling to the living. For example, a spouse or family member may not receive a dream visit, but a casual friend does. The absence of a reassuring dream visit can be quite distressing to the grievers, who may wonder if they are being punished or why the dead choose not to visit them. Some wonder, "Why did I have this dream?" while others wonder, "Why did someone else have a dream that was meant for me?"

The answer to this mystery lies in the unknown reaches of consciousness. Visitation dreams usually occur where strong emotional ties exist, but emotional ties do not guarantee a visit. Likewise, desire to have contact cannot cause a visit to happen. Dream messages and visits from the afterlife seem to occur under a complex set of circumstances. People who have innate psychic ability and who meditate are more likely to have lucid and out-of-body (OBE) dreams, but those qualities also do not guarantee a visit from the dead. And, people who have had no marked prior psychic experiences may have intense dream visits.

Despite the variables and unknowns, it is possible to improve the conditions that enhance dream visitations.

The boundary that divides the world of the living from the afterlife is a powerful one. We do not know the conditions that exist on the Other Side that must be engineered for pathways to open, even in dreams. When the dead visit, they often tell us they have limited time, as though the window of opportunity is narrow.

Another factor is the way a person dreams. All humans may share the dreamscape and the act of dreaming, but there are unique factors for each person that are beyond our present comprehension. Thus, a dream visit is like electricity that finds the path of least resistance. There is an intended visit, a push from the Other Side, and a pull from the side of the living. The dream is attracted to the best channel, which may account for friends receiving visits instead of family members.

The following dream experiences of a middle-aged woman illustrate how this may happen:

> I have had two dreams about loved ones who have died. The first was my grandmother. The second was my mother-in-law. Both dreams could be described more as "visits" than dreams. What I mean is both times the women were talking to me more than they were part of a dream sequence. Both times the women were reassuring me and telling me they were with me. Both times I woke up happy and grateful that I had seen them.

Both dreams were very vivid. The second time (after the one with my mother-in-law) I wrote down every detail I could remember—it was about four pages long. What struck me as odd was that I can remember thanking her for visiting me. She just smiled. She wanted me to reassure her son (my husband) that she was with him. I asked her why she didn't just visit him and she replied that she couldn't "because of the way that he dreams."

The dreamer was not certain what her mother-in-law meant by that remark, which implied that an obstacle existed that prevented access to her husband's dream states. The wife acknowledged that she was naturally intuitive and sensitive to the thoughts and feelings of others. She also had frequent precognitive and lucid dreams, which she could control. She enjoyed dreaming because it was "sort of like enjoying a good book or a movie." Consequently, she may have been easier to reach from the Other Side.

Can we initiate dream visits from the dead?

The occurrences of dream visits from the dead have no reliable predictors. Grief, longing, emotional intensity and desire for reunions play a part in the experience, but do not guarantee a dream visit. As noted earlier, the dead sometimes indicate it is difficult to bridge worlds.

We may be able to improve our opportunities for reunions by setting intentions prior to sleep for contact dreaming. Also, providing for the presence of the ancestral dead in daily life provides on an ongoing energetic link to the dead that may encourage dream visits. The presence of ancestral dead can be honored through home altars, prayer and petitions for guidance.

The benefits of afterlife dreaming

Dream visits and messages from the dead can alleviate grief and facilitate closure, and should be integrated into any counseling. Visitation dreams should be evaluated for both their symbolic content and their integrity as real events. In particular, therapists and counselors should honor these dreams as real experiences and not dismiss them as wish fulfillments, thus robbing the dreamer of the power and beauty of the dream experience.

Dream visits from the dead also can help the living process beliefs and concerns about dying and the afterlife. Natural concerns and questions arise throughout life, as we ponder the meaning of why we are here, where we came from, and where we are going when our time is done. Visitation dreams are direct experiences, the most powerful way to acquire spiritual knowledge and wisdom.

Understanding Afterlife and Angel Contacts

Karen Herrick, Ph.D.

Karen E. Herrick is the director of the Center for Children of Alcoholics, Inc., in Red Bank, New Jersey. After finishing her master's degree in social work from Rutgers University, she began to educate families on the disease concept of alcoholism. She developed a successful private practice, eventually seeing all types of people with psychological problems, including addictions.

Her book *You're Not Finished Yet,* encapsulates her private practice work. The book includes two chapters on spirituality and spiritual experiences inspired by her Holy Spirit experience during holotropic breathwork training.

She attended more educational sessions in California through the Spiritual Emergence Network and eventually completed a Ph.D. at the Union Institute & University in Cincinnati, Ohio. Her thesis was entitled *Naming Spiritual Experiences.* Of the 133 mental health professionals she researched, 75% stated that they believed further education about spiritual experiences, near-death experiences (NDEs) and/or after-life experiences would be beneficial to them personally and professionally. During her therapeutic practice, she encourages some clients to visit with mediums to aid in handling their grief and loss of loved ones.

She was ordained at the Cathedral of St. John the Divine and uses her Interfaith ministry to be actively involved in using the Spiritual Psychology of William James, Carl Jung, and Abraham Maslow with clients and people everywhere. She is presently the first female president in thirty-seven years of the Academy for Spiritual and Consciousness Studies (ASCS). She has recently completed requirements for certification with the American Center for Integration of Spiritually Transformative Experiences (ACISTE). The mental health professionals she researched indicated they needed more networking opportunities. One of her purposes now is to educate these professionals by first welcoming them into the ASCS organization as members.

For more about Karen, go to karenherrick.com.

Spiritual Experiences Don't Mean You're Crazy!

Usually when people tell me of a spiritual experience, they'll start by saying, "I don't have the words to describe this to you," or "You're going to think I'm crazy when I tell you this, but . . ." And then they tell me what happened to them. One definition of the word "crazy" is being of unsound mind or being mentally imbalanced, deranged or insane.

When I was married to my alcoholic husband, the more emotions I showed outwardly, the more he called me crazy. The more he called me this, the more I felt crazy because I was the only one in the relationship admitting to feeling anything.

Many times people who come to me who are considered to be the crazy one in the family are just having a lot of feelings and are showing them outwardly. They might also feel crazy because of something that has happened to them like the spiritual experiences described below.

Basically the differences between someone who is having a spiritual experience and someone who is mentally ill are as follows:

- A mystic, someone who has experienced God, is humbled by the experience. A mentally ill person brags, is grandiose, or is inflated about what he or she has heard and seen.

- A person having a spiritual experience can tell you about their experience over and over again. The story won't change much as the person tells you. This is called having a good ego and inner strength to explain the experience.

- The person has or had a "life" before the experience, which in psychological terms is called "good pre-episode functioning."

- Mostly in telling you about spiritual experiences, the person describes something visual. (They can hear also, but the most experiences my clients have described have been visual experiences.)

- The spiritual experience usually gives an answer to the person having it.

- These are not signs of mental illness. The main forms of mental illness are schizophrenia, paranoia, and mania. They have these characteristics:

~ Usually someone who is mentally ill is hallucinating.

~ The person is grandiose or inflated in bragging about what they are hearing or seeing. (Statistically, mentally ill people usually hear voices or what they are describing. They can see things but don't usually.) They are not humbled by what they are describing.

~ The person cannot repeat the same story coherently.

~ They have not had good pre-episode functioning.

~ They cannot move out of the hallucinatory state they are in unless they are medicated.

Also, it's important to note that someone who is mentally ill could also be having a spiritual experience. It would take a team of professionals who understand both dynamics of psychotic and spiritual experiences to determine a treatment plan for this person.

Only 35% of the mental health professionals who were researched during my survey stated they were able to recognize the difference between spiritual and psychotic experiences. The low percentage shows that more training is needed in the area of recognizing the above differences.

I have had clients often tell me that before they came to see me, no doctors, ministers, or priests had been able to help them understand these spiritual experiences. I believe that understanding and becoming educated about these vast ranges of experiences will be a movement for many professionals in the near future.

Sane Hallucinations—Seeing the Deceased

Mental health professionals need to know about the term "sane hallucinations" used in the 1880s by colleagues of William James, sometimes called the father of American psychology. Unfortunately, America followed Sigmund Freud instead of James, so sex is used to sell us everything from toothpaste to cars.

In 1898 at the International Congress of Experimental Psychology, researchers described research that had been conducted since 1894 in five countries: the United States, England, France, Spain, and Russia. The highly statistically significant findings were that some people saw their loved ones in a time period of zero to twelve hours after the loved ones' death. They usually appeared in early morning hours while the person was in bed. The deceased loved ones had come to say they were fine, that they were going "home," not to worry about them, and that they loved the person to whom they were appearing. They usually wore clothing that the person recognized as having seen them wear the last time they were with this person. These experiences were called sane hallucinations. We need to bring this term back to the profession of psychology!

People See Angels

Perfectly sane, ordinary people report seeing angels. This is an example:

> At a time when my father was dying after a long illness, I was feeling very frightened, overwhelmed and not able to cry or release my emotions because I was being strong for him. One night in my bed, I sensed a tremendous

presence of light and another presence that
must have been an angel. When the second
presence sat down on the edge of my bed and I
felt the indentation and weight on my
mattress, I attempted to scream which seemed
to release the fear in me. I was then able to cry.
The release was so wonderful. I was so
thankful for the angel who sat on my bed.

This is another example:

My husband was in the hospital and I was half
out of my mind. I felt the presence of angels in
my bedroom upon my return home. I never
felt anything like this before. I saw nothing but
I felt they were with me. I was comforted
because I knew I was on a different plane than
usual. I will never forget this experience
although it's very difficult for me to explain it.

Massage Table Aid from Angels or Others

It is very common for massage therapist and Reiki
practitioners to report spiritual connection experiences with
clients. This is an example a therapist reported:

When I'm doing massage on a client, my hands
start to go towards an area that needs healing. I
am sort of in a trance. I just know that my
client is getting healing and that their pain is
leaving. I sense someone else in the room. It
could be God, Mary, or angels. I don't say
anything to my clients about these feelings or
knowings, but sometimes after the session they
will tell me that they felt a presence or the

presence of angels in the room when I worked
on them.

This is another example described by a person receiving a
massage:

The first time I was re-birthed, it had been a
year after my husband died. I was on a
massage table and he appeared over the table.
He was telling me how to raise our young
sons. He would come to my bed at night and
kind of float over the bed. He has been in my
bed where I can feel his back. I also feel him
following me around on some days.

Many of my clients report experiences on a massage table
whether the massage therapist is aware of it or not.

Dream Visitations from the Afterlife

Many people describe dream visitations from loved
ones who have passed. This person describes dream
visitations from people living in the afterlife.

My mother, father, uncle, grandparents and
cousins have come to me in bed at different
times. They appear when one of the family
members they were particularly close to is
having a problem here on Earth.

Another person had a dream visitation from her mother.

I had a dream and I liked it very much. My
mother was in it. She was sweet, nice and
happy, which is unusual for my mother. Her
happy state showed me that we might have
gotten her in a better place, where she is now,

because of the therapy work that I have done
about my family of origin.

The visitations can be from spirits not known to the person,
or from angels.

During the dream, I sat up in my bed and
someone was sitting on the edge of my bed as
real as could be. I felt like I was awake but I
didn't wake up and jump up. I sat up and
someone was there. I was not afraid. And then,
the spirit or angel disappeared. It felt like no
other kind of a dream I have ever had. My
dreams fade, but this dream is as real today as
the night that I had it.

Reconnective Healing and Meeting Spirits

Reconnective healing practitioners use energy to help
the client or patient reconnect with the ground of being. This
is a practitioner's description of unique experiences.

I successfully accompanied a patient of mine to
the other side at the time of his death because
he was so terrified. Also, in distant
Reconnective Healing, I have learned to leave
my body, connect with God's energy and
travel to what is called "the Gap." This is a
place between Earth and the other side. My
spirit meets with the spirit of the person I am
working on from a distance and healing takes
place. (During this time of healing I have my
patients, who are at a distance from me, lie or
sit down at an appointed time with dimmed
lights and listening to peaceful music.) It's

interesting that they all report having felt weightless and that healing energy was being swirled through their body during their distanced healing. They have also reported positive results from the healing.

Spontaneous After-Death Communication

I've had clients tell me many different stories about communication with relatives or friends who have died. During these communications, they feel cold air around, then hear a voice in their heads, or dream of the relative or friend. These dreams are more vivid than the usual dreams they have and are usually only of that person. The person is typically around thirty years of age and is free of any physical ailments or sickness he or she experienced while here on Earth or at the time of death. The loved one usually tells my client that he or she is well and the client is left with a warm and loving feeling.

I've had several older men come and report to me about the death of their wives where they have smelled their wives' perfume in the house long after their wives have passed over. They also feel the presence of their wives in their bedrooms at night, or they have felt "soft breezes" at different times, perhaps when a favorite song came on the radio. These men do not want to throw away their wives' clothing or remove their articles from the home and are often in conflict with their adult children because the children feel they are not "getting over" their grief fast enough. I encourage them not to be rushed in their grief. I sometimes suggest a visit to a medium, which aids greatly in overcoming chronic grief.

Approximately two-thirds of widows have an experience after the death of their husbands that they interpret as a reunion with their spouse. Since women tend to outlive men, a large number of females have experienced this.

When I asked a couple of my aunts whether they had experienced such visitations from their husbands (my uncles), the answer I received was, "Oh, yes, he returned to visit me and it was wonderful." If I hadn't asked, I would never have known they experienced a visitation.

Guardian Angels Visit with Messages

One day in August 2000, I was reading an article in the *Two River Times*, our local newspaper, a portion of which I have included below.

> Have you felt this before? That time in your life when something miraculous happens? The event fills you with joy, hope and overwhelming happiness. You think you're going to burst, an explosion from the chest outward, like some supernova erupting through your sternum, into the galaxy. Energy radiates from within, working its magic through your whole body. You're overcome by the feeling that there is good in the world.
>
> That "wow" moment consumes space and time. It lingers, and then it's gone. Some people experience it at the birth of their first child. Others grasp the feeling during a great personal achievement like finishing the New York marathon. For others, a "wow" is simply

witnessing a yellow-breasted finch's flight from the flower garden.

I got "wow-ed" when I was twenty-four. My gas kitchen oven blew up in my face, leaving second and third degree burns on the better part of my visage. Clean and to the point, the blowout left me with no eyebrows, clump eyelashes and an unsolicited dermabrasion facial. It brought new meaning to the term "mug shot." My roommate of three days was overwhelmed, to say the least. My girlfriend cried. The doctor said never go out in the sun again without an SPF 500. Great. Just what a twenty-something, beach hopping maven wants to hear. I had just broken up with my boyfriend and my life was officially over.

As I left the emergency room, the resident insisted I wear this giant, white sock over my head. "It'll keep the infection down," he offered. The shroud was really to keep me from falling down. I almost passed out when I encountered my first mirror. I was gruesome. I still opted out of the sock, a more obvious if not dubious choice.

My first "wow" was a reversal. I imploded. My heart sank. Dread veiled my spirit. How was I going to get through this one? I wondered. With silver oxide cradled in one hand and a couple of Percasets in the other, I skulked home. My single-girl party ship was capsized. I was alone, swollen and lipless. I saw no sweet kisses in my future. I finally understood the true purpose for big, red, wax lips.

I crawled into bed, leaving the light off. My roommate did the best he could, half-joking he'd leave me lip balm and sunglasses for the morning. I cocked him a one-eyed "Good night," my stubbing lashes entangling themselves in mid-blink. I lay there wondering my next career move. Circus sideshow, a sales rep for some heavy-duty make-up line, spokesperson for Scab Pickers Anonymous. Was it worth sticking around for? Would I ever look the same? Then my real "wow" moment hit me.

For at the edge of my bed stood three guardian angels. Three, I was told, because I was such high maintenance they had to take shifts. I half-smirked at the thought of the poor soul appointed to my wee-hours-of-the-night crusades. Amazingly, none of them was scorched. Guess you guys missed the call about two hours ago, I thought.

The tallest angel, shrouded in friar's garb, told me to slow down. He said nothing, but I knew what he was saying without saying a word. Bizarre, I thought; this must be really good medication. The second and smaller angel simply looked on. His gaze ping-ponged fervently between the Robe and me. He must have been the one sleeping on the job. (I found out later, from my roommate's description that I was blown out from the gas kitchen oven like

a ten-year-old's birthday cake. One minute I
was on fire, the next, extinguished and
slumped against the cabinets some ten feet
across the room. Guess the middle guy had
some lungs after all).

Holding no grudges, I looked to the third. My
little cherub propped his elbow on my bed,
reached over, and touched my face. Supernova
whooshed over me at warp speed. "We'll keep
an eye on you. It's not your time." I grinned a
sunburned smirk, my cracked lips split with
relief. And the angels were gone.

Was that all a high-grade pharmaceutical
hallucination? Or did the drugs launch me into
the astral plane? Could it have been my inner
survival mechanism kicking in, keeping me
from initiating the Big Dirt Nap on my own?
Think what you may, but my "wow" has kept
me going ever since. Life is filled with good
and bad times. But knowing I've got an angelic
A-Team of three in the wings, figuratively or
otherwise, keeps me in good stead. Never
underestimate a "wow" moment or the power
of symbolically placed images. Real or not,
they serve their purpose."

The author of this Red Bank column, Tara Collins,
included her email at the end of this story and asked for
comments. I wrote her telling her about spiritual experiences
which sometimes happen when someone is desperate and is
in a life crisis. I said that I definitely thought her angel story
was a spiritual experience. Here is what Tara wrote a couple
of weeks later in her next column:

Funny how two people can have totally different reactions to a story. In my column on August 24, I described one of many "wow" moments I've experienced over the years. My father e-mailed me the week after the oven story and told me how frightening it was. Frightening? That surely wasn't my intention. But from a father's perspective, no doubt, his thought of losing his only daughter in a fiery blaze not linked with a plane crash could surely be perceived as frightening. I assured him it was better for me to have told him fourteen years after the fact than the day it happened. He would have MADE me get on a plane that day and fly home with the "sock" over my head. I would have preferred to go down in a fiery blaze. I now chalk that story up to one of those Tijuana jail stories; some things are better left unsaid to a parent until WAY after the fact.

Two days later, I got an email from Karen Herrick. She was enthralled with my story; no mention of "frightened, " scared or even mildly spooked. She was, however, surprised at my willingness to share such an intimate moment. Geez, I had briefly thought about that one. But then I decided, "Eh, you all think I'm crazy (Here's that word again!) anyway, so why not?"

She wanted to talk. Herrick is a social worker, psychotherapist and founder of the Center for Children of Alcoholics on Broad Street, who is also working on her doctoral thesis. A bit skeptical, I considered my options. I wondered if I wouldn't walk out of our meeting with a pack of Paxil in one hand and a script for a frontal lobotomy in the other. She assured me I was not crazy, at least on the seeing angel's part. We met over lunch at Juanito's on Monmouth Street. The extra-hot hot sauce masked my sweaty brow. Her doctoral topic? Near-death and spiritual encounters. Wow. Were those angels trying to tell me their own little Tijuana story?

We talked about the work of Raymond Moody, the connectedness of the world and our place in it. Apparently, people who have these experiences can go one of two ways. They either become very at ease and trusting with life and what it offers. Or they become very distraught with the incongruity of what they've seen vs. what they believe and try very hard to "forget," which only increases their anxiety in life. Confronted with that celestial head-trip, I found the Paxil and lobotomy much less frightening. After talking, I realized that many people have these experiences but never talk about them. They fear being misunderstood, deemed crazy or too frightened to speak of the event. I found Herrick understanding, sane and willing to listen to the stories I had.

Spiritual Interventions That Saved Lives

My very first client to tell me about a spiritual experience came to my office in the form of a 29-year-old man who had just left a meaningful relationship. He wanted my help in understanding why this relationship had failed. He was VERY nervous.

Most first-time clients are nervous, but his fear level was extremely high. I asked him all types of questions to try to discover why he was so afraid, but to no avail. When he returned for his second session, I put down my pad and told him, "You have as much fear today as you had during our first session. I feel there is something you are afraid to tell me; and, if this is so, I need you to explain it to me now."

He stated that something had happened to him, but his priest had told him never to tell anyone. He had been instructed to just "forget it." I asked, "Can you forget it?" "No," he said. I replied "Well, I hear a lot of very strange stories, so I'd like to hear this one."

He began by again stating that he lived with his parents and his father was an alcoholic. His father had never physically abused him in any way; however, they would fight verbally sometimes when his father had been drinking. One evening he came home and his father was in the kitchen and had been drinking. An argument ensued and his father picked up a carving knife from the table and threw it at his son.

My new client said, "When I tell you this you're going to think I'm crazy, but something like a sheet of Plexiglas, but it wasn't Plexiglas, came down in front of me and the knife bounced off of it." I told him that I was qualified to decide whether he was crazy or not and that he wasn't. I said that he had had a spiritual experience. I also said that it was obvious that his priest never had, but that the priest was trying to protect him from some people in society who would label this as a "crazy" story.

I said I would give him some information about spiritual experiences. He hadn't come to me to learn about these and so I stated that someday when he was older, he might want to look into the information about them. I suggested that he not talk to just anyone about these experiences, but when he felt safe with some people he might meet in the future who had also had something "weird" (as they are explained in our society) happen to them, he could then share his story.

I also told him that we could not count on this sheet of Plexiglas coming down again to protect him so I suggested he not fight with his father anymore when his father was drinking. He was to ignore him and leave the room, which he agreed to do.

In my Ph.D. research, there were verbatim responses from eighteen attendees who had checked the box "Other types of spiritual experiences I and/or my clients have had." This is one answer I received: "Car hurled toward me out of control and I felt an invisible barrier. The car seemed to bounce off this barrier and then right itself." When I spoke to this person during my telephone follow-up interview, I asked her about this experience. She said "Yes, it felt like a sheet of Plexiglas just came out of nowhere and stopped my car from going down the mountain."

Spiritual Experiences You Could Have

There are many different types of these experiences that you could have that are meaningful to you or that you have trouble adjusting to afterwards. For more information on this subject, please go to our web site at or contact me personally at Karen@karenherrick.com or www.spiritualexperiences.info. Once your experience is understood and integrated into your life, you will find yourself happier knowing more about your soul's purpose in life.

Honoring Spirit's Efforts to Reach us

Rhonda Schwartz

Author of *Love Eternal*, Rhonda Schwartz grew up in a spiritual household. She was taught from an early age that God is Love, Life, Spirit, Eternal, and that mankind is made in his likeness. It wasn't until her mother passed in 2001, however, and she began having communication from her that she learned firsthand what that could mean for those who have lost a loved one—namely that they are still with us. They still love and care about us and are able to communicate with us if we realize this possibility, pay attention, and listen.

Her compelling journey was further enhanced when she met, fell in love with, and married her scientist husband Dr. Gary E. Schwartz, author of *The Afterlife Experiments* and *The Sacred Promise*.

Together they are continuing their efforts, along with a team of people both here and in spirit, to scientifically build a bridge between here and there. It is their belief that by showing that consciousness survives death, and by giving spirit a voice, not only can much grief be eliminated, but humanity as a whole can be benefited—and perhaps saved. Rhonda's website is at rhondaeklundschwartz.com.

Honoring Spirit's Efforts to Reach Us

Excerpts from the book, *Love Eternal*

by Rhonda Schwartz

> *Just when the caterpillar thought the*
> *world was over, it became a butterfly.*
> - Anonymous

Who that has lost someone that they deeply loved and shared their life with hasn't sat in the numb, lingering, persistent silence left by that person's mysterious and seemingly permanent disappearance, and wondered: Where are they now? Are they okay? What are they doing, and do they still remember and love me?

The thought of losing my mother I knew would one day leave me in that dark agonizing place, pondering those deep questions. My life and hers had been so full of light, so intertwined, so connected; and even though I had relocated across country, had a job and friends, and had built a life for myself, I couldn't imagine what life would be like without her — it was beyond my comprehension.

Then when that unimaginable, fateful day was actually upon me, what was even further beyond my comprehension was the possibility that our relationship, communication and interaction wasn't actually over. At no time had I entertained the idea that we might, somehow, still be involved in each other's lives after that moment of seemingly definitive closure — death.

How would you feel, however, if at such a time of inconceivable and profound grief, questioning, and soul searching, you suddenly began having experiences indicating to you that your loved one was still very much alive—continuing to express their concern and love for you and wanting you to know that they were still with you?

What would you think if someone you thought had just been snatched from your life, that you imagined you would never have the chance to be with again, started communicating with you in very tangible ways as though nothing catastrophic had happened or changed? Signaling and interacting with you in ways that left little or no doubt in your mind as to their continuing presence?

What would you then do, in a world where science, religion and popular thought offer very few answers about what comes next, if indeed anything comes next, and yet you knew what you were experiencing was real?

Before I tell you what I did, let me share with you one event that so defied everything I had come to expect following such a significant loss that I was metaphorically brought to my knees, left stunned and in a state of reverent shock, amazement and wonder.

It was the Thanksgiving holiday and I was home visiting my mom from Seattle. My dad had passed three years earlier, and I'm an only child, so it was just the two of us, hitting our favorite restaurants, visiting people I always liked seeing when I came home, shopping at the mall together and just enjoying each other's company. We were best friends.

On Thanksgiving Day, we had gone to church in the morning and then out for a late afternoon meal with a friend: a turkey dinner with all of the trimmings. Upon returning home to the warm, memories-filled house I had grown up in, my mom said that she was going to lie down for a little while. She had been subtly preparing me in ways that I recognized were her way of letting me know that she sensed she may not be with me much longer. Although she didn't like to talk about it explicitly, I felt she wanted to ensure that I wasn't taken completely by surprise when the time came.

Though I didn't expect her to pass that night, I couldn't even fathom such a surreal possibility, I sat close by her room at the dining room table, quietly reading and praying.

An hour and a half or so later, she came out and said that she would like me to come and sit with her. I sat down on her bed, and she said there were three things she wanted to tell me, but that she could only remember two of them. One, was to "love that man," and she explained that meant to love everyone. The other was to "see the good in this world."

We sat together for a time, and she passed a short while later. The next few hours were one of those times in life when you take care of business because it's what has to be done, but every fiber of your being is fighting against what is unfolding, because it is exactly opposite to what you want to be happening. My heart was broken and the thought that I was going to have to live the rest of my life without her was unfathomable.

I think to some extent we can choose when we depart this world if we are near that transition point. I've heard of people sometimes waiting until a loved one leaves the room before they pass, so as to have privacy for that moment. Looking back on it, I think the fact that I was home and that we were together might have made her feel safer in a way. Passing while I was still there meant that she wasn't alone, we were together, and I was spared the shock of receiving a phone call from a stranger with the news. As it turned out, she was teaching me right up until the end, or at least what I thought was the end at the time; but she had even more to show me—more than I could ever have imagined. And I wouldn't have to wait very long.

Although I remembered very little instruction given by my church about afterlife communication, I did recall a strong claim that life is eternal. I rationalized from that standpoint that if life is eternal, then death is an illusion, and consequently there was no reason continued communication shouldn't be possible—at least theoretically.

Already having a belief that life continued after death, I made a point to talk with her, thinking she may still very well be with me even though she was no longer in her body. I thought that if she could hear me, it would be comforting for her to hear my voice and to know that I knew she was still alive.

We were so close that there was nothing left unsaid. I was simply thanking her for all she had done for me and others over the years and expressing my appreciation for the beautiful, thoughtful, selfless, giving person that she was. I was also getting my mind around the fact that this was a life-altering turning point; my life would never be the same again and I was losing the most precious thing in the world to me.

That night I slept, though not very well, in the bed that she and I had shared the previous nights that week during my visit. There was only one bedroom in the house, as the room that had been mine growing up, she now used as her office and study.

I couldn't help but think of all the similar slumber party-like times we'd had over the years, whether we were on family vacations when I was a young girl, on annual trips we enjoyed taking to Milwaukee, or visiting relatives in

Florida. It was always fun to have girl talk before we fell asleep. But tonight, it was very quiet.

I would manage to drift off to sleep, but would wake up every hour or so. Then about four o'clock in the morning, all of a sudden I became aware that one corner of the room, up near the ceiling, seemed to be unusually bright. I had had my eyes closed and I actually opened them to see where the light was coming from. I decided, well, maybe it was the night light in the bathroom shining into the bedroom, and that it had been that way all along and I hadn't noticed it until just that moment. But it was strange.

Not giving it too much thought, I went back to sleep. When I got up about three hours later, it was already light outside, so the effect wasn't visible, but when I walked out of the bedroom and into the hall, I was startled to see that the light in my mom's study was on. It apparently was the source of the light that had been shining into the bedroom, and it had come on precisely at the time she would normally have gotten up to begin her metaphysical reading and prayer for the day.

I remember standing in the hall just outside her office, cautiously peering in, eyes wide, looking around, and saying aloud, "Don't scare me now!"

It was at that moment that I realized that what we call "death" isn't necessarily the permanent discontinuation, or even temporary interruption, of communication with loved ones that we think it is. Far from proof and just the beginning, I knew I was on a new and unexpected path of adventure and discovery.

But this isn't the event that I said shook me to my core and forever changed how I would come to think about life after death and define how I would live my life from that day forward. That would happen three days later.

I had arranged with my boss to stay in Illinois for another week. There were a lot of things that needed to be handled before I headed back to Seattle. The plan was to deal with what needed my immediate attention and then I was simply going to button up the house for six months and come back in the summer to take care of all the rest. That would at least give me time to decide what to do with the house and every memory-filled thing in it.

One of my first tasks that I knew I needed to do was to contact my father's previous employer. When my dad passed, I remembered my mom showing me some paperwork for a small annuity from a retirement plan that she had made a particular selection for called a "ten-year certain" policy. It stated that if she passed before the ten years was up, it would continue to come to me for the remainder of the ten years and then stop.

Before calling, I looked through every drawer and file in the house for the papers, but couldn't find them anywhere. I didn't give it too much thought because I was sure they would have a record of it in their files. I called the company to inform them of my mother's passing, and of my recollection of the policy and the option my mom had elected.

They informed me, however, that they had no memory of such an agreement and that they had nothing on file indicating such a selection had been offered or made.

Yeah.

Okay, hmm, now what do I do?

I hung up the phone, very aware once again of how quiet the house was.

I sat in the living room at mom's desk trying to decide what I should do next. Normally it would have been so easy to ask her, but nothing was normal anymore. I thought to myself what my natural reaction would have been: to doggedly rifle through every drawer and file in the house again until I found those papers. But with so many things to do, I really didn't have time for that.

Over the last couple of days, I had gotten in the habit of praying to God and talking to Mom. Praying to God was a familiar practice, talking to Mom when she didn't appear to be in the room or on the phone—was not. However, she had already given me some indication that she was still around, and being in her home that was so filled with her essence and where we had had countless conversations over the years, it seemed natural to reach out and call on her.

I remember getting up and standing in the archway between the dining room and living room and saying, out loud, "God, I know you know where those papers are, and if you can reveal their location to me, I would really appreciate it. And Mom, I know you know where those papers are as well, and why I need to find them, so if you can show me where they are, please do."

Well no sooner had I spoken those words, than in my head, I heard, "Go into my study, and in the closet, on the floor, behind Dad's folded flag, you'll find those papers."

It was so clear.

I stood there for a moment in the silence following those words a little stunned. But I knew I didn't have to stop and analyze or question the validity of the words I'd just heard; it was so easy to go check. All I had to do was to walk into the next room and look.

I took a deep breath and marched toward the open door. Stepping into her study filled with books and memories of her—a very beautiful, spiritual woman, a loving wife and Mother, and someone devoted to God and her church—I knew our life together had been special. As I turned and saw the partially closed door to what had once been my closet as a child, I felt like that young girl: small and vulnerable, and with so much to learn about life, the universe, and the greater spiritual reality.

Reaching for the doorknob, it was as though everything was moving in slow motion. As the door eased opened, my heart began beating faster as light from the room flooded the tiny space, revealing my father's folded military flag leaning against the wall on the floor. More amazing yet was the sight of several loose sheets of paper curling up behind the flag.

I stood there for a moment, seemingly frozen in time, considering what all of this meant. If those were the papers I had been looking for, and if I had been led to them by my mother who had passed on three days earlier, then everything from that second on was changed. Everything from that moment forward was different.

I reached down, fully aware of the gravity of the moment and gently lifted up the few, loose pages. My thoughts were racing, not yet having time to fully consider the implications as I scanned the familiar words of the document that my mother had shown me three years earlier. These were indeed the papers I had turned the house upside down looking for. And now, in a sense, my life was being turned upside down by how I was seemingly led to them by my deceased mother.

I was now on a quest, a journey in search of answers to what I had just witnessed. If my mother's transition was death and she was still able to so clearly communicate with me, then death wasn't anything like what I had been taught and thought it was.

So, what I did was to begin documenting my experiences in a journal. What I couldn't have known, however, early on that Monday morning, was that I was about to discover that my journey with my mom had only just begun.

There weren't enough hours in the day that first week after mom passed. During one morning, my first stop was at the lawyer's office and then on to an appointment with my mom's financial investor. We had met a couple of times before, so we weren't complete strangers. She expressed her condolences and said that she too had lost her mother, but that she had been 61 when her mother passed. I was considerably younger.

I remember a shockwave of sadness hitting me, and struggling to fight back feelings of having been cheated out of years together, and of it all being too soon. I don't think I was very successful in trying to conceal my surge of emotions as we both instinctively hurried to complete our business and I left as quickly as possible.

I rushed out to the car and immediately burst into tears. I shouted, "I wanted to have my mom that long!" Then, much to my amazement, I heard her words, inside my head, saying, "This will give you time to fly."

It startled me. The stream of tears stopped flowing and I sat motionless in the silence that followed. Her words were distinctly different from those of a normal thought that comes to mind. They were spoken in the first person and abruptly cut into the scene that I felt I was playing out all by myself. It was as though she were sitting right there in the car with me and simply spoke her mind in response to what she saw me going through.

I remember thinking, can this really be happening? Is this what it's going to be like now? Now that my mom is dead, she's going to be able to be with me and to talk to me telepathically? Is that how it works? Why didn't I know about this before? Why hadn't anyone told me? Is this a common occurrence? Do other people experience this, or is it just us? Or, am I just fooling myself?

I had a lot of questions.

Exactly one week after my mom's passing, I was wrapping up loose ends and preparing to go back to Seattle. I had been running around town all day and was completely exhausted, so I decided to get some carry-out food from a local Swedish restaurant for dinner. Kroppkakor was a traditional Swedish dish that had always been one of my favorites, and it was fall, so I knew it was in season. I had fond memories of my dad on dark, frosty evenings, taking one of our pans from home and bringing back the round potato dumplings stuffed with salt pork and looking like dirty snowballs. My Mom would then heat them up on the stove, causing the windows throughout the house to steam over, creating a cozy barrier from the cold outside.

Being November, it was dark at 6:30, and some people had already strung Christmas tree lights on the outside of their houses. As I drove home along the familiar streets, so peaceful and beautifully decorated, streets that for years my mom and I had driven along together, I reached over and put my hand on the passenger's seat next to me as though I were holding her hand.

I began talking to her just as though she were in the car with me (because she had shown me that she might very well be). I pointed out certain landmarks as we drove by them and commented on how festive the colored lights were and how cool the fall air felt.

When I arrived home, I couldn't wait to have a nice quiet dinner without interruptions. I took the phone off the hook and poured my dirty snowballs out of their Styrofoam container and onto my plate. I took them into the living room, turned on an ice-skating show that I had been looking forward to watching all day, and sat down thinking I would enjoy a few peaceful minutes while I wound down from a hectic and wonder-filled day.

As I began eating, I started sharing with my mom the notion that because of our seeming, continued connectedness, maybe she and I could somehow bring down the veil between here and there, because to me, over the last week it appeared to be pretty thin. What I sensed next, and this was just an internal feeling, was that she was excited and agreeable to this proposition.

Then I felt her say, "You just relax and enjoy your dinner now. You have enough to do." I would come to recognize that she would often give responses that were surprising and not what I would have expected. I thought she might have come back with an enthusiastic, "Yes!" and then offer some ideas on how we might go about doing that.

This led me, even more strongly, to think that I was actually communicating with her, and that it wasn't just my imagination or wishful thinking.

As I sat there, pleased and amused with this latest communication, I became distracted by an annoying noise coming from the kitchen. This entire time, the telephone in the kitchen had been persistently making that alarm that it makes when it's letting you know that it's off the hook. It was still blaring away and was making my "quiet time" anything but.

I had already watched one skater complete her routine and another had begun hers. I thought the phone must be electronically stuck somehow, although I had never known that to happen. Irritated, I got up and went into the kitchen to see what the problem was. As I reached for the receiver, the buzzing immediately stopped. I didn't adjust it in the cradle; I didn't push any buttons; it just stopped.

Again I was I frozen in my tracks. I felt strongly that somehow my mom had been able to make that happen, that she wanted me to know that she had been with me in the car on the way home that evening, and that she knew I had heard what she had said about my interest in continuing our connectedness in the hopes of maybe proving for others that life and love do continue after death.

This was the first time I experienced an example of what I would later come to call a punctuation mark — a punctuation mark being a sign following a previous sign or event, or series of events, caused or facilitated by spirit. The punctuation mark serves to indicate to the person who experienced it, that what you witnessed really was a communication from the other side — so don't miss it! And don't dismiss it as mere coincidence.

It had been less than a week, but I already felt as though I was beginning to learn a little about how communication with the other side works. I would be returning to Seattle soon, however, and I didn't know whether my leaving the area might somehow short circuit the energetic connection we had — if that was what it was. I was thinking of it in those terms because of the way lights and other devices that rely on electricity seemed to be able to be affected.

I had been home exactly one week when I received confirmation that my mom was not about to leave me and that she was bound and determined to let me know that she would always be there if I needed her.

This night I had decided was going to be a nice quiet evening at home, alone, or more accurately, a nice quiet evening at home — with Mom. I planned to make a simple supper, relax, and watch a rerun of a made-for-TV movie called *A Promise Kept, THE OKSANA BAIUL STORY; The True Story of a Solid Gold Triumph.*

You may recall that Oksana Baiul was the Olympic gold-medal figure-skating champion from Ukraine who defeated Nancy Kerrigan of the United States in the 1994 Winter Olympic Games in Lillehammer, Norway. She was only 15 at the time and fairly new on the senior-level skating scene. Her win over Kerrigan was something of an upset, but her personal journey was one of those captivating and heartwarming stories that define the spirit of the Olympics.

At thirteen, her divorced mother, Marina, died, leaving Oksana alone without any other family members to care for her. Although her coach stepped in and looked after her for a time, he soon emigrated to Canada, leaving Oksana behind. Once again, she was left alone and was actually sleeping on a makeshift bed at her skating rink.

Mercifully, Galina Zmievskaya, a world class figure-skating coach from Odessa and mother-in-law of Olympic champion Viktor Petrenko, took Oksana under her wing. And it was under her guidance and training that Oksana, skating to Swan Lake, skated to Olympic gold as the ugly duckling that turns into a swan.

No doubt it would be a moving and uplifting success story to watch. But I couldn't even imagine what it must have been like for such a young girl to lose her mother and to be so alone in the world. I knew how difficult and painful it was for me. I could certainly relate. But I was forty-five, not thirteen. I had had many years with my mother. We had shared so many of life's experiences together, I had so many memories of her, she had taught me so many things, and I was a grown woman with a life that was on track.

Suspecting that there may be some sort of message of comfort for me in this movie, I could never have predicted precisely what form it would take.

When I first learned that the movie was going to be aired that evening, I said out loud to Mom, "Oh, the Oksana Baiul movie is going to be on television tonight. You saw it when it was originally on and I remember you telling me about it and that you liked it. But I've never seen it."

Talking to Mom in a very natural way as if she were right there in the room with me was my way of honoring her efforts and seeming continued presence in my life. If she was actually there, I wanted our relationship, although altered, to be as normal as possible.

By telling her about the movie that was going to be on that night and that I was looking forward to watching it, I was simply making conversation, much like we would have done on any Sunday afternoon.

It must be so frustrating for those on the other side if they try and try to let us know they're here and we don't realize, recognize or acknowledge their attempts. I didn't want my Mom to suffer that disappointment, especially since she seemed to be so good at making her presence known.

I suppose I was also hoping that my talking to her and keeping her in the loop, so to speak, of my life might act as an invitation for her to continue to stick around and not go off somewhere and disappear forever.

It seemed to be working so far, although I don't know that she would have needed any encouragement.

The movie was just starting, so I turned on the television in the living room and began making dinner in the kitchen. On the menu that night? The ultimate comfort food—macaroni and cheese. Even though I could see the TV from the kitchen, I wasn't giving the program my full attention; I was busy timing the pasta and pouring my soft drink.

For the first time since being back in Seattle, I was beginning to get a strong sense of her presence. I felt that she wanted me to sit down with her and for us to watch the movie together.

I was planning to do so, but I remember telling her that I wanted to finish making my dinner first.

I then felt something that I had never experienced before—a new kind of communication that I would feel again in the future at a time when I needed to make a very important decision in my life. What I was feeling, in my whole being, was a sense of urgency. I was experiencing a sense of her being impatient with me that I wasn't in watching the show with her.

How was it that she was able to make me feel, almost physically, an emotion? Before if she had been in the room, maybe I could have picked up on a look or a posture that would have given me a clue about what she was thinking, but now, how was she able to do that?

You would think that question might have stopped me in my tracks and that I wouldn't have rested until I'd analyzed the phenomenon and gotten an answer, or at least given it some serious consideration. Curiously, instead, I responded much like I would have if she had been standing in my living room, arms crossed, tapping her foot, telling me to hurry up or I'll miss the good part.

I remember telling her that I would be in in a minute, but that I wanted to take the garbage out first. That way the kitchen would be cleaned up and I could sit down with my dinner and just relax and enjoy the show.

I was a little amused because I felt her impatience intensify. She really wanted me to come in right then. You know that feeling when a parent is expressing disapproval of something you're doing, or in this case not doing? I sensed that feeling at that moment as strongly as I had ever felt it in my entire life.

But I had lived alone for a long time, and I was used to doing things in my own home in my own way, and it had been many years since my Mother had told me what to do— So, I took the garbage out anyway.

When I came back in and started dishing up my macaroni and cheese, I could feel my Mom eagerly wanting me to join her in the living room. If she had had a body at that moment, I imagined she would have been saying, "Come on, hurry up," and waving for me to come in.

I remember saying to her, "I'm coming, I'm coming." I took my plate and sat down on the sofa, leaving a place next to me for Mom to sit. Now, mind you, I would never have thought to do this if she hadn't made her presence so apparent to me. I would have grieved, gone on with my life, and cherished my loving memories of her. But she was there, so it seemed, and it was perfectly natural. It actually would have seemed a little rude not to have included her in that way.

No sooner had I taken my seat, mac and cheese in hand, that I realized why she had been so insistent that I not wait to come in.

There was a scene in the film she wanted me to see. A message she wanted me to hear.

The movie was at a point in the story where Oksana's mother is dying, and thirteen-year-old Oksana is at her bedside holding her mother's hand. Marina says to her beautiful and talented daughter:

I am so sorry. You are so young. Oksana listen
to me. I had so many dreams. Promise me. . . .
listen to me. You have a gift, a wonderful gift.
It will always be a part of you. It will never
leave you. Promise me you will be strong.
Promise me you won't give up your dream.
Please do this for me. Please promise me. I
promise I will always be with you, watching
you. Never forget that. When you need me, I
will lift you up and set you down as softly as a
feather. You will make me so proud.
Remember that.

What a beautiful message for a mother to share with
her daughter, and my mother, I believe, found a way to say
those words to me too. Now I knew why she had been so
insistent on my watching at that moment. And I almost
missed it.

Like most mothers and daughters, my Mom and I
loved to shop, and we particularly liked shopping together. I
was about to be shown that this too didn't have to stop just
because she had passed. If we live forever, why shouldn't
we continue to do the things we enjoyed doing before we
passed with the people we love?

I was at a mall one day wandering through The
Museum Store. I couldn't help but think of my mom as I
admired all the pretty objects d'art that were temptingly
displayed. They were the types of things we would always
keep our eye out for as gifts to buy for birthdays and
holidays. I felt a little sad that I could no longer give her gifts
and share in the love and joy that comes from both giving
and receiving.

Leaving the store, I turned and was struck by a print in the window. It was of a painting by artist Jack Vetttriano entitled *Dance Me to the End of Love*. The atmospheric scene was a romantic depiction of an elegant, 1940s couple ballroom dancing on a beach.

I was reminded of my parents' love of dancing, and I knew my Mom would have admired Vettriano's capturing the essence of her passion. As I stood taking in its beauty, I began to wonder if my mom might not be there with me. I was beginning to notice that sometimes when she was around, there would be a buildup, a kind of perceptual slow-rolling thunder of awareness in advance of my being certain of her presence. The hairs on the back of my neck might feel like they are going up or I may feel like someone is watching me.

I continued down to another shop, my attention trained on my next task of finding a special pair of earrings. I scanned the entire jewelry counter and was disappointed because they didn't appear to have the particular ones I was searching for. Not wanting to give up too easily, I continued to mill about hoping I might stumble upon them.

Then I began feeling an intruding thought, a nudge that seemed to be saying to me, "Keep looking. You are missing them. They are here." Was it really a thought outside of myself communicating to me? I had sensed that my mom might be with me. Or was this just my own mind trying to make something out of nothing?

I pressed on and continued looking, even though I thought I had already looked at every pair—some twice. The feeling came again, "You are missing them. They are here. Look again." Curious as to whether I was really receiving disembodied direction, I kept looking. I felt a little like I was playing a game of hide and seek; only who I was playing with was just as hidden as the object I was searching for. I continued to scour the displays, but no earrings.

The strong feeling persisted, as did I, and then, right in plain sight, there were the exact pair of earrings I had been wanting.

I felt both the intimacy and seemingly insignificant nature of this occurrence to be important. It was sweet that she was there with me at that moment, and important because it showed that after-death communication isn't reserved solely for life or death situations. Simple, everyday interaction apparently is possible and normal.

Receiving and Understanding Signs

Joe Higgins

Joe Higgins is an Amazon bestselling author and intuitive medium who has had the ability to communicate with those who have passed on since an early age. Joe has completed and taught classes in mediumship and advanced mediumship as well as becoming a certified Reiki master. He has completed the Morris Pratt Institute training and a residential course in pastoral skills in Lily Dale, New York. He has published three books: *Hello...Anyone Home? A Guide on How our Deceased Loved Ones Try to Contact Us through the Use of Signs*, *The Everything Guide to Evidence of the Afterlife: A Scientific Approach to Proving the Existence of Life after Death* (Everything Series), and *Always Connected for Veterans: Deceased Vets Give Guidance From The Other Side*.

Joe's fourth book, *Always Connected: Understanding Signs From Deceased Loved Ones*, will be published in July 2014. Joe has become a leading authority on the process of Signs. His website is at josephmhiggins.com.

Receiving and Understanding Signs
With channeled excerpts from the book
Hello...Anyone Home?
By Joseph M. Higgins

Editor's note: *The following introduction has been channeled by Joe. The presenter is an entity from the next plane of life. Hence, when the entity refers to "you" and "your side," it is a reference to us on this side of life and to the Earth plane. The entity describes the problems we have on this side of life with receiving signs of communication from the next plane of life.*

After loved ones have passed, they often wish to send a sign to their loved ones on the physical plane that they are truly still in existence and can connect to them. By talking directly to the deceased about how you miss them, love them and wish they were still around, you open up the channel for communicating with our side. You have set the intention by your thoughts and your actions to open a line of communication with your deceased loved one. Our reaction is to go through the necessary protocol in order to teach your passed loved one the dynamics of interacting with your side. This puts into motion a whole series of actions and investigations on how to best contact you. Sometimes, the signs of contact go unseen, as they might be confusing, mixed too well into the background of your daily lives, or maybe just because you're preoccupied with other things on your mind.

It seems you all have a tendency to be very protective about your space and any energy around it. It is because you are truly a spiritual being that you are quite aware of your surroundings and how you feel in certain situations. You all have had experiences, such as knowing when someone is standing behind you, or perhaps you feel uneasy about entering a certain location. You might not have any proof to base this feeling on, as it's just a gut feeling. This is the sense that you are tapping into this part of your divine makeup, which helps with communication.

So the first thing to learn is how to tap into this protective field that you have around you and to begin to look and listen for the signs that you have asked for. When we mentioned a protective field, we meant this in the sense that it is used on your physical plane—to give you extra information concerning your environment. In the past, it was used, to a higher degree, in order for survival. Today, it might be used to tap into in order to make specific decisions or when seeking guidance.

Another main theme is to let go of the everyday worries and responsibilities that seem to occupy your mind at all times. It is difficult to look or listen for signs from us when you are preoccupied by the activities of your daily living. This is one reason we make contact while you sleep, as you have relaxed and it is easier to make the connection. So put aside all the thoughts and questions that your mind tries to process in what seems like every minute of the day. Pursuing techniques such as meditation will help you to relax your mind and to make it much easier for us to tap into, to place a thought, a physical object, or to create the sign that you have been looking for.

End of the introduction

The speaker from the afterlife is explaining that they repeatedly attempt to communicate with us. The following stories were reported to me, Joe, by people who have had these experiences in which loved ones from the other side have made efforts to give signs of communication to people on this side of life.

Story 1: Two Months Later

Joe: This is the story about a loved one sending signs from the other side that was reported to me.

Today, I was reading one of my aunt's pocket calendars. She kept detailed notes of her ongoing schedules throughout most of her life. Some might call them journals; but for someone who had a busy work schedule all her life, the daily pocket planners were the way to go.

Looking at some of her final months was interesting, because she tried to keep a schedule, even though her physical body was starting to give out. "Today I went to Stop and Shop; in the afternoon called a friend." As she started to feel more run down and the weather became colder and more unpredictable, many of the notations showed her staying in most of the day.

Frequently, it would say "doctor appointment in morning," "stayed in the balance of the day." "Had my hair done," "stayed in the balance of the day." "Went food shopping in morning but returned due to weather, stayed in the balance of the day."

I found that expression odd, since I have never heard of any expression like that in my 50 years. So, whether she went to the market or the doctor, she would very often end her entry "stayed in balance of the day."

That night, before I went to bed, I said, "Gee, you have not contacted me in a while, I wonder why.

The very next morning, as I was driving to work, I began to think about her notes in her daily calendar, and within two minutes, as the weather man on the radio was wrapping up his report, he said that it would be partly cloudy and humid for "the balance of the day."

I began to smile and a warm feeling come over me, knowing that I had received another sign from my loving aunt.

Comments on Story 1 by the Channeled Entity

We use various methods to connect with your side, including sounds, smells, and electrical manipulation. They will vary from the simple sounds of someone's voice to the more complex meetings within a dream.

Many times, people have a close relationship with the natural surroundings of the physical plane. Within these boundaries are methods of contact that can be arranged to show a sign. We have the ability to intercede in the action of the animal world as well as with plants and the weather. If someone would recognize a sign more easily through the action of an animal, or a significant flower or breeze, then this would be implemented in the choice of contact.

We are not limited as to the methods of contact, and we have vast, interacting abilities within the physical plane.

But the most important thing to remember is that you're not losing your grip on reality, that these events and signs appearing around you are actual communications from your loved ones on the other side.

We have used this sign communication since the beginning of human time. You are not the first to experience these types of contact, nor will you be the last. You see, as spiritual beings, you are always in contact with the other side, as this is where you originally came from; and this is where you'll return to. After you leave the physical plane through the transition called death, you will be able to connect with your loved ones who remain on the physical plane. As spiritual entities, you are connected to all those who are here with you and to others on the other side.

You only think that you are limited by your physical being to be able to connect with others. Once you are free from limitations of your physical body, your consciousness and spirit are free to interact with many others at any time or place.

We just happen to choose a particular method that we think might gain your attention in the easiest and most efficient way. If you're thinking of a loved one and a favorite song of theirs comes on the radio, and it makes you think, "That was strange," then the message, the sign, was successful. The most important thing is not to doubt the sign when it comes across your path, as it has been intended for you to receive that communication at that particular time in that particular place. The fact that you pick it up and wonder about it is evidence that the communication was clear enough to stop you in your daily thoughts to have you concentrate on what has just happened. We've grabbed your attention.

Story 2: Listen to the music

Joe: This story also was reported to me, by a woman:

After being widowed for about two years, I had recently met a man I really liked. We talked on the phone for a while and went out together a couple of times, so the relationship was very new. While on the phone one day, he asked me if I wanted to go see Fleetwood Mac in concert; and, I, in turn, asked him if he would accompany me to a friend's wedding. These events were not to happen for at least another month; so, although the relationship was new, we were making "long term" plans.

While driving later in the day, I began to panic, asking myself, "What did you just do?" I thought I had to be crazy for making plans a month away, when we really did not know each other. Although I felt ready to move on with my life, the thought of a new relationship after being married for twenty-five years was downright scary.

Doubt and confusion began to creep into my brain. Although it sounds crazy, I began "talking" to my deceased husband, asking him for help with all of the questions I had running through my brain. "Is he really a nice guy?" "Is he good for me?" "Is this the right thing to do?" "What do you suggest?" I remember thinking, "I wish you could tell me what to do; I'm scared."

The radio was on in the car; and, at that moment, my husband's favorite song by Matchbox Twenty came on the radio. I remember thinking, "There you are." He loved all kinds of music, and was always listening to something. Hearing his favorite song at that moment made me smile to myself; and I felt somewhat comforted. However, it was the song that played right after the first one that absolutely let me know he was there listening and answering my questions. It was a Fleetwood Mac song! I knew without a doubt that he had heard me and was using music, a medium that he loved so much, to answer my questions. He was letting me know that everything was all right, that it was OK to move on with this relationship and my life.

Just in case I thought that the two songs were a coincidence, after running my errands, I returned to my car about an hour later and playing on the radio was a Fleetwood Mac song and right after that, a Matchbox Twenty song. He was making sure that I definitely got his answers to my questions. It could not have been any more obvious.

As I thanked him for answering me, I had tears in my eyes. Getting that sign made me feel so much better, less confused, and at peace with all of the changes happening in my life.

Comments on Story 2 by the Channeled Entity

Sometimes the sign can be quite obvious. Very often, we will have to repeat a sign multiple times before someone finally believes what they had thought in the first place, that it is a true contact with their loved one. We understand this and that is why we continue to give you a sign, even if you are having difficulty accepting it because of your doubts or fears.

This is the way we try to communicate with you; and, at times, it can be subtle, while at other times, it can be quite obvious. Once you start to connect the dots, you'll begin to see a pattern of how this all works: Your thoughts about a passed loved one, the sign coming through, how appropriate it might be for that time, how it relates to a current situation in your life or perhaps some insight that is needed to help resolve or deal with a particular problem . These are all reasons we come to you, and at times we will use a friend or loved one to make the connection due to the surrounding events that are happening at that time.

Story 3: The Wig

Joe: This is a story about receiving signs that comes from my own life:

A good example of how a loved one can come through a friend or family member in order to pass on a message is related in the following incident that happened to me. One evening, while I was preparing to meditate, I encountered a personality coming into my thoughts; and, as a medium, I identified it as someone who wanted to come through and pass along some information. I immediately recognized who the person was, because I had met this woman the year before. Jane was the aunt of a close friend of mine. She had passed about six months prior to this event.

Since I was trying to be very disciplined with my meditation training, I accepted her into my consciousness, said hello, and welcomed her. I told her that I would be able to connect with her at another time but that I was in the midst of meditating and training myself, and I did not want to be disturbed. When you are a medium, you have to set guidelines as to when anyone can come through or your mind will be cluttered with conversational thoughts all day long. However, if someone comes through whom I immediately recognize, out of the blue, then it usually means something very important and I need to pay attention.

She was persistent, just as she had been in her life on our physical plane. Therefore, I stopped my meditation and allowed Jane to come through with the information that needed to be passed on to her niece.

She immediately told me that she was doing fine, that she was no longer in pain; she was smiling broadly and moving about. Now, the strange part: As she was telling me that she was in good spirits, no pun intended, she reached up to her head and removed a wig. She then placed it back on her head. She did this repeatedly. Then she removed the wig and shook it in her right hand while smiling broadly and laughing out loud. Next, she grasped the wig and held it with two hands to her heart and placed it back on her head. Jane then mentioned that she did not want to keep me from my scheduled meditation, but she only wanted to come through so I could pass the message along that she was happy and healthy and to say "hi "to her niece. When I asked her about the wig, she just looked at me and smiled with the widest grin imaginable; but she did not comment.

At that point, I wished her much love and peace; I thanked her for coming and told her that I would convey the message to her family. Then her energy pulled away and I continued with my meditation.

After my meditation, the force of the message that had been brought through to me was so strong that I felt I needed to connect with the family to let them know that their aunt had come to me, telling me that she was fine and no longer in pain. I immediately went to my computer and started to compose an e-mail message. I had not spoken to or been in any contact with her family in over three months. As I prepared the e-mail message, Jane's face kept appearing in my mind as being happy, joyful, and actually laughing. As a result, I was looking forward to passing on this message to her family. I completed the e-mail message and sent it off to her niece. I closed out of my computer and turned it off for the evening.

In less than ten minutes, my phone rang; I had a strange sensation that it had something to do with the e-mail I had just sent. When I answered the phone, I recognized the voice immediately. It was Jane's niece. She was happy to hear from me, since we had not chatted for a long time. She said she just received the e-mail message and had to call me right away because of the events that had occurred at her house that same afternoon. It seems that Jane's husband, who lived next door, had been in quite an emotional state while talking to the niece and her other aunt. He was looking for a specific wig that his wife loved to wear when she went out in public, because he wanted to give it to his new girlfriend. When I say new girlfriend," I am being kind, because, as I found out, he was quite friendly with her before his wife had passed. As he stood in the niece's living room demanding to know where Jane's wig was stored, the niece and the other aunt were astonished at his request.

They just couldn't believe that he was so petty and thoughtless as to demand a wig that had been used by his wife while she was battling cancer, just so that it could be given to this other woman. Throughout that afternoon, they looked through the two houses in every closet, every box, and everywhere imaginable for the wig that was so coveted by the husband of the deceased.

When the niece told me this story, I found it very curious that the message had come through that evening concerning events that happened during that same afternoon. She could not believe how strange it was, and I couldn't understand the meaning of the message until the niece explained to me what happened next.

After thoroughly searching both homes and not finding a clue to the whereabouts of the wig, the niece came up with an idea and picked up the phone. She thought that there might be a slight chance that someone else would know the location of this so valued wig. An older gentleman answered the phone, remembered meeting the niece, and of course meeting Jane. He remembered these details because Jane had only recently passed away and he was the owner of the funeral home. When the niece asked if perhaps the wig was stored somewhere at the home, the owner explained exactly where the wig was located.

It seems that while setting up and organizing her own funeral, Jane had requested that one particular wig be buried with her, since it had brought her so much comfort and peace during the last few months of her life.

Now, it all came together. Now, I understood why Jane had come through that evening to show me that she actually had the wig with her, and it was not going to get into the hands of her husband's lover. That is why she was dancing joyfully and holding the wig close to her heart. She knew that she had gotten the last laugh!

Jane's niece and sister were so overjoyed with the message that had come through that they laughed and cried, knowing that their loved one had truly come through with an appropriate sign for that exact situation at just the right time.

Joe's Comments on Story 3

This is a perfect example of when a loved one needs to come through with a specific sign at a specific time and cannot get through directly to his/her loved ones. At such a time, they may come through to a friend.

In order to try to get that sign through, Jane probably tried to get through directly to the niece but was not successful. Therefore, going through me, a medium, was the perfect second choice. She knew I would relate the message as soon as I received it and she was correct.

Comments on Story 3 by the Channeled Entity

If a loved one needs to come through, they will find a way; just be open to any possibilities.

Accepting a sign can be very simple for some people; and, to others, it can create a complex maze of emotional and physical turmoil. What we mean by this is that someone might say, "Oh I just received a sign from Uncle John." Others may become confused and think that something out of the ordinary just happened but that it might not be an actual connection from their uncle.

To accept a sign, first you must be in the right emotional and physical state to be aware that an actual sign has been presented to you. One of the main ingredients is your willingness and openness to receiving a sign. This is simple in its explanation, but, at times, it is difficult to practice. Just be open to the possibility, remember to say "thank you" when you realize that communication has been made, and we will know that you truly have accepted this invitation to communicate.

Story 4: One More Time

Joe: This is a story that comes from my own life about the need to be open and remove doubt:

I have actually seen this in person from a woman who attended a local charitable fair while I was donating mediumistic readings. She came to me about two family members who had passed, and I mentioned that they had been trying to send her signs that they were around her. She finally admitted to me that, yes, she had seen the signs, but doubted them. She kept asking for more signs without accepting any of them. Her relatives on the other side informed me that they would send one more sign to her; and, if she did not accept it, there would be no more. They told me it would be large and obvious.

One month later when I ran into the woman, she smiled and told me they had come through and that this time, she finally accepted the sign. I was happy for her and asked how they did it. She said that she had been thinking of her father as she pulled up to an intersection on a busy road, wondering if she would be given the opportunity again to witness a sign from him and to be able to say "yes" and thank him for it. As the light turned green and before she could pull out, a tractor trailer passed through the intersection. She began to cry as she saw the advertisement on the side of that huge truck had the same childhood nickname her father used to call her throughout her life.

Comments on Story 4 by the Channeled Entity

Sometimes, after receiving a sign, you may confide in friends and family and tell them what has happened. Or you may keep this information to yourself, as you're afraid of being ridiculed and called crazy. But, what you may not realize is that many, many people have had the same type of experience and were made to feel exactly as you are feeling when you try to figure out what is happening, what has happened, and whether it will happen again. Don't think that you are alone in these circumstances; millions of other people have experienced the same thing. The bottom line is to be joyous that you have had the ability to pick up the communication that has been specifically prepared just for you. You are the main part of a successful contact attempt. Without your understanding and acceptance, that communication from your loved one will simply go by your consciousness and will never have the impact that it was intended to have.

Story 5: In the News

Joe: This is a story told to me a few years ago:

I can remember that about one month after my aunt's death, I was reading the *Boston Globe* on a Sunday afternoon and decided to look at the obituaries. Sometimes they are of famous people, or perhaps someone's parent from work or school might be listed. I started to read one on the death of a woman forty-five years old, and I thought how young she was to pass over. Then, I wondered why I was doing this. It was unfortunate, but I didn't know her. I then proceeded to read the next page of news.

Something made me turn the page back to the woman's obituary. But when I did, I continued to read the obituary but on a different column. It was not about the forty-five-year-old woman. Instead, I was reading about a ninety-five-year-old man. Right there, as I was reading, my aunt's name appeared, because the man's sister had the same first and last names as my aunt. Also, his mother had the same name as my aunt's mother. I knew that this was not a coincidence, but clearly a sign.

Comments on Story 5 by the Channeled Entity

The reason these specific methods of contact were chosen was to give you an idea of the variety of ways that we can go about trying to communicate with you. We have noticed that most people possess the ability to recognize signs once they have understood these explanations. It is not our intention to try to make the connections more difficult than they can be. We like to use familiar things that you interact with in your daily lives. It is also our intention to relate to the vast majority of people who have witnessed contact from these methods. Depending on the individual, specific methods may be used.

Joe's Closing Comments

When I have talked to people about the subject matter for my research and listened to their stories, there seemed to be a common thread. Initially, most of them thought that they might be imagining what was happening. I, too, have had this reaction and I should know better. We all experience doubt, because this is just a natural self-checking mechanism we all share. Knowing that millions of others believe in the concept of connecting to our departed loved ones brings some solace by helping us recognize that we are not alone in our experiences; many others have actually received a sign.

Tips for Initiating a Sign

1. Ask for a sign.

2. Put no conditions on the time or method.

3. Believe and be open to receiving the sign.

4. Know that accepting the sign will create more signs.

5. Keep a dream journal next to your bed.

6. Emotional highs and lows and a chaotic lifestyle can be disruptive to the process of receiving signs.

7. Meditate. It will help in receiving and understanding signs.

The Threshold Room

Herb Puryear, Ph.D.
Anne Puryear, D.D.

Herb Puryear, Ph.D., is a clinical psychologist who graduated from Stanford and the University of North Carolina. He has been consultant to psychiatric hospitals, a professor of psychology at Trinity University, director of research and education at the Cayce Foundation in Virginia Beach, and president of Atlantic University. He is the author of eight books, including *The Edgar Cayce Primer*, *Reflections on the Path*, *Sex & The Spiritual Path*, and *Why Jesus Taught Reincarnation*. He was the host of two series for PBS, and lectures worldwide about his research on spiritual truths.

Anne Puryear, D.D., received her ministerial degree in Washington, D.C. She began a research center investigating paranormal experiences and teaching students to develop their ESP. A Gestalt Therapist, she was co-founder of Life Guidance Foundation, and later began giving life readings in a state similar to Edgar Cayce's state. She gave over 10,000 readings for the A.R.E. Clinic in Phoenix, Arizona, in special medical programs, and in her private practice and at The Logos Center. Anne is the author of *Stephen Lives! My Son Stephen, His Life, Suicide & Afterlife* and *Messages from God*.

The Threshold Room

We co-founded The Logos Center in 1983 in Phoenix, Arizona, based on the teachings of Jesus, Edgar Cayce and other spiritual leaders. In the Logos Center was a 10′ X 10′ fully dedicated meditation room we called "The Threshold," because it was a space between two dimensions. We carefully designed The Threshold Room using our knowledge about connecting with people in the afterlife and the effects of physical configurations on psychic ability.

In March 2014, we sold the building containing our Threshold Room, but continue the Logos Center, meeting in other locations and broadening our Internet presence. However, the Threshold Room was very successful and is a viable method of enhancing afterlife connections we encourage others to duplicate. This is the story of The Threshold Room.

Dr. Moody's Work: The Catalyst for The Threshold Room

My son Stephen passed into spirit when he was 15. After his passing, I began to talk frequently to him, and he answered me back. He dictated the book *Stephen Lives! My Son Stephen, His Life, Suicide and Afterlife* to me. So I had a high level of confidence in communicating with him. But I had not <u>seen</u> him since his passing. I wanted to see Stephen.

One day, I read Dr. Raymond Moody's *Reunions: Visionary Encounters with Departed Loved Ones*. Dr. Moody explained that people are able to see a loved one who has passed away by gazing into a mirror. After reading the book, I decided on a whim to give it a try. Highly doubtful that it would work, I placed a small rectangular makeup mirror on the top shelf of one of my bookcases in my office, closed the blinds and door, turned off the lights, and sat in my chair looking into the mirror, waiting to see what would happen. I kind of half prayed and half meditated while I asked Stephen to appear if he could.

Nothing happened.

A half hour passed and I could not even hear Stephen, which I usually could. I started to turn on the lights and chalk the experience up as a failure, but decided since I had worked at it this long, to give it a few more minutes. I sat back down and continued gazing upward at the mirror. In a short time, a purple light appeared in the mirror and grew bigger. Then it moved out of the mirror to the right side. I blinked my eyes but the purple light stayed. I kept looking at the light. Stephen's face appeared. His face turned to the right, making a side view, but it wasn't like a photograph. It was moving like when he was alive. I think I gasped, and tears filled my eyes. The vision in the mirror lasted only a minute or so but I said out loud, "There is something to this. I saw Stephen like when he was alive!"

I rushed into the bedroom and told Herb what happened. We began to discuss how to set up a room to help people communicate with loved ones who have died. We discussed Faraday cages, pyramids, mirrors, stones, gems and various designs. Those discussions evolved into The Threshold Project. Herb designed the room and oversaw each segment that was built.

The Design of the Threshold Room

We knew that a room shielded from extraneous sounds and electromagnetism could enhance psychic activity. This type of shielded room is called a Faraday cage. In the late fifties, Dr. Andrea Puharich and psychic Peter Hurkos demonstrated that a Faraday cage could increase psychic accuracy significantly. Sometimes Hurkos could correctly identify information not known to him using his psychic ability with 100% accuracy while sitting in the Faraday cage.

So we built a Faraday Cage in the Logos Center. It was a 10' X 10' fully dedicated meditation room. The room was fully lined with copper screening and deeply grounded with a copper rod. The metal door was also grounded. The walls, ceiling and door were insulated to be as soundproof as possible.

We also surmised that a pyramid made of copper could enhance psychic ability. During the 1970s, a great deal of research was conducted demonstrating the effects of different spaces on psychic performance, such as the shape of an egg, a pyramid, and others. This research led to the expression "pyramid power," because it was apparent that the pyramid shape enhanced abilities.

As a result, inside The Threshold was a copper pyramid, also 10' X 10,' with proportions of those of the great pyramid of Giza.

Surrounding the pyramid was an amethyst grid. Dr. Richard Gerber, author of *Vibrational Medicine* gave us the instructions on how to establish a powerful energy pattern by placing an amethyst at each corner and at the apex of the pyramid.

We prepared the inside of the room to enhance psychic abilities and afterlife communication. Bill Roberts, highly respected Monroe Institute facilitator, provided us with appropriate Hemi-Sync® CD's, for our Bose player, designed to enhance higher states of consciousness.

Using what we had learned about mirror gazing from Dr. Moody's *Reunions*, we mounted a mirror high on the wall so that the experiencers could see into the mirror but not see themselves. With the power brought to this room by the sincere seeking and meditations of the subjects, this room became truly a sacred space.

Studies of The Threshold Room's Effects

We asked for 25 volunteers, including believers and non-believers, to participate in very intensive six-week research projects in three research programs that were held two years apart to see if The Threshold Room would enhance their ability to connect with a loved one who had died. We always had far more than 25 people who wanted to participate each time we performed this study. In each of the three programs there were slightly more women than men.

The participants were given a required-reading list before they were accepted in the program so they would better understand experiences they might have. These books were *Hello from Heaven* (Bill Guggenheim's research with over 3,000 people who had various experiences with loved ones who died), *Reunions* (Raymond Moody's wonderful, informative book), *There is a River* (the story of Edgar Cayce's journey and psychic gifts), *Stephen Lives!* (Anne's book), *Journeys out of the Body* (Robert Monroe's amazing book of out-of-body experiences), *Opening Doors Within* (Eileen Caddy's book of her messages from God or that still small voice within), *Conversations with God* (Neale Donald Walsh's first book on his talks with God), and *The Edgar Cayce Primer* (Herb's best-selling book with specific chapters about what Edgar Cayce received in his readings).

Each of the 25 participants in the three programs filled out an extensive form of 33 questions about their backgrounds, fields of study, and books that had the most impact on their lives. They were required to write a one-page review of each of the required-reading books. They were given a sheet of 20 required preparation activities for the six-week research program that they were to study and complete. They were required to commit two hours a week, for a total of 12 hours. They had to agree that they had a sincere desire to attune to someone in the spirit plane and a willingness to experiment, persevere, and be open to experiences . They were required to refrain from taking any stimulants (coffee, tea, alcohol, chocolate, colas, and sugars) for four to eight hours or more before each session, because stimulants can make it more difficult to attune.

The instructions included ways in which to prepare for better attunement, including meditation, prayer, breathing exercises, relaxation techniques, setting the intent of expecting to have an experience with a loved one who died, and taking into the Threshold Room a photo, piece of jewelry, or something else that belonged to the person who died.

They filled out a lengthy, detailed form before each of the 12 sessions with questions about their state of mind: whether they were anxious, nervous, and so on.

When they were in The Threshold Room, participants were allowed to have a light that could be dimmed, or they could attune and meditate completely in the dark. They were given the choice of two Hemi-Sync® CDs to have playing while in the room or no music, and whether they wanted headphones or not.

A facilitator was always available to let them know when their session was over, but they were asked not to speak to the facilitator or anyone else until they filled out another lengthy form about their experiences and emotional states after the session. They had to list what music they played, what objects they brought into the room, including any stones and gems, and their choice between two aroma therapy oils available to enhance meditation.

In the Threshold Room a green chair that reclined almost completely flat was under the pyramid, facing east. The person could recline or sit up.

If they chose to meditate in the dark, their eyes would soon light adapt and they could look up and see the mirror placed high up on the wall. The edges of the mirror were covered with black velvet to make gazing into it easier and less distracting. According to our friend Richard Gerber, M.D., author of *Vibrational Medicine*, who instructed us in a specific and complicated way to set an amethyst grid, we would take fifteen minutes before each week's sessions to set the grid and re-set it each following week. There were very large amethyst geodes in each corner, actually shaped like angel wings, and a small amethyst point at the apex of the pyramid. Behind the chair was a very large double terminated quartz crystal, which helps in out-of-body travel, according to many stone and gem experts.

Herb and I and several others are Pranic Healing graduates, so after each participant finished, the room, chair and stones were sprayed with Pranic Healing spray (see Master Stephen Co's book, *Your Hands Can Heal You* for instructions on how to make and use the spray) to clean out any energies from the previous participant and have an energetically clean room for the next person.

Participant Experiences

Sometime between a few seconds and 20 or 30 minutes in the chair making their personal attunements and asking to communicate with someone in Spirit, the following experiences happened.

Parents had actual physical experiences with their children who had died, being touched by them and talking with them. Some could hear them speak aloud; some could hear them inside their head as if they moved their thoughts aside and spoke. Several felt their presence and saw movement in the mirror—faces and colors. One woman felt her son's hands touch hers and move them together in a dance movement they did when he was alive. This experience lasted over 20 minutes.

Many dog lovers saw their elderly dogs that had died years before, romping in fields like they did as puppies, completely healed and well. A man trying to contact his father who died smelled the aroma of the cigarettes his dad smoked and felt his presence. Many men and women heard and saw loved ones who had died, appearing as they were in the prime of life. Frequently, people asked for a message for themselves or another family member, and were amazed at what they heard, such as advice about health, relationships, and how they needed to do specific things in their lives or for a loved one. Others trying to contact a specific loved one, instead were visited in the room by another family member or friend who had died. In all of the programs, 100% of the subjects saw a rainbow of colors and movement while looking into a mirror. Almost as many saw past lives like watching a movie of how they lived and died in times past, where they recognized friends and relatives.

Results of the Three Research Programs

When results were tabulated and combined for the three research programs, 72% of the 75 participants had had an encounter with a loved one who died. These encounters were in five categories of experiences: actual touch, hearing a voice, feeling their presence, seeing a loved one in the room or in the mirror, and smells associated with a loved one. There were a dozen other categories, such as seeing an animal who had died, learning about past lives, and getting intuitive guidance, which over 72% also experienced.

It took many volunteers and staff hours of work to facilitate these projects and it is not an easy job to do. Hearing people's experiences and seeing their faces after having an encounter they had so hoped and prayed might happen but were unable to experience before is priceless, as they say. Almost 95% said they were helped by the experiences and felt more relaxed and confident about contacting someone who had died.

An Experience with Orbs in The Threshold Room

A lovely woman whose son had died desperately wanted to have a contact with him. When she learned about The Threshold Room, she wanted to schedule sessions to connect with her son, but we had sold the building and were getting ready to move out. When she found we were moving, she quickly scheduled some sessions in it. After two sessions, she had not established communication with her son and was discouraged. Yet she came for one last session before we turned the building over to the new owners. Before she came, I went into the room and prayed and asked that God please let her have an experience with her son to help her in the grief process, because this would be the last session she could have in the room.

She came out of the room, her eyes wild with excitement, and showed me some videos on her cell phone. She had called on her son and turned on her cell video recorder. Orbs moving at a fast speed (much much harder to capture on film) came from where she was sitting and moved quickly up through the pyramid. You could clearly see them! It happened over and over on several videos. It was amazing and she and all of us believe her son communicated in this most unusual and evidential way.

You Can Build Your Own Threshold Room

You can build your own Threshold Room. It doesn't have to be as large as the one we used for 12 years in the Logos building. In fact, years ago a person made his bathroom into such a room and it worked beautifully for him. We are currently drawing up plans to add a limited version of The Threshold Room to our home in which to meditate daily and contact our loved ones.

There are many ways to hear from those in Spirit. We have just personally found this unusual room, this sacred space, makes moving across the threshold and back a bit easier and more evidential.

Love Language
of the Afterlife

Susanne Wilson, M.A.

Susanne Wilson has a B.A. in management with an HR concentration, M.A. in public administration, and certification as a senior professional in human resources (SPHR). She has been a manager of compensation and benefits in a company, vice president of a company, founder and administrative director of the Center for Leadership and Innovation at Florida Gulf Coast University, and administrative manager of the Stanford University Medical Center. She is a member of the International Association of Reiki Professionals and is a Usui Reiki Master Teacher. She works with a global clientele providing readings, intuition-development lessons, and Reiki classes. Susanne is currently writing her first book about her evolution as a medium and how anyone can make a direct connection with the afterlife.

You can learn more about Susanne on her website at carefreemedium.com.

My name is Susanne Wilson. I am known as the Carefree Medium mainly because I live and work in Carefree, Arizona. I believe that no matter what happens, any of us has the potential to feel carefree. This is because the peace that surpasses understanding is always available, when we make inner peace our priority.

I am often asked "When did you first know that you are a medium?" I knew I was different as soon as I started school at age five in the Head Start program. Head Start is a federally funded program to help promote school readiness for low-income children. My five-year-old self was terrified during those first weeks at school. I saw spirit lights, colors, and faces around the teacher and my classmates. One day before school started, I hid in the back of the classroom behind a big rocking chair toy that was turned upside down and leaned against the back wall. The teacher marked me as being absent that day, until I emerged from my hiding place at snack time. I must have been hungry.

My grandfather was a Protestant minister and mediumistic himself. He often talked with me in a comforting way about Spirit. Eventually I stopped being afraid. I learned it was better to hide my abilities. When I was 14 years old, my grandfather's spirit visited me immediately after he passed. No one in our home had yet been notified of his passing. It was late and I was in bed. My grandfather awakened me. Smiling, he held out his hands and we danced elegantly as we had many times. He explained that God had called him home. He told me, "You are going to be all right." Then he disappeared and I cried. A moment later I heard the phone in the kitchen ring several times, followed by my mother answering it and then sobbing. She had just been told on the phone that her father (my grandfather) had passed unexpectedly at age 56.

As an adult, I spent many years focused on living a so-called normal life. I built a successful career and made a good living. I earned my bachelor's and master's degrees from traditional universities and found my life partner, Carl, whom I married in 1987. From the early 1990s, I was secretly studying psychic development and doing mini readings for friends and acquaintances.

I often say that mediumship is a calling, not a choice. I did not choose to work as a professional medium. In 2007 the universe gave me a wake-up call that literally took my breath away. I had an allergic reaction known as anaphylaxis and I had stopped breathing. I was surrounded by white light. I heard beautiful spirit music that washed waves of peace through me. I felt the arms of my grandfather enfolding me. I heard a voice say that I had to go back and start my work. When a shot of epinephrine was injected into my arm, I felt myself being vacuumed painfully back into my physical body. My near-death experience was the one minute that changed my life. I realized we are here to bring a bit of heaven to earth. I found my calling.

I provide readings and teach Reiki and intuition development classes and private lessons. Clients always want to meet their spirit guides during an intuition lesson, and thus I developed and fine-tuned a meditation designed for meeting your spirit guide. While conducting these meditations, I found to my surprise that more than guides were showing up for my clients. They were also connecting with their loved ones in the afterlife. The first few times this happened during my guided meditation, I thought it was because loved ones can sometimes act as helper guides. They show up in our lives at just the right time. But it started happening over and over until finally I realized: Spirit wants me to teach people how to make their own direct connection with the afterlife. Today I teach visualizations and methods to "make a date" to connect with your loved one in the afterlife. I feel that all people have the potential to make this direct connection. We can learn to dialogue through signs, symbols, synchronicities, dreams, and meditations. It is a unique and wondrous syntax, the love language of the afterlife.

Following are true accounts from two of my clients.

Children in the Afterlife

My name is Elizabeth Veney Boisson. I am a wife, mother of three children and formerly a university lecturer. I am also president and co-founder of an international grief support organization, Helping Parents Heal.

On October 20, 2009, my son Morgan died at the Base Camp of Mount Everest in Tibet. It was the most devastating day of my life, but at the same time it was the moment that I realized that love never dies. I was able to speak to his roommate by cell phone and asked him to put the phone to Morgan's ear. He had stopped breathing and was undergoing CPR. I told him that we loved him, not to be afraid, and that we were very proud of him. At the exact instant that Morgan stopped breathing, I felt him with me, hugging me from the inside. It was a warm, calming feeling that washed through me. I realized that he was comforting me and that he wanted me to know that he would always be with me.

Before Morgan died, I did not believe that it would be possible to carry on without one of my children. However, I realized in an instant that I had to carry on, not only for my two daughters who needed me, but more importantly for

Morgan, whose only wish is to see us happy. I knew we had to live and thrive for him.

My strongest desire after his death was to somehow communicate with him. I didn't know how this would be possible—I had never been to a psychic medium. Morgan took matters into his own hands. I had been practicing yoga at a studio for years, and Morgan had sometimes gone with me. Angie, the owner of the studio, decided in January 2010 to interview a psychic medium who had recently moved to the area and was looking for rental space. Angie's way of evaluating the psychic medium, Susanne Wilson, was to ask Susanne to "read" a photo of my kids included in our annual Christmas card. Angie provided no other information to Susanne.

Susanne connected with my son, communicating his personality and mannerisms. Susanne gave Angie numerous validations—including details that were not public knowledge and not known to Angie (who diligently wrote everything down). I will share a few highlights. Susanne said a young man showed her a big teddy bear and bottle of Captain Morgan. My son's name is Morgan and we affectionately call him Big Bear. We have a dog named Captain, Morgan's second nickname. Susanne saw Morgan shouting through a megaphone that he was *OKAY*—very significant because Morgan was a cheerleader at the University of Arizona, and his megaphone was at his service. Susanne saw him on a mountain, lying on his back. She saw a black box at his ear; that he had listened intently but had been unable to speak. He told Susanne to say, *"Mom, I heard everything you said and I love you back."* I was comforted to know Morgan had heard me when the phone was held to his ear.

Susanne further told Angie that my son and his two roommates were a "band of three," that they were like brothers. Although Morgan was close to all the students who helplessly watched him die that morning, his two roommates were especially important to him. Colin and Matt accompanied Morgan's body to Lhasa and waited with him until my husband was able to finally get a visa to enter Tibet six days later. Perhaps most stunning—Susanne told Angie that we would receive a special rock from the place that Morgan died and she sketched the rock. We made no mention of this detail to anyone. Several months later Colin delivered Morgan's Rock upon his return from China, exactly as Susanne had said.

Within a month after Morgan died, I founded a local parents' support group and an Internet site to honor our children. A few months later I had my own reading with Susanne in which more validations came through, including that Morgan and I would work together to help parents connect with their deceased children in the Afterlife. I later met Mark Ireland through Susanne and two years later with the help of several other bereaved parents, we co-founded Helping Parents Heal (HPH), which currently has 15 chapters in the U.S. and one in Canada.

Susanne has spoken at our HPH Scottsdale meetings on three occasions. The most recent occasion was last October. Susanne talked about the methods that anyone could use to make his own direct connection to a loved one in the afterlife. She then gently led our group through a 20-minute guided meditation to make the connection. Afterwards many attendees reported excellent results, as they were able to see their children and feel their presence. Unfortunately, I was preoccupied that day and found myself frustrated as I was unable to meditate.

Recently, Susanne invited me to experience a one-on-one guided meditation with her. I am overjoyed to say that I easily connected with my son, Morgan. Susanne led me through the steps to meet with Morgan at our favorite place: on our boat in the middle of Bartlett Lake. I could feel myself sink down into the seat on the boat as I was seated directly across from Morgan. I could feel the heat of the Arizona summer sun and smell suntan lotion and marshy water. The boat quietly bobbed as we were anchored in the "no-wake" zone. I could feel Morgan hug me from the inside and I could clearly see his laughing eyes. He is doing so well and participates with us in every aspect of our lives. The meditation brought tears of joy to my eyes. I was sad to leave Morgan, but I now know that it is possible to connect with him whenever I want to using Susanne's method.

I know in my heart that Morgan is working diligently in the afterlife to help children get messages through to their parents. I am incredibly proud of him.

Finding My Soul Mate, Again

My name is Danielle. My journey led to Susanne's office in October 2012, eight months after my husband died by suicide. Before he died we had separated to work on our marital issues, and he took his life six months later. Early in our relationship he had asked me what I thought about suicide, and he even made comments that if I ever left him he would "die." He denied being suicidal or that he would die by suicide, but his life was reckless, so as to die accidentally.

When he died I felt at peace that he was no longer suffering, but I could smell him strongly and had several vivid dream visits. There were many "signs" that I hoped were signs, but I also worried they were only wishful thinking. I searched for a connection and finally found Susanne's website. When I saw her photograph I felt that I knew her, and on my first visit to her office she asked if we had met before.

Thomas came through with vigor, strength, a touch of arrogance, and his awesome sense of humor, just as he would enter any room while on the Earthly plane. His validation through Susanne could not have been more clear, with specific information that no one, especially Susanne would have ever known about the two of us. There was a specific name he called himself privately, there were his family members in spirit with him, there were comments about things I have done, privately, that he relayed to Susanne. He answered questions I had for him, he provided family information, and he spoke of memories of our dogs. He validated the signs I had received and now we use them to communicate. My Thomas is very much still alive!

Susanne has guided me into deep meditations and has provided the knowledge and practice of the tools I needed to communicate with spirit, and specifically with my Thomas. I have invited him into dreams, but I admit I struggle to remember the details of dreams. Therefore, I have gone on several "dates" with my husband in meditation. Some have been in the presence of Susanne so that I could receive immediate validation, but several have been done alone in the privacy of my home. It is an amazing experience to travel and spend time with the love of my life. The memories of my meditative journeys are as alive in my memory as any Earthly interaction I have encountered, but filled with unconditional love and acceptance.

Thank you, Susanne. You have made an enormous difference in my life, and I believe that joy cascades down the river of my spirit to touch and nourish those around me. As a nurse, I have become more spiritual in my care. As a mother of two beautiful sons, I am gentle and loving with their needs. Through Thomas, I have gained more insight into what happens when we "die," and I no longer fear life. My children have seen a change in my approach to life, and they are doing the same. My youngest son struggled the most with the loss of his stepfather. Through a reading with Susanne, he was reunited with Thomas and his grandparents.

As I work with Susanne to develop my intuitive abilities, Thomas usually makes a visit and offers insight. He loves to answer questions, and most importantly, he kisses my cheek while teasing me the way he always did. I miss him dearly, yet we have a bond beyond anything I could have imagined. Since there is no death, there cannot be "'til death do us part."

People in Spirit Materialize to Speak

Victor Zammit, Ph.D.

Victor James Zammit, B.A. Grad. Dip.Ed. M.A. LL.B. Ph.D., worked as an attorney in the Local Courts, District and Supreme Courts in Sydney Australia. For many years, his main interest was in human rights and social justice. Around 1990 he began to experience spontaneous clairvoyance and clairaudience, which led him to begin a systematic investigation of the afterlife. He was astonished to discover a hidden world of research that he felt provided overwhelming evidence for life after death. Since that time, his priority has been sharing his discoveries on his website where an earlier version of his book, *A Lawyer Presents the Evidence for the Afterlife,* was viewed by more than a million people. His book is acknowledged as one of the most complete books on the afterlife and afterlife communication. His website is at victorzammit.com.

Reunions Through Physical Mediumship— an Old Practice Being Rediscovered

By Victor Zammit

If you died, and months or years later had the opportunity to come back in a temporary physical body for a few minutes to talk to your loved one in front of a group of people, what would you say?

I can tell you from personal experience that this is the most amazing thing I have ever experienced in my life. Imagine that you are sitting in a totally pitch black room. Darkness is necessary because ectoplasm—the whitish, smoky looking substance taken from the medium's body to make materializations happen—is extremely sensitive to light. You are holding hands with seven other people you know very well. And suddenly there is an extra person in the room. It is materialized William, the spirit convener of the Circle of the Silver Cord. To show that he is fully materialized he stamps his feet and claps his hands. He comes and puts his large hand on your shoulder. He talks to you and answers questions about the spirit world for about twenty minutes like an old friend.

You know it's not one of the other sitters because all sitters hold hands when someone is materialized, and you can hear where the other sitters are when they speak. You know it's not the medium because he is tied into his chair with one-way cable ties, has a gag around his mouth so he cannot speak, and is deeply unconscious in trance.

I must emphasize that although the meeting is in darkness, it is not frightening or spooky. The session begins with a brief prayer and there is a lot of exciting, uplifting music. This is done to raise the "vibrations" of the sitters. When the spirit people begin to speak and materialize one at a time, there is a lot of humor and good-natured fun. They move objects, touch people gently and people are talking to each other and asking questions.

After the preliminaries, William tells you that he wants to bring through a loved one for someone in the room. He leaves and there is a sudden whooshing sound as the new person materializes. You hear a faint voice as the newcomer struggles to get used to speaking in this way. He or she calls the name of someone—usually a loved one—in the circle. When that sitter answers, you hear footsteps as the materialized spirit moves across the room and then you hear an intimate conversation.

Nick's reunion with Sarah

Here is an example. The audio version is on my website at http://victorzammit.com. The medium, David Thompson, is immobilized and in trance. Several sitters are in a circle. A voice comes from the afterlife with personal information known only to one of the sitters. The voice belongs to Nick, who died five months before. He asks to speak with his partner Sarah, a guest sitting with our Circle. Nick materializes and speaks very softly—but with great emotion—as is common with many first-time communicators.

Nick: Can you hear me?

All: Yes we can hear you. You're OK. You're fine.

Nick: Oh My God. I'm a bit frightened of this.

All: It's OK, You're OK...you're among friends.. You're OK, just remain calm. Relax. It's OK.

Circle member: It's just a bit strange.

Nick: You're right it is a bit strange.

All: It's OK.

Circle member: Take a moment to adjust.

Nick: I never thought I'd do this.

Circle member: It's wonderful that you have come.

Circle member: Can you tell us who you are?

Nick: My name's Nick.

All: It's Nick, Hello Nick.

Sarah: Baby.

Nick: I can't. It's Sarah, I want to see Sarah.

All: You're here to see Sarah.

Sarah: Darling I'm here. I love you baby I love you so
             much.

Nick: I love you too.

Sarah: Don't ever leave me OK. I know you're with me.

Nick: I spend as much time with you as I can. I'm always
             with you to help.

Sarah: OK my baby, just stay close. I love you so much and
             you know how grateful I am to you for doing this.

Nick: You know something.. all those things that you
             bought?

Sarah: Yeah.

Nick: They're gone, they're lost. They was lost.

Sarah: Yeah?

Nick: Don't worry about them.

Sarah: Really?

Nick: I knew you was there. I knew you was there

Sarah: Did you darling?

Sarah: I just, was I enough for you? I just . . .

Nick: Listen to me, listen to me; we haven't got long. Listen to me.

Sarah: OK my baby.

Nick: Always remember . . .

Sarah: Yeah?

Nick: I love you with all my heart.

Sarah: OK.

Nick: I told you that just before I left you.

Sarah: I know.

Nick: I'll always be with you. I'll always be with you.

Sarah: OK my darling.

Nick: Promise me something. I want you to be happy.

Sarah: I will for you. I will for you. I'll make the best of what I've got here. For you.

Nick: Remember, whatever happens we'll always be together 'til we meet again.

Sarah: You promise me that?

Nick: I promise you.

Sarah: You . . .

Nick: From the bottom of my heart, I promise you.

Sarah: OK my darling.

Nick: I want you to be . . . happy!

Sarah: I will try. I am trying. I'm trying so hard. It's just such a shock, you know. But I'm trying hard. I'm doing better, Darling.

Nick: You are girl, and you're doing fantastic.

Sarah: As long as I've got you with me and I know I do. I just hope I did enough for you.

Nick: Yes you did, you were everything I ever wanted.

Sarah: I was... good. I just wanted to be enough.

Nick: That's why I died peacefully.

Sarah: You...Oh thank goodness.

Nick: That's why I had that look of peace on my face.

Sarah: Yes. Yes. Did you see me when I went to see you?

Nick: I did. And everything you put into the coffin. I saw it all.

Sarah: Oh, thank you darling. I tried to do right by you. I tried to do everything I could. I really tried hard.

Nick: You done more than any man could ever want. More than any man could ever want.

Sarah: OK my baby because you know you were worth it. Don't ever doubt how much I loved you and how much I will continue to love you. Don't ever doubt it.

Nick: Don't ever doubt my love for you.

Sarah: OK my baby.

{Nick places his hands around Sarah's face in an embrace}

Sarah: Oh!! Oh I love you. I love you.

{Sharp whoosh sounds of dematerialization}

Everyone in the room is caught up in the intense emotion of the reunion. We all feel privileged to have witnessed a very special event, a meeting between two worlds.

Reunions - the Ultimate Evidence of the Afterlife

For me, physical mediumship with its spirit lights, bangs and raps and movement of the cone-shaped light weight "trumpets" used to amplify voices is extremely fascinating. But what is absolutely conclusive evidence that we are communicating with the afterlife and not some unknown function of the human psyche are the reunions between people in the room with people they had known while they were alive.

When the energy is right in these demonstrations by physical medium David Thompson, up to three loved relatives or friends will materialize one after the other. Each then walks across the room to greet the person he or she has come to contact in the room. In the seven years my wife Wendy and I have been members of David's circle, we have been present at more than 100 of these reunions. Among many others, Wendy's father materialized, my sister materialized, the husband of one good friend, the father of two other good friends and the Chinese grandfather of one of Wendy's friends materialized. The talk is always intimate, of things that no one on Earth could know except the person concerned. People have spoken in several languages unknown to the medium.

The most common messages they bring are

- I love you.
- Be happy.
- Thank you for all you did.
- Don't blame yourself.
- I'm so proud of you.
- I see things differently now.
- I'm sorry I didn't tell you I loved you.

While usually it is relatives who materialize for reunions, that is not always the case. In David's Circle of the Silver Cord, quite a number of physical mediums and investigators materialize and speak to people who knew them while alive. Montague Keen, the well-known British investigator from the Society for Psychical Research, came through immediately after his death with a speech that was read at his memorial. He afterwards materialized again and talked to and embraced his wife Veronica, who confirmed his identity.

While we were in New Zealand, Gordon Higginson, the English medium who was head of the famous Arthur Findlay College, came through to talk to Ken Pretty whom he had known in England. This is a transcript of their meeting:

GH   My name is Gordon Higginson.

KP: Hello, Gordon. It's Ken Pretty here.

GH: Yes I know. That's why I'm here, you know. (Laughter)

Circle member: You're very clear.

GH   Well I hope so. I used to do this work when I was upon the Earth.

KP   Absolutely.

GH   I did, didn't I?

KP: Yes, you did.

KP: How wonderful to hear from you. I worked in your church in London Road, Stoke on Trent. It was a long time ago. Way back in the early 60s, I think.

GH   But did you not work at Castleford?

KP   Oh Castleford. Oh yes that's right. I do apologize.

KP   Don't forget.

On one unforgettable occasion a young female police officer (daughter of a member of the Circle) was sitting as a guest with us. She had been distraught about an incident when she had tried unsuccessfully to resuscitate a doctor who had drowned in a boating accident. He came through to thank her for her efforts and to reassure her that he had already passed before she started to work on him. He also told her that being in the light of her aura had been a big help to him in crossing over.

How Do You Know the Spirits Who Materialize Are Who They Claim to Be?

People materialize with the features they had while alive — they are recognized by their loved ones by voice and by touch. On the website of the Circle of the Silver Cord (http://circleofthesilvercord.net/), you can see a video testimonial by a young lady whose big brother, Jeff, materialized in a meeting in Florida in 2010. Afterward, she said tearfully, "He came through this evening and gave me hugs around my neck and pressed his face against mine . . .

and I could feel the stubble of his beard pushed against my face and I asked him to please kiss me. And he took both his hands and held my face and kissed me three times on my forehead. And I know it's my brother that came through because I could smell him and if you looked around the room this evening there was nobody in there that had any sort of facial hair and I could feel all the individual hairs of my brother pressed into my face. I have absolutely no doubt in my mind that I met my brother again tonight. And that was the most special thing that has ever happened to me."

On another occasion a young man recognized that his grandfather's materialized hand was missing the finger that had been amputated when he was alive.

Children sometimes materialize. One member of the spirit team, Tim, died at the age of nine and regularly shows his small moving hand in the light of an object coated with luminous tape. Another spirit child would frequently walk around the home circle touching people. David Thompson says that the thing that kept him going in physical mediumship at the beginning was an occasion when a young child materialized and climbed onto the lap of her grieving father. The father was able to feel her face, her dress and her hair—and his life was forever transformed.

Animals occasionally materialize. In England a husband and the family dog materialized. On the recording, you can hear the materialized pet dog barking and running across the room to put its paws onto the knees of the wife.

Many of the people who attend David's sessions are mental mediums. Frequently they will get confirmation of previous contacts through mental mediumship. When Wendy's father came through, he confirmed that he had spoken through David via mental mediumship the previous night. And immediately after the session, he came through to me clairaudiently with a further message for Wendy, asking her to get in touch with an estranged family member and actually giving his address.

Something very evidential is when the same person materializes for the same sitter through different physical mediums. This has happened when the father of Elizabeth Pretty in New Zealand materialized through another physical medium in England and confirmed to her their earlier meeting through David.

David Thompson has been a medium for more than twenty-five years and is one of the most highly developed physical mediums demonstrating publicly in the world today. He started off as an excellent mental medium and one day his guide asked him to allow himself to be put into trance. His mediumship includes

- mental mediumship
- deep trance, where he becomes totally unconscious and William or other members of his spirit team take over his body and speak for extended periods of time. They coat his vocal cords with ectoplasm so their voices are the same as when they materialize.
- physical mediumship, where loud sounds and raps occur, objects are levitated and moved around the room
- direct-voice mediumship
- full materialization
- trance healing mediumship (where a spirit doctor takes over his body)

Can I Get David Thompson to Bring Through My Whole Family?

David Thompson does travel to Europe and the United States to demonstrate on a regular basis. In a public demonstration where perhaps 40 people are present, there may be three reunions as well as the experienced communicators in the spirit team.

The people who come through are chosen by the spirit team on the basis of need. A good example of this was a séance in Sarasota where a man's son materialized for a very special reason. The son had been killed two and a half years before—run down on the sidewalk. The driver was high on drugs and ended up walking out of court with a $350 ticket. In a video testimonial on the Circle of the Silver Cord website the father—after the séance—said,

> And I vowed to my son that I would seek revenge. Only he and I knew that. You know it's not something you brag about. He came through tonight and he held me and he told me "Daddy try to forgive him and promise me that you won't do anything." And those kind of things are not something that you can read in the newspaper ... I feel a relief now. There is a burden lifted from me. I promised him that I wouldn't do anything—in front of 34 people. ... I've been to a lot of mediums and...this was ...an experience.

Another woman gives her video testimonial about David Thompson's materializations. Her husband was a Baptist minister who was brutally murdered. She attended one of David Thompson's demonstrations two months later and her husband came through. She said,

> He walked across the room...I could hear his shoes...he put his hands on my face and they were his hands...and he bent and kissed me and talked to me in his voice...and the evidence coming through nobody else could have even dreamt it. So that to me, it basically changed the whole pattern of grieving...the anger at what had happened to such a wonderful man. And it made an incredible difference in my life.

Another thing that influences who will materialize in a public demonstration, is who will make the best communicators. Some of the spirits who have materialized through David say that it is like trying to talk with your head in a bucket of water. They say that their mind is temporarily clouded in a state they say is similar to coming out of an anesthetic. They have to try to remember what they looked like and what their voices sounded like as well as focusing on the main things they want to say. Some people in spirit are just unable to handle the process, especially if their relatives are highly emotional or unresponsive; sometimes they try and only manage a few muffled sounds.

The number of reunions in a given sitting is also affected by the amount of harmony and goodwill in the sitters. Sometimes when David goes to a city to give several demonstrations, the reunions in one will be brilliant with a lot of energy because the people present are harmonious and giving. At the following demonstration, the energy might be flat because of the presence of disharmony, negative emotions of a "prove it to me" attitude. On these occasions, it may not be possible to bring inexperienced communicators through. Some groups are fixated on physical phenomena rather than giving out the loving vibrations that make reunions possible.

Why Can't They Turn on the Lights?

One of the key properties of ectoplasm is that some of its forms are extremely sensitive to light and other electromagnetic energy, so much so that even turning on a flashlight drives the substance back into the medium's body with the force of snapped elastic. Bruises, open wounds and hemorrhage may result. There are many examples in the history of physical mediumship where mediums were cut, bruised, and severely injured by sitters trying to grab materialized forms, which simply dissolved in their hands. Because of this sensitivity to light, most physical mediums have to work in the dark or with occasional use of low, red light, and those responsible for their safety have to use absolute care in selecting sitters who can be trusted to stay still and hold hands during materializations.

During a materialization experiment with David Thompson in Sydney, Australia, I was present when one of the sitters was startled by the medium's chair being levitated and dumped in the middle of the room at the end of the session. She let out a sudden scream. When the lights came on, the medium's face showed a swelling near his eye and a number of small cuts that had not been there before the session. As he put it, a sudden noise creates an effect similar to glass shattering. On another occasion, William had to withdraw the ectoplasm quickly as a curtain over one of the windows was beginning to fall down. When David regained consciousness, he knew what had happened by tenderness in his stomach area. On a third occasion during a demonstration in Adelaide, a woman inadvertently touched the ectoplasm and it whipped back into David leaving a cut on his hand. He still has the scar today.

The members of the Circle are very keen to be able to take videos of the materializations, but until now this has been vetoed by the spirit team because the energy of the infrared camera could harm the medium. However, William has assured us that this is a goal for the future, and experiments are ongoing in the home circle.

On rare occasions, when the conditions are right and the ectoplasm has been stabilized by the spirit team, we have been able to turn on a low red light for a few seconds and film the ectoplasm flowing from David's mouth. It is an amazing sight. White and shimmering, glowing moving and alive.

Reunions Through Direct Voice Mediumship

Direct voice mediumship is also part of physical mediumship and is a wonderful thing to experience. Here the spirits don't fully materialize, but use ectoplasm to create an artificial voice box that sits on the medium's shoulder. Sometimes William will do this to save energy. At other times, the voices seem to be disembodied and come from anywhere in the room. I have heard William's voice coming right up close to my left ear and then a minute later beside my right ear and then from the top of a 12-foot ceiling and then instantly on the other side of the room. Some of the voices are incredibly loud and some just a whisper.

In the United States, the most famous direct voice medium was Etta Wreidt from Buffalo, New York (died 1942). She was also able to do materializations, but is most remembered for the voices. She was always conscious during séances and often joined in the conversation with visitors. Voices were heard in her sessions speaking in Dutch, French, Spanish, Norwegian, and Arabic.

Just as William looks after David, Dr. John Sharp looked after Mrs. Wriedt. On several occasions, Mrs. Wriedt was engaged to sit with royalty. Lady Warwick, who had been the mistress of King Edward VII, claimed that she had heard the late king talking to her in his unmistakable German accent and that she conversed with him, partly in German. After the Titanic sank, she brought through William Stead, who talked to his daughter (see Michael Tymn's book *Transcending the Titanic: Beyond Death's Door*, 2012).

Leslie Flint (died 1994) was a brilliant English physical medium who tried materializations a few times but didn't like the feeling, so he restricted his mediumship to direct voice. You can listen on the Internet to audio recordings of the many famous people who spoke through him.

The Anni Nanji recordings are especially impressive. These are 66 recordings of casual conversations between one of Leslie Flint's regular sitters and his wife Anni who had died. Anni was a Swedish lady who died of cancer, and her Indian husband was a doctor from Bombay. She was speaking to her husband in direct voice through Leslie Flint between 1971 and 1983. They talk in casual conversation like any married couple. The wife tells her husband that he comes to visit her very often when he is asleep and cannot understand that he does not remember visiting her. Dr. Nanji said, "This wasn't someone impersonating my wife. It was my dead wife who knew so many things unknown to the medium, Leslie Flint." You can listen to these remarkable

tapes online at
http://www.leslieflint.com/recordingsnanji.html

Why Are There So Few Physical Mediums Today?

Once you experience this rare kind of mediumship for the first time, the obvious questions you ask are why don't people know more about it and how can it be developed?

Physical mediumship takes time and patience to develop and there needs to be someone in the group who has the necessary physical predisposition—possibly a reason why many of the great physical mediums of the past had siblings who also had the gift. Sometimes a circle will have to sit for years before getting the first voices. Leslie Flint, the famous direct voice medium, sat with a group weekly for seven years before the voices came through clearly.

After the Second World War, physical mediumship was almost entirely replaced by mental mediumship. It was quicker to develop, much safer, and could be practiced in lighted conditions. Some people speculate that the proliferation of electrical energies in radio, television, computers and mobile phones, all of which give out electromagnetic energy, has made it more difficult to get the incredible materializations in red light that happened in the pre-war years.

Energy-Based Physical Mediumship

Since about 1950, and increasingly since 1990, a number of circles have been developing mediumship based on group energy, either on its own or with ectoplasm. The most famous of these was a dedicated group of psychic researchers in Norfolk, UK, known as the Scole Experimental Group, led by Robin and Sandra Foy. They had 500 sittings from December 1992 to November 1998, working in co-operation with a wonderful team of spirit scientists, guides and helpers.

The phenomena that were developed were energy based and breathtaking. It did not require a single physical medium as such, although two of the group members remained in deep trance throughout. Every member of the group contributed to the phenomena. There was no danger involved to sitters or mediums by working in this way; it could be developed quicker and was more versatile. Many more groups have gone on since to achieve spectacular phenomena in a similar energy-based way.

How to Develop Your Own Physical Mediumship Circle.

If you have the patience and dedication, you may be able to create a home circle for the development of physical mediumship that includes both direct voice and materialization. This is possibly the most exciting form of spirit communication possible. At the moment, there seems to be a resurgence of interest in physical mediumship, and we have heard of new groups sitting in England, Scotland, Austria, Australia, Germany, and the United States.

There are several excellent guides to developing a home circle online. The Noah's Ark Society Guide is useful: http://physicalmediumshipdevelopment.blogspot.com.au/

John Butler's excellent book *Exploring the Psychic World* (1949) contains instructions on how to develop direct voice in six months (p. 119-126). We have reprinted them at http://www.victorzammit.com/articles/directvoicecircle.htm.

Robin Foy also sells a *Basic Guide to Developing an Energy - Based Physical Circle*, a 72-page book dictated by the Scole Spirit Team. Learn more about it at this link: http://www.scoleexperiment.com/index.php/the-basic-guide-v15-8

As well, there are a number of websites and forums on physical mediumship where you can get help and advice.

While some authors claim that a medium is not needed to start a circle, especially for energy-based mediumship, others say that having someone who is a medium, especially if they are able to go into trance, is a huge help. In some circles, someone in the group will spontaneously go into trance without training.

Here is a basic idea of what is required:

1. Get together a small group of people who are equally excited about the possibility of spirit communication. The normally recommended number is between five and nine. The members should be chosen with care, as group harmony is the most important point.

2. Decide on a place to meet. It should be the same place all the time, ideally a small room with no furnishings that can be completely blacked out and which is totally dedicated to the purpose. There should be some means of heating in winter or cooling in summer.

3. Decide on a time for sitting—exactly the same time every week for about an hour. People must be committed to not missing except in exceptional circumstances.

4. When people arrive, avoid any discussion of controversial subjects and go into the room after about 15 minutes.

5. The members should sit in a circle and open with a prayer to focus the energies and tune into the spirit world.

6. Immediately after the opening prayer, there should be music—either quiet singing in unison or recorded music. The music does not have to be religious. Some circles use popular songs that everyone loves. One of the functions of the music is to help the medium go into trance. The other is to raise the energy.

7. At the conclusion of the designated time, close the circle with a prayer.

Harmony—the most important element

John Butler claims that the reason most circles fail to get results is lack of harmony. He writes:

> In our own home circle we got very speedy results because we purposely set out to cultivate harmony among the sitters. We saw little of each other immediately before the sitting so that no controversial conversation might take place. We did not permit criticism of anybody or anything. We consciously tried to see the best in each other, and avoided being irritated by mannerisms. We became, if you like, a mutual admiration society, but we preserved harmony. There was not a shred of malice or unkindness or envy or jealousy, or even questioning amongst the whole lot of us. Tolerance and harmony reigned supreme.

This seems to be a crucial lesson for anyone who is interested in contacting the spirit world.

Where Can You Witness David Thompson's Physical Mediumship Today?

David Thompson is based in Sydney, Australia, but regularly conducts public demonstrations in England, especially at the Banyan Centre in Kent, and in Europe. You can find details on the Circle of the Silver Cord website: http://circleofthesilvercord.net/

He travels to the United States approximately once a year and is open to demonstrating in more venues as part of a package involving demonstrations of deep trance and trance healing. For the physical mediumship, you would need to have a venue that can seat up to 40 people in a secure room that can be totally light-proofed. It must also be clean (no cobwebs) as anything left around can be absorbed into the ectoplasm. You would need to be able to vouch for the sincerity and honesty of the people who are going to sit. He can be contacted at silvercordcircle@gmail.com.

Victor's website is at victorzammit.com. Subscribe to the free Friday Afterlife Report for weekly interviews, videos and updates on afterlife research.

The Future for Afterlife Communication

R. Craig Hogan, Ph.D.
Editor

Monsignor Robert Hugh Benson, speaking from the world unseen through the medium Anthony Borgia said, "The day will assuredly come when our two worlds will be closely interrelated, when communication between the two will be a commonplace of life, and then the great wealth of resources of the spirit world will be open to the Earth world, to draw upon for the benefit of the whole human race."

We are seeing the blush on the horizon from the dawn of that day. Today, humankind knows more proven methods by which anyone can communicate with loved ones in the afterlife than at any time in history, and more are being given to us as quickly as we are able to mature into understanding them. People are learning how to have rich, fulfilling, continuing relationships with loved ones now living just out of eyesight, but close enough for us to hear their messages.

In the near future, everyone will know someone whose life has been revitalized and fulfilled by exciting, new relationships with those they thought they had lost. A short time later, communicating with our loved ones living in that nearby realm will be as commonplace as speaking on the phone to family members in another country. The stages of life we describe will extend beyond childhood, adulthood, and old age into a stage of life we might call "rejuvenation," characterized by loving reunions, joy, perfect health, and time for reflection. What we call death will be seen as a natural passage into another stage of life.

Because of these changes in society resulting from afterlife connections, people will grow to have the conviction that our purpose for living in this Earth period of our eternal lives is to learn how to love and serve together, in peace and brotherhood. The knowledge of our eternal natures will stop society's headlong, self-destructive plunge into the abyss that is the inevitable result of the suffocating embrace of materialism.

Those are the benefits Monsignor Benson predicted would come to humankind on the day when communication between our two worlds has become a commonplace of life. We are now seeing the first light of the dawn of that day.

20572541R00177

Made in the USA
San Bernardino, CA
28 December 2018